HOW TO
KEEP YOUR
SAVINGS
SAFE

HOW TO KEEP YOUR SAVINGS SAFE

Protecting the Money You Can't Afford to Lose

WALTER L. UPDEGRAVE

CROWN PUBLISHERS, INC.
New York

TO MARY

Published by Crown Publishers, Inc., 201 East 50th Street, New York, New York
10022. Member of the Crown Publishing Group.

CROWN is a trademark of Crown Publishers, Inc.

Manufactured in the United States of America

Library of Congress Cataloging-in-Publication Data

Updegrave, Walter L.
    How to keep your savings safe : protecting the money you can't afford to lose / by
    Walter L. Updegrave.
    Includes index.
    1. Investments.   2. Finance, Personal.   I. Title.
HG4521.U63   1992
332.024'01—dc20   91-36900
                                                                    CIP

ISBN 0-517-58734-3
10   9   8   7   6   5   4   3   2   1
First Edition

CONTENTS

ACKNOWLEDGMENTS

There are a number of people whose cooperation made this book possible. Walter Frank, Mary Sue Hoban, and their colleagues at the Donoghue Organization were instrumental in helping me develop criteria for picking the safest money funds. Mary Novick of Standard & Poor's mutual funds ratings group was extremely patient in answering my many nitpicking queries about money funds. For their help in providing safety ratings and financial information on insurance companies, I am deeply indebted to the insurance ratings divisions of A.M. Best, Moody's Investors Service, and Standard & Poor's. I would also like to thank Paul Bauer of the Bauer Group for providing me with his organization's safety ratings of banks and credit unions and Warren Heller of Veribanc, Inc., for conscientiously returning my calls when he knew he'd have to answer still more questions about bank safety and bank reform. Finally, thanks to my editor, Jane Meara, for her guidance and wise counsel, and to my agent, Rich Pine, for enthusiastically embracing this project.

PREFACE

A Lesson for the 1990s

WE used to take comfort in the notion that government regulators were benevolent Big Brothers who worked to protect our interests. We believed that bank examiners kept vigilant guard over banks and S&Ls to prevent them from taking liberties with our savings. We assumed that state insurance regulators would make sure insurance companies made good on their guarantees.

But the 1980s largely proved those trusting notions wrong. As the S&L crisis developed into a huge taxpayer bailout and troubles with banks and insurance companies threatened to push us into an even deeper hole, it became obvious that this quaint idea of government regulators as protectors was little more than a fantasy. Too often, regulators seem more concerned about the industry they're overseeing than about the consumers whom they're supposed to be protecting.

So the lesson from the 1980s that you should take with you into the 1990s is this: Don't be lulled into a false sense of security by the idea that the federal or state government is acting as a watchdog to protect your savings. You must assume the responsibility for your money's security. You must rely on your own research, your own judgment, your own vigilance. The onus is on *you* to keep your savings safe.

This book will tell you what you need to know to take on that responsibility so that you can protect the money, whether in banks, insurance companies, or money-market funds, that you simply cannot afford to lose.

1

SAFE SAVING: A TREND FOR THE NINETIES

The Age of Uncertainty

YOU don't have to be a Nobel laureate in economics to see that the U.S. financial system is on exceedingly shaky ground, possibly in its worst shape since the 1930s Depression. We already know that savings-and-loan associations have been devastated, done in by mindless deregulation, congressional neglect, and the greed and incompetence of the S&L officers themselves. And we've pretty much reconciled ourselves to picking up the tab for that fiasco, a bailout that, at last count, could cost U.S. taxpayers an estimated $750 billion to $1 trillion.

But, over the last year or so, it has become apparent that, far from getting better, things are getting worse. The S&L disease is spreading rapidly, infecting institutions once thought perfectly healthy. Banks and credit unions, former bastions of financial probity, are failing with disconcerting regularity. Insurance companies are reeling with losses from junk bonds and bad real-estate loans. Suddenly, the very places we put our money when we want to be *absolutely, positively* sure we aren't putting our cash at risk don't seem so safe anymore. Everywhere we turn, the safety net provided by federally insured financial institutions seems to be tearing apart. In short, the financial system has become much scarier and less secure than it used to be. Banks, S&Ls, and insurance companies are still making the same promises of safety and security, but the words ring hollow.

1

To get an idea of just how precarious our former safe refuges have become—and why it's important for you to begin developing new strategies to keep your savings safe—let's take a look at a few stats:

Banks Have Been Failing at an Alarming Rate: Between 1985 and 1990, 1,016 banks went belly up—that's 218 more than went bust in the previous fifty years. In early 1991, federal regulators figured another 340 banks would fail over the next two years. But, in the face of a devastated real-estate market, even that gloomy outlook proved too optimistic. In June 1991, then Federal Deposit Insurance chairman William Seidman boosted his estimate to 440 bank failures for 1991 and 1992. Recent failures range from small banks like Harlem's Freedom National (where some $15 million spread over 120 accounts held by charities was not federally insured) to regional behemoths like the Bank of New England, one of the largest banks in New England. There are also plenty of bank-failure candidates in the future. As of mid-1991, the FDIC's list of problem banks—those still operating but with an above-average chance of failing—contained more than a thousand names.

There has been a move to overhaul and strengthen the banking system by letting banks get into other areas of business. But, ironically, this may put you at *greater* risk. The banking reforms proposed in 1991 by the U.S. Treasury Department and embraced to varying degrees by some members of Congress would allow banks to get into real estate and insurance as well as underwrite and sell stocks, bonds, mutual funds—in short, banks could become one-stop financial supermarkets. To anyone with an iota of sense, though, these proposals are, in the words of Yogi Berra, déjà vu all over again. Don't the regulators remember what happened when S&Ls were deregulated and immediately went out and blew depositors' money on lousy real-estate investments and windmill farms? If another round of freewheeling deregulation is a cure, we may be better off with the disease.

The FDIC Bank Insurance Fund Is Headed for Bankruptcy—If It's Not Already There: At the end of 1990, according to the FDIC's own figures, the fund that backs up insured bank deposits had only one-third the amount of reserves required by law. Unfortunately, even these pathetic figures are probably wildly optimistic. The General Accounting Office, the investigative arm of Congress and one of the few government organizations capable of doing credible research, said that the FDIC fund probably only had one-fifth of the legally required reserves and, worse yet, predicted the fund could be $5 billion in the red by the beginning of 1992. In an even starker assessment of the FDIC insurance fund, a private research company that assigns safety ratings to banks, Veribanc, Inc., claims that if the FDIC truly recognized banks' problem loans and other problems, the bank-insurance fund could be $4 billion to $8 billion in the hole. By the summer of 1991, things were looking so bad that the head of the GAO, Charles Bowsher, specifically warned a congressional committee that the FDIC fund might need a large taxpayer bailout. The unavoidable irony: The fund that doles out money to repay depositors when a bank fails is itself in need of a handout.

The U.S. Treasury Has Been Trying to Cut Back Deposit Insurance: Now, just when consumers are most worried about the safety of bank deposits, the brain trust at the U.S. Treasury spent much of last year trying to convince Congress to cut back on deposit insurance and, in some cases, *eliminate it entirely*. As this book went to press, Congress was balking about going along with most of the Treasury Department's recommendations to scale back deposit insurance. But since there is always the chance that some version of these cutbacks might make it into law—if not now, perhaps in the future—it's important that you understand these proposals and how they affect the safety of your money. This book will examine the potential reductions in deposit insurance and tell you how to protect your money under almost any scenario Congress might conjure up.

Insurance Companies Are Looking More and More Like an S&L Disaster Waiting to Happen: Remember when you thought of insurance companies as anchors of financial stability? Institutions as solid as the Rock of Gibraltar? No more. Bad junk-bond investments and lousy real-estate loans have become a ticking time bomb at many insurance companies. In July 1991, we saw the largest insurance-company collapse ever in the U.S. when mounting losses in real-estate loans led the New Jersey Insurance Commissioner to seize Mutual Benefit Life, a Newark-based insurer with $13.5 billion in assets. The commissioner immediately froze cash withdrawals on individual policies for an indefinite period. Some 400,000 individuals had policies with the company and another 200,000 or more were in pensions funded by Mutual Benefit annuities. Mutual Benefit's demise followed by just two months the 3 failure of another major insurer, Los Angeles–based $13 billion First

Executive Corporation, which caved in under the weight of hundreds of millions of dollars' worth of losses in junk bonds. The result: hundreds of thousands of people whose own savings or pensions were invested with First Executive's insurance subsidiaries initially suffered a 30 percent cut in their pension and annuity payments. How much policyholders will ultimately lose is still uncertain. Mutual Benefit and First Executive aren't alone. Other large insurance companies, including at least one industry giant, are skating on thin financial ice. So what does that mean to you? A lot if you own a whole-life-insurance policy or annuity or if, like millions of workers, you have retirement money invested in guaranteed investment contracts issued by insurers.

Money-Market Funds Are Cracking at the Seams: Safety and high returns—that's the irresistible combination money-market funds have touted for years. But, to woo new investors into money-market funds (which, in turn, leads to higher fees for the companies who run these funds), some funds have been sacrificing the safety side of that combination. Within the last two years, more than a dozen funds have seen securities they own go into default. So far shareholders haven't lost money because the fund company has reimbursed them or earnings have erased the loss. The Securities and Exchange Commission has tightened the rules a bit; still, several money-fund experts predict that losses can—and will—eventually occur.

Even Supposedly Risk-Free Treasury Money Funds Aren't Totally Safe: To capitalize on savers' fears about safety, mutual-fund companies have been aggressively marketing—and investors have been flocking to—funds that hold only government securities. But many of the savers desperately seeking safety probably don't know that even Treasury funds can lose money and that some supposedly pure Treasury-bill funds actually *hold no Treasuries at all.*

Given this age of uncertainty, a time when the safety of even the most secure investments is being called into question, it's important to develop a safe savings strategy—that is, a strategy that emphasizes safety without sacrificing a reasonable return. And if you are dealing with money that you definitely cannot afford to lose—retirement savings you'll need in a few years, money for a house down payment, college tuition funds, savings for an emergency, mad money you've put aside for the day you decide never to return to work from lunch—then the need to practice safe savings is even more crucial.

This book will help you develop a safe saving strategy in three ways. First, it will alert you to hidden risks, both large and small, in supposedly unassailable safe havens. Only by knowing what those risks are can you decide whether you are being adequately rewarded for taking them or, indeed, whether you want to take such risks at all.

Second, you will learn how to evaluate the safety and stability of banks, insurance companies, and money-market funds. This will help you identify those institutions and investments you can feel comfortable doing business with—and shun those that exceed your appetite for risk.

Finally, this book will highlight institutions and investments that have been thoroughly examined and judged safe by appropriate experts.

Does that mean this book will give you a 100 percent iron-clad guarantee against all risk? Of course not. No one, not even the almighty U.S. government, can guarantee to wipe away all risk, nor would you want all risk eliminated, as you'll see at the end of this chapter. But this book can help you avoid risks you weren't otherwise aware of and, in so doing, make your savings and investments far safer.

To fully understand, however, why safe saving will become so important in the 1990s, you've got to go back for a moment to the 1980s, when safety was the last thing anyone thought about when investing money.

MOPPING UP THE EIGHTIES MESS

After any wild party, there's usually lots of cleaning up to do. The traditional morning-after-the-bash routine of rounding up half-empty beer bottles, wiping glass rings off the top of your $3,000 Ethan Allen Early American dining-room table and vacuuming potato chip and Ritz Cracker crumbs off your prize Bokhara rug.

Well, in a financial sense, the 1980s weren't much different from a wild, debauched decade-long party. Intoxicated with the lure of easy profits, companies and corporate raiders took over other companies, expanded wildly into areas of business they knew little or nothing about. To finance their spending spree, they issued billions of dollars in what they insisted were perfectly safe "high-yield" bonds but the rest of the world rightly called junk bonds. Banks, insurance companies, and savings-and-loan associations got into the act, too, investing in those junk bonds, making loans to ridiculously overextended companies, and plowing money into ill-conceived speculative real-estate schemes. There were a few lone voices in the financial community who warned that all this would come to no good. But, if the junk bonds failed, the corporate raiders were off the hook because it wasn't their money that would be lost. Those losses went to the people who bought the junk bonds. And the investment bankers who were selling the junk were raking in billions—so they weren't about to expose the junk-bond market for the Ponzi scheme it often was. By the time the 1980s blowout reached its height, the financial community's fundamental values had become so twisted that the people who were the equivalent of the party animal who dances on a table with a lampshade on his head were revered, almost beatifed. Think back for a moment. Drexel Burnham junk-bond king Michael Milken was thought of as a financial whiz kid, not a soon-to-be convicted felon with a bad toupee. And, ridiculous as it now seems, many otherwise sane people actually considered Donald Trump a visionary entrepreneur, not somebody who couldn't just say no when borrowing money.

The upshot of all this is that the 1980s debauchery called for an industrial-strength cleanup. Companies that assured everyone they could make good on their promise to repay their debt were now defaulting on their junk bonds. An astounding number of banks and S&Ls could be placed into three categories: failed, failing, and hoping desperately not to fail. Insurance companies were also wobbly because, during the 1980s fling, they giddily consumed junk bonds and made foolish real-estate loans that have come back to give them a very severe financial hangover.

But, you may object, you didn't go to this party. You didn't buy junk bonds. You didn't invest in vacant office towers in Houston or Dallas. You didn't ask Donald Trump to build that Castle of Kitsch, the Taj Mahal. No, you stuck with good old boring bank certificates of deposit or, feeling a bit venturesome, maybe stuck some spare cash in a money-market fund or stashed retirement money into a deferred annuity. So, surely, you shouldn't be dragged into this mess and, worse yet, be asked to pay for it. Only the scoundrels and incompetents who caused the damage or the lunatics who tried to capitalize on the 1980s mass hysteria should have to face the consequences.

Unfortunately the harsh reality is that almost anyone can get hurt in the fallout from the 1980s madness. All you need is a savings account or CD in a bank that fails, or shares in a money-market fund that owns securities of a company that defaults on its debts or a whole-life-insurance policy or annuity with an insurance company that played in the junk-bond pile or rushed into risky commercial real-estate mortgages. It's that simple for what happens on Wall Street to come back and haunt Main Street.

Let's take a look at a few people who were inadvertently sucked into the financial black hole created by the roaring eighties.

A BANK FLEECES ITS CUSTOMERS

A gift from heaven. That's exactly what Mabel Dickson, a retiree in her early sixties living in Cahokia, Illinois, thought she'd received four years ago when an officer of Germania Bank, a savings-and-loan association in St. Louis, phoned her at home to tell her about a wonderful deal being reserved for special customers of the bank. If she merely switched her money out of federally insured certificates of deposit yielding 7 percent and into the bank's uninsured subordinated notes paying 11 percent, Mabel could earn thousands of dollars a year more in interest. When Mabel went down to Germania to check out this incredible deal, she found the bank lobby plastered with posters touting the 11 percent rate. To make the subordinated notes more palatable to savers like Mabel, the bank had even given them a cute name: "schnotes." It sounded better, more cuddly, less like a potentially dangerous investment than "subordinated notes." Then, right there in the lobby, a helpful bank representative took out his calculator and punched in the numbers to show Mabel that she could earn exactly $600 a month more in interest than she was currently earning on her CDs. *Six hundred a month!*

Recovering from cancer of the lymph system and facing medical costs upwards of $4,200 a year, Mabel was anxious to stretch her savings. So the extra cash looked awfully good. Still, she didn't want to sacrifice the safety of the money she had earned during some twenty years running a restaurant and a doughnut shop. "I told him I was sick and couldn't afford to lose a penny of my money," says Mabel. "He assured me over and over again that it was safe, that Germania was doing real well and needed the money to build more branches."

Trusting the word of a representative of the one-hundred-year-old bank with whom she and her father before her had banked most of their lives, Mabel moved her money out of federally insured CDs and into the "schnotes." Eventually she poured every cent she had saved for retirement—some $229,000 in all—into the Germania bonds.

Unfortunately what she originally considered a heavenly gift turned her life into a hellish nightmare. Three years later, in June 1990, Mabel received a note from the Resolution Trust Corporation, the federal regulators overseeing the S&L bailout, telling her that interest payments on the schnotes had been frozen. Huge losses in real-estate loans had so depleted the bank's capital that RTC took over management of the bank.

Now, as she struggles by on her Social Security payments, her life savings gone, Mabel Dickson questions whether there's *any* financial institution out there she can truly place her faith in. "If you can't trust a bank," wonders Mabel, "who in this world can you trust?"

Good question. And one that, in the case of Germania, Mabel is unfortunately not alone in asking. It turns out Mabel was not the only person who had been lured into the bonds with promises of no risk and high returns. Ralph Asbury, a fifty-seven-year-old former steelworker, and his wife, Dorothy, fifty-one, put $5,000 into the notes. "The salesman assured us that it was safe and that the bank wasn't having any financial problems," says Dorothy Asbury. "But I kept asking 'What if?' And he said if anything did happen we still didn't have to worry because we'd get our money back before the stockholders in the bank." To persuade another CD customer, Marie Zarlingo, sixty-three, the Germania saleswoman mentioned that Laclede Gas, the local utility company, had invested $5.5 million in the schnotes. The saleswoman also promised that the schnotes would be paid off in three years. "I figured if it was good enough for Laclede and we'd get our money back in three years," says Marie, "then it was safe." She transferred $20,000 from federally insured CDs into the schnotes.

Altogether more than eight hundred bondholders, many of them elderly retirees like Mabel Dickson, the Asburys, and Marie Zarlingo, had invested upwards of $10 million. Many, if not all, feel they have been unfairly victimized, duped by an institution that capitalized on their trust and lured them into the kind of risky investments one usually doesn't associate with a bank. Though Mabel and other bond owners are part of a class action suit to reclaim their savings, it's unclear how much, if any, of their money they will reclaim. And even if the suit is successful, they will inevitably have to shell out some of their settlement to their lawyers. As of June 1991, none of these Germania "schnote" holders had gotten back a cent of their money.

8   Of course, though the Germania schnote holders were clearly victimized by their bank, it's also true that they had strayed beyond fed-

erally insured bank accounts. But even if you stick to institutions and accounts fully covered by federal deposit insurance, there are a variety of ways you can either lose money outright or suffer the emotional trauma of being separated from your savings for extended periods of time. And some unlucky depositors have suffered both these fates.

VICTIMS OF RED TAPE
AND BUREAUCRATIC SNAFUS

In 1985, John Calandro, a financial planner in Dallas, Texas, thought he'd found the perfect low-risk, high-return investment for safety-conscious savers: federally insured CDs paying 10 percent interest a year for ten years at Resource Savings in Denison, Texas, a town near Dallas. The CDs were ideal for conservative clients of his who wanted to stash their cash somewhere safe, yet still get a good, predictable stream of income from it. Altogether, twelve of his clients bought $1 million worth of the CDs. And then, figuring he'd also follow his own advice, Calandro put $250,000 of his own in the Resource CDs. Wary of exceeding the $100,000 federal-deposit-insurance ceiling, Calandro was careful to set up his own and his clients' accounts so they were fully covered. As a financial planner, Calandro also knew that once a client's $100,000 CD began earning interest, the amount over $100,000 would *not* be insured. So, instead of letting the interest accumulate in the $100,000 CD accounts, Calandro set them up so that each month's interest would go directly to the client. This way, the CD balance would slip back to the $100,000 insurance ceiling at the end of each month. "The idea behind the CDs, the fact that they were federally insured and the way that I set them up," says Calandro, "was that they were virtually risk free. It's hard to imagine a safer investment."

But on November 19, 1990, Calandro and his clients received a "Dear Depositor" notice from the Resolution Trust Corporation. The notice said that federal regulators had shut down the thrift and were paying off customers. The notice also noted that depositors could come in the next two days to claim their money in person. Otherwise they could get their money by mail in about two weeks.

Anxious to get his hands on his and his clients' money as soon as possible, Calandro went to the bank at 9 A.M. on November 19. He found a line of depositors already stretched around the block. He joined the line and waited for three hours, until noon, but Resource Savings didn't open. When Calandro returned the next day, the bank was open, but there was also a huge line. Fearful he wouldn't make it into the bank that day—the last day he could personally claim his money—Calandro went back to his office and started calling congressmen to complain about the fact that Resolution Trust obviously didn't have enough staff to handle the large number of depositors. The offices of the congressmen he reached said they couldn't do anything.

In desperation, Calandro went back to Resource Savings at 6:45 that night and pounded on the door until the RTC personnel going over the bank's records let him in. He explained to them that he had $250,000 of his own money and about $1 million of clients' money in the bank and that he wanted it, now! Even though he had proper documentation, the RTC people told him he'd have to claim his money by mail. "At that point, I'd had it," says Calandro. "I told them, 'I'm not leaving until I get the money. You can arrest me, but I'm not leaving.' " Two state policemen standing in the bank seemed more than willing to haul him away and throw him into the slammer. But, wary of the publicity that might result from throwing a depositor in jail, the RTC people huddled together a minute and decided they would return his money. But not his clients'. They wrote out a check for $250,000 to Calandro and told him to beat it. Even though he got the $250,000, he didn't get paid for the $2,000 or so in interest that had accumulated on the CD but had not actually been paid.

Immediately Calandro made sure each of his clients had the proper documentation and filed the correct forms to claim their money. He figured it might take a week, maybe ten days for his clients to get reimbursed. After all, the RTC had been in the business of closing down failed thrifts for quite a while now and must have an organized system for paying off depositors promptly and efficiently. But one week stretched into two and two dragged on to three and suddenly a month had gone by and many of his clients had not gotten a check from the RTC. So Calandro began hounding the RTC officials working at Resource every day, asking them about the status of his clients' accounts. The financial planner quickly found that, even though the RTC had essentially been running Resource for almost a year before they closed it down, the place was a bureaucratic nightmare. Every time he called he got a different story. The check's in the mail; we need more documentation; the check is being processed—no one seemed to know what was really going on. "It was unbelievable to me how disorganized they were," says Calandro. "They were totally incompetent." One day Calandro called and asked to speak to the official overseeing the payout at

Resource Savings only to be told by a temporary employee that no RTC officials would be at Resource for an entire week; they had all been assigned to handle another bank closing in the area. When Calandro specifically asked about the $145,000 claim for one client, the temp said she thought the claim had been processed but she wasn't sure if the check had been mailed.

Finally, after five long weeks, Calandro's clients got their money. "In some cases, the checks had been sitting around the office and the RTC just never got around to sending them out," says Calandro. During the time the RTC sat on roughly $1 million of his clients' money, the twelve clients were paid no interest, not to mention that interest that had accumulated on the accounts but had not been paid had put them over the insurance-ceiling limit. Altogether, in both interest earned but not paid as well as interest lost while the RTC diddled around with the bank records, Calandro figures his clients lost about $12,000—a $12,000 effective loss in insured bank accounts. The episode completely destroyed what little faith Calandro had in government agencies as effective regulators. "These guys were the biggest schmos I ever saw. They had no compassion for people and their organization skills were nil," sums up Calandro. "Overall, it was the biggest circus I've ever seen."

THE MORAL IN ALL THIS

The lesson in the stories of people such as Mabel Dickson and John Calandro is simple. If you're dealing with money that you can't afford to lose, then it's critical that you limit yourself to ultrasafe, highly secure refuges that can survive all manner of economic turmoil—deep recessions, rampant inflation, anything short of financial Armageddon. (Obviously, you will have to periodically monitor the health of these safe havens. After all, the infamous Charles Keating's Lincoln Savings was once a healthy, thriving savings-and-loan association before it was run into the ground at a cost of $2 billion to U.S. taxpayers.)

Exactly which type of safe haven you choose will depend both on your tolerance for risk and your financial goals. For the cash you'll need for immediate use or emergencies, a top-quality bank or money-market fund is probably the best place. If you think interest rates are headed down, you may want to lock up a high rate with a CD at a safe bank. If you're convinced rates are headed up, then you're better off in a high-quality money-market fund whose rate of return will track that of rising interest rates. For longer-term goals, such as saving for retirement, you may want to consider a low-risk tax-deferred single-premium annuity, which has the advantage of letting your money earn interest free of taxes until withdrawal. (Besides income tax, there's a 10 percent penalty if you withdraw your money before age 59½.)

Of course, in the case of banks at least, even if you screw up and choose one that bites the dust, you will still have federal deposit insurance to bail you out—assuming, of course, that your bank or credit union *is* federally insured (not all are) and that the type of account you have is actually covered by federal insurance (banks are pushing more noninsured products than ever before) and that the amount of money in your account or accounts doesn't exceed the federal-insurance ceiling. These conditions are becoming even murkier than ever because of the current move to overhaul the nation's banking system as well as the federal deposit-insurance program. Thus, while it's nice to have federal deposit insurance and you certainly ought to know the rules so that you're fully covered by it, risk-averse investors realize that, above all, you don't want to put yourself in the position of having to fall back on it. As for those places where the safety net is flimsy or perilously close to the ground or doesn't exist at all—as is the case with insurance companies and money-market funds—then the need to stick to top-tier funds and highly capitalized institutions is even more crucial. This book will not only help you find those institutions, but help you protect your savings by alerting you to the hidden risks in many investments that are being touted as ultrasafe.

THE RISK IN TRYING TO ELIMINATE *ALL* RISK

It is not, repeat *not*, the aim of this book to totally eliminate risk. First of all, that would be impossible. Any move you make with your money involves some kind of risk. Invest $10,000 of your savings in thirty-year Treasury bonds and, assuming the U.S. hasn't been overrun by a Mideast potentate or other foreign power, you're sure of getting your principal back in thirty years. But if you need it *before* then, you are at the mercy of interest rates. When interest rates go up, the value of your Treasury bond goes down. If interest rates go up two percentage points from the time you buy your Treasury bond, you could lose $2,000 when you cash your bond in. (For an explanation of exactly why rising interest rates cause bond prices to fall, see chapter 6.) To avoid that risk you could always stick the $10,000 under your mattress.

Depending on your household arrangements and whether or not virtues like honesty run in your family, it would be there thirty years from now. But inflation would have eroded most of its buying power. Saving and investing, much like living, simply can't be done without taking some risks.

Second, even if you could eliminate risk, it wouldn't be wise to do so. Savvy investors know that by taking on additional risk, you can often earn a higher rate of return and thereby increase your wealth. Investing in stocks, for example, is far riskier than putting your money in short-term CDs, but over periods of twenty or more years, stocks produce far higher returns. Of course, as anyone who's ever watched the value of a stock or mutual fund plummet during a stock-market meltdown, higher risk can backfire too, at least in the short term. That's why smart savers and investors divvy up their money into several baskets of varying risk. This allows them to take advantage of the high rates of return offered by some investments without blowing their entire wad should those investments backfire. This process goes by the grand name of asset allocation, but it's really quite simple. Some baskets represent higher-risk investments like stocks, bonds, or mutual funds that invest in stocks or bonds. Usually that's money you're sure you won't have to dip into for at least three years and more likely five years or so. This is also money with which you can afford a temporary setback because you know that, in time, you'll recoup your losses. The other baskets are reserved for that cash on which you can't afford to take even a temporary loss. The money in this basket goes into things like bank accounts and CDs, money-market funds, and retirement savings vehicles such as deferred annuities and guaranteed investment contracts. *This book deals specifically with that portion of your money you don't want to lose even temporarily—the basket you can't afford to drop.*

No book, despite any claims its cover might make, can eliminate the risk in investing and saving. But this book can do something far more important—let you know when you're taking risks and tell you how to keep them to a minimum.

2

OUR SHAKY BANKING SYSTEM

See the bank. See the bank run.

To most Americans, the idea of a bank run—thousands of panicked depositors descending en masse on a bank to demand their money immediately because they're fearful for its safety—had become little more than a fading memory of an earlier age, an image associated with breadlines, ramshackle Hoovervilles, and other scenes of economic devastation usually glimpsed in grainy newsreel footage from the 1930s Depression. With the Federal Deposit Insurance Corporation protecting individuals' bank accounts, the notion that people would run scared to their banks and flee with their money seemed about as likely to happen today as, say, rock-star Madonna joining a cloistered order of nuns.

But, just as other vestiges of the Depression such as soup kitchens and homelessness have made a comeback, so, too, in the wake of the wild, careless lending spree of the 1980s, have formerly unthinkable bank runs become frightening realities.

In the first weekend of May 1991, for example, depositors at the First National Bank of Toms River, New Jersey, a 110-year-old national bank, swarmed into many of the bank's branches in communities along the New Jersey shore and began cashing in CDs, closing savings accounts, drawing down on checking accounts—in general grabbing as much of their money as possible as quickly as they could. In some branches, the scene approached pandemonium, as long lines of people at tellers' windows and in the lobby clamored for their money. The alarm was triggered by a story in the local newspaper, *The Asbury Park Press*, reporting that a huge write-down of bad real-estate loans had wiped out the bank's capital, putting First National $21 million in the red. In other words, if all the bank's assets were sold at that moment, there wouldn't be enough cash to pay off creditors and depositors. Within a few hours, the run snowballed so quickly, that Kenneth Motz, a lanky, dapper senior vice president of marketing, was dispatched to allay depositors' fears and, most important, to get them to stop pulling out their money! The biggest withdrawals were coming from branches where elderly retirees accounted for the bulk of deposits. "You could look in their eyes and see the fear," says Motz. "Many of these people had their life's savings in the bank and they were afraid of losing their money." So Motz launched into what Donna Flynn, a reporter at *The Asbury Press* who followed Motz from branch to branch one day, called his "George Bailey" spiel. As movie buffs will recall, George Bailey, played by actor Jimmy Stewart, was the owner of a Building and Loan Association on the verge of bankruptcy in the Frank Capra classic, *It's a Wonderful Life*. In one memorable scene in that movie, Jimmy Stewart pleads with the depositors to have faith in the building-and-loan association and to limit their withdrawals to only what they need to get by on for the next few days.

Motz's plea wasn't too different. "I climbed up behind the teller's windows and basically told people that their money was safe and that there was no cause for panic," says Motz. "Then I walked among them and reassured them that it wasn't all doom and gloom." Motz delivered his spiel at about fifteen branches in two days, speeding from one to the next with reporter Flynn and her photographer doing their best to keep up with the fast-moving, smooth-talking banker. "It was actually kind of scary at times," says Flynn of Motz's run from bank to bank. "He was doing fifty-five miles an hour in forty-mile-an-hour zones on these rain-slicked roads and we were trying to keep up. At one point, I looked at my photographer and said, 'This guy's going to get us both killed.' "

Despite his ambitious driving, Ken Motz's pitch wasn't nearly as effective as Jimmy Stewart's. Maybe it was because Motz didn't have Jimmy Stewart's downhome aw-shucks charm, or because First National's depositors weren't trusting, forgiving souls like the movie characters in Bedford Falls, or maybe it's just because Motz didn't have the benefit of a Frank Capra script. Whatever the reason, First National's run didn't have a happy Hollywood ending. In just four days, account holders sucked $75 million in deposits out of the bank. First National submitted a plan to raise capital to the Office of the Comptroller of the Currency, the federal agency that regulates national banks, but the plan was rejected. On May 22, the FDIC closed the bank and on May 23, First National was acquired by First Fidelity Bank of Newark.

While a run spurred by retirees at a relatively small and hapless New Jersey bank might lead one to question the competence of its managers, it certainly wouldn't shake one's faith in the banking system as a whole. Except that First National was neither the only, nor the most publicized incident of the year. At the beginning of 1991, a much, much larger bank underwent a much, much larger run. The Bank of New England, once part of the thirtieth-largest banking company in the country, suffered a similar fate on Friday, January 4, after the bank announced an expected $450 million loss for the last quarter of 1990—a loss large enough to wipe out its equity, which is its cushion against further losses. But this was a major-league run. Over the course of two days, everyone from individual depositors to large corporations withdrew an estimated $1 billion in deposits. Some customers were reportedly carrying out brief-cases and pocketbooks bulging with cash.

Wait a minute. What's going on here? The whole idea behind launching the Federal Deposit Insurance Corporation in 1933 was to prevent runs and the crises of confidence among depositors that cause them. And for more than fifty years the system worked. People understood that occasionally a bank might fail, but that the U.S. government stood behind the bank ready to pay off depositors whose accounts were federally insured.

But recently that sense of trust, the feeling that despite problems now and again everything was basically all right, began to erode. In a *Time* Magazine/CNN poll taken in January 1991, for example, only 7 percent of the one thousand adults surveyed said they felt very confident about the soundness of U.S. banks while 59 percent claimed they were only somewhat confident or not confident at all. And once that bond of trust between depositors and their banks begins to unravel, the public's confidence in a bank can snap faster than you can fill out a withdrawal slip. Suddenly, in the face of negative press coverage or mere rumors of trouble, people began to wonder if, maybe, even though there is deposit insurance, just maybe they might be better off simply clearing out of a bank that seemed to be headed for problems.

16

One indication of just how jittery depositors can get occurred in early

January 1991 when the governor of Rhode Island shut down forty-five banks and credit unions because of problems at a state-chartered deposit insurance company (For more details on the Rhode Island fiasco, see chapter 5). When reporting on Rhode Island's banking crisis, Cable News Network used videotape of a branch of Old Stone Bank as a backdrop. Even though Old Stone Bank was not in trouble and, since it was federally insured, not connected in any way to the Rhode Island mess, the mere association of its name with the state's banking crisis caused a mini-run on the bank.

While Old Stone Bank was obviously the victim of faulty judgment by CNN and snap decisions by fearful depositors, some people, bankers in particular, also consider the runs at places like the Bank of New England or First National Bank of Toms River as the knee-jerk reactions of unsophisticated depositors. After all, bankers argue, why pull your money out of an institution if it's covered by federal insurance? That's irrational! But is it? "I don't think it's irrational at all," says Warren Heller, president of Veribanc, Inc., a Wakesfield, Massachusetts, company that rates the safety of banks, savings-and-loan associations, and credit unions across the country. "Even if my money is insured—and it's possible not all of it is—why should I go through all the hassles of a bank shutdown? I don't want to go to the ATM on Friday night and not be able to get my money out. I don't want to have checks bounce, have to open up new accounts and reorder checks. These are hassles most people would just as soon avoid."

WHO CAN YOU TRUST?

While no one is suggesting that bank runs will become as commonplace in the 1990s as they were in the early 1930s when some eleven thousand or so banks permanently closed their doors, a fundamental change has clearly taken place in the way people think of financial institutions, including banks. A bank used to be a place you approached with more than a little trepidation, much like a child approaches a stern parent. You went into a bank almost as a supplicant, hoping you could convince the bankers you were worthy of their trust. Now, the reverse is more likely true. It's the bank's reputation that's in question and the bank must prove its trustworthiness to you. And in extreme cases, à la Motz and First National, the bank might even be reduced to pleading with you to stick with it, to trust the bank, to give it another chance, 17 please.

Given this reversal of fortunes, it's time to adopt a safe savings strategy when dealing with banks and savings-and-loan associations. The aim: to eliminate as much risk as you can to assure that your money is totally safe—namely, that it is covered by federal deposit insurance and sits in a bank or savings-and-loan association that isn't going to tumble when the first economic ill wind blows.

The first step in that strategy is to get a better idea of the ills afflicting our banking system as well as the FDIC's bank-deposit-insurance fund and to understand why both seem so hell-bent on self-destruction. The rest of this chapter will fill you in on that. Now that Congress and the U.S. Treasury have begun toying with the critical insurance that covers bank accounts, it's a good time to review the current rules, examine how those rules might be changed now or in the future, and look at ways of keeping your money safe under almost any deposit-insurance program Congress is likely to come up with. Then, in chapter 3, you'll learn to evaluate the safety of banks so you can choose the safest ones— those least likely to become casualties of the banking crisis. By sticking to the most solid institutions, you should be able to sidestep the hassles of dealing with a failed bank. That way you won't have to be one of the guinea pigs who has to test how well and how quickly deposit insurance works.

WHAT'S BEHIND THE RISING TIDE OF BANK FAILURES?

There's a good reason very few people in that *Time*/CNN poll could muster up any confidence in their bank. The fact is that banks have lurched from one crisis to another during the last decade. In the 1980s and early 1990s, banks have been failing at the fastest clip since the Great Depression. From 1934, the year the Federal Deposit Insurance Corporation commenced operations, through 1990, a total of 1,701 banks in the U.S. failed. But get this: Some 1,300 of those failures took place after 1979. In other words, of all the bank failures that took place during the last fifty-seven years, more than 75 percent occurred in the 1980s and 1990. What's more, though that frenetic pace may have peaked in 1988 and 1989, years in which more than 200 banks collapsed, many more sick banks will expire in the years ahead. In early 1991, the FDIC projected that 340 banks would fail in 1991 and 1992. But we already know that number is too low. In June 1991, the FDIC revised that projection upward to 440 failures. Even that number could be too

18

modest. In 1991, the FDIC's list of troubled banks—those operating with a very low capital margin, or facing heavy losses or saddled with a high percentage of bad loans—had 1,046 institutions on it. In other words, as of 1991 there were 1,044 banks that the FDIC felt were in bad enough shape that they deserved special scrutiny. Of course, if this torrent of failures were happening at a time when all was going well with the rest of our financial system it would be alarming enough. But, as we well know from our tax bill, the banks' troubles come on top of a worse problem with the S&Ls. In the 1980s, roughly 1,200 S&Ls failed or were taken over by other institutions. What's more, even as Congress pumps more money into the S&L bailout, thrift institutions continue to founder. Of the 2,543 S&Ls still in existence as of the end of 1990, 523 were "liquidation insolvent" according to Veribanc. Which means that if all the thrifts in the country were closed down and their assets sold, one-fifth of them wouldn't have enough cash to pay off their depositors and other creditors.

How did the banks get in such terrible shape, especially considering the S&L fiasco was already a huge red warning flag? How did bankers, during a decade marked by prosperity and the biggest stock-market boom in history, manage to run a relatively healthy industry into the ground? To be fair to the banks, some of the problems that helped do them in during the hectic eighties weren't of their own making. In some ways, banks, like dinosaurs, were the innocent victims of a radical change in their environment, although, in the case of banks, that change wasn't a shifting of polar ice caps but a basic change in the way companies financed their activities. In the good old days, when a blue-chip company needed to borrow money, it met its friendly banker at the club or on the golf course, and they worked out a loan, usually at the going prime rate. The result was a tidy, relatively risk-free profit for the bank. But in the 1970s and even more so in the 1980s, companies found they could borrow more cheaply by sidestepping the banks and going directly to Wall Street. There, companies issued commercial paper—basically a corporate IOU—or long-term bonds, sometimes junk bonds. As banks found themselves being deserted by their best customers, they had to go out and drum up new ones, often customers the banks might have previously considered too risky. Some new customers the banks came up with were Third World countries—places like Brazil, Mexico, and Argentina—to whom they lent billions in the 1970s. By the 1980s, these countries had defaulted on much of that debt, racking up considerable 19 losses for the banks.

These losses didn't break the banks, but they did put pressure on bankers to drum up new business that could recoup the losses and invigorate the banks' financial health. So, in search of quick profits, the banks effectively joined forces with Michael Milken and other junk-bond wizards and tried to capitalize on the wave of takeovers, corporate raids, and restructurings that swept Wall Street in the 1980s. You see, in a typical corporate takeover, junk bonds alone couldn't provide all the financing necessary to complete the transaction. That's where the banks came in. They made up the shortfall with bank loans. Because these deals were generally risky and involved huge amounts of debt, they were called "highly leveraged transactions" and became better known simply as HLTs. Unfortunately, when billions of dollars in defaults rocked the junk-bond market in 1989 and 1990, the HLTs didn't turn out to be the savior bankers once thought they would be. Still, the banks did manage to get good collateral on their loans this time—as opposed to Third World loans, where the collateral was essentially the country's word. So, even though the HLT loans didn't bail out the banks, they didn't drown them, either. No, that task was left to the loans that really did banks in—commercial real-estate loans.

In the go-go eighties, real-estate prices, particularly in the Northeast, began to go crazy. As prices spiraled ever upward, lemming-like, real-estate developers began putting up office buildings, shopping centers, malls, apartment buildings, industrial parks, any structure that could be rented out, as fast as they could get the money to build. Now, this kind of mindless herd mentality is expected of real-estate developers. They're like very young children whose appetite is limited only by what they can get their grubby little hands on. It is a well-known fact that developers will build and keep on building until they spoil their own market with a glut of new developments. In this sense, Donald Trump is only the best-known example of the species, not its worst offender.

But the standard for bankers is supposed to be higher. They are supposed to provide the voice of reason. They are supposed to bring developers' fantasies up short with a dose of reality. They are, after all, lending *your* money. But in the 1980s a funny thing happened. The bankers in many cases outfantasized (if that's even a word) the real-estate developers. The bankers opened up their coffers and poured money into office buildings, condo projects, shopping centers, casinos, and hotels. No project, it seemed, was too big or too small, too risky or too outright dumb. Banks were actually elbowing each other out of the way to make loans that, in a saner era, would have been rejected flat out. "They worked on the assumption that real estate will never decline in value," says Paul Bauer, owner of the Bauer Group, a company that monitors the performance of banks and assigns them safety ratings. "The banks were too interested in growth. They made loans on questionable appraisals that inflated the value of the real estate. They thought it would be all right, though, because they never expected the bubble to burst. But when it did they got caught with real estate that wasn't worth what they thought it was." The real irony here is that these freewheeling, shoot from the hip banks willing to lend millions on risky real-estate ventures were the same institutions that require thirty-eight pages of documentation and financial disclosure if you so much as want a $10,000 college tuition loan fully secured by your car, home, and all other tangible possessions. By the time 1990 dragged to an end, banks had made some $969 billion or so in real-estate loans—of which $45 billion were behind in payments or in default and on which the banks had repossessed about $25 billion worth of property.

While much of the current banking crisis can be traced to lousy management and bad loans, banks weren't exactly slouches when it came to good old fraud, self-dealing, and other shadowy practices. A 1991 General Accounting Office investigation of thirty-nine banks that failed in 1988 and 1989, for example, noted that at one failed bank "regulators attributed the bank's high losses to insider abuses with possible organized-crime connections. Fraudulent activity, falsification of records, and a $5 million kiting operation [kiting is a fraudulent check scheme] were also cited." GAO went on to say that this bank's current and former presidents were arrested for money laundering and other illegal acts and were removed from the bank in handcuffs. In other cases, bank directors—the people who have a fiduciary duty to safeguard the bank's assets—helped push an ailing bank over the edge into insolvency. In several of the failing banks, for example, directors voted to continue dividend payments on the bank's stock even though the payments exceeded the bank's income. In some cases, dividends were paid even when the bank had a loss. While this practice zapped the bank's capital and made bankruptcy almost a certainty, the dividend policy did benefit someone—the directors who also happened to be major stockholders in the bank and, therefore, got the dividends.

True, U.S. banks have yet to produce anyone comparable to the Charles Keatings or David Pauls or other sleazeballs who oozed out of the S&L debacle. But the banks are trying. In one of the biggest banking scandals since the S&L days, the largest bank in Washington,

D.C., First American Bankshares, was being investigated for allegedly having been secretly controlled by a shadowy foreign bank, the Bank of Credit and Commerce International (BCCI), otherwise known as the Bank of Crooks and Criminals International. What makes the First American–BCCI tale especially juicy is that it's got something for everyone: international intrigue (former Panamanian dictator–drug runner Manuel Noriega laundered his drug money through BCCI); ties to U.S. intelligence and terrorists (the CIA banked at BCCI and the organization of Palestinian terrorist Abu Nidal allegedly operated out of BCCI's London office); and, a necessity for any Washington, D.C., story, a political angle (Clark Clifford, an adviser to several Democratic presidents, was chairman of First American and claimed he didn't know there was a link between First American and BCCI). As of August 1991, startling revelations were still unfolding about the BCCI empire—the U.S. National Security Agency allegedly funneled money for the Iran-Contra deals through BCCI, for example—so the chances are good the banks will come through with a riveting financial scandal with a D.C. twist that will rank right up there with the best of the S&L scams.

JUST WHAT HAPPENS WHEN A BANK GOES BELLY UP?

Considering that more than a thousand banks with several million depositors have failed in the 1980s and early 1990s alone—and given that hundreds more banks and possibly millions more depositors will go through this financial trauma in the next few years—it pays to take a look at exactly what takes place when the bank goes bust. This way, should you be unfortunate enough to have an account in a failing bank, you'll know what to expect and how to get your money back as quickly and painlessly as possible. The FDIC has three basic ways of dealing with a failed bank. Here's a brief explanation of each.

Purchase and assumption: This procedure, which is used in about 85 percent of all bank failures, is the easiest and most effort-free for depositors. The FDIC finds a healthy bank to assume *all* the deposits, both insured and uninsured, of the failing bank. In other words, all your accounts are covered, insured or not. But even then the process isn't completely pain free. Usually the FDIC swoops in and closes the bank on a Friday, which means you probably lose access to your money over the weekend at the very least. Many people find this out when they try, unsuccessfully, to get cash from an ATM. In the best-case scenario, the acquiring bank would have all the accounts of the failed bank up and running by Monday. Which means you would have access to your accounts then—either at the same branch where you banked before or at branches of the acquiring bank. Also, any checks you wrote on your old account before it shut down should continue to clear through the acquiring bank. If the accounts of the bankrupt bank are in horrible shape, however, it could take the FDIC and the acquiring bank longer to straighten out the records and during that time you would not have access to your money, nor would checks clear. Most purchase and assumptions do go off pretty smoothly, though.

Even if the procedure unwinds without a hitch, however, you should be prepared for a few unpleasant surprises, such as having the interest rate on CDs and other accounts lowered. The acquiring bank can even put your money into a low-interest-rate passbook savings account or a checking account that pays no interest. If the interest rate on a CD, for example, is not lowered, you do *not* have the right to withdraw your money from the acquiring bank without paying any penalties that might apply. The theory here is that the new bank is sticking with the deal the old bank offered you, so you, too, must abide by the old deal.

Deposit transfer: Under this arrangement, used in about 10 percent of failures, the deposit accounts in your failing bank are transferred to a healthy bank. Unlike in a purchase and assumption, however, only *insured* deposits are transferred in a deposit transfer. If you have $125,000 in a CD, for example, you would only get $100,000 of it. As with a purchase and assumption, the acquiring bank would continue to clear your checks. In a deposit transfer, however, the new bank won't automatically open accounts for you. Your money has only been parked there temporarily. If you want to establish accounts, you'll have to sign up the same as any other new customer (In a purchase and assumption, you don't have to do anything if you want to keep your money in the new bank.) The acquiring bank has the right to lower the interest rate on your accounts and you have the right to withdraw your money if they do. In fact, unlike a purchase and assumption, you can withdraw your money without penalty even if the bank keeps the same rate you had before. The reason is that the new bank is only being used as a convenient way to pay off depositors of the failing bank. The new bank isn't actually acquiring the deposits.

Depositor payoff: This is the most troublesome process for depositors, which, thankfully, is used in only about 5 percent of failures. In a depositor payoff, the FDIC shuts down the bank and then, usually within a few days, opens it up and pays off depositors by check for *insured* deposits only. Depositor payoffs can involve hours of standing on line to get your money and, possibly, considerable haggling with the FDIC over exactly how much is owed you and how much is insured. In the meantime, any checks you wrote on the account in the failed bank will bounce. So if you had written a check to pay your credit card bill or some other creditor, chances are those creditors will charge you a returned-check fee.

The fastest way to get your money is to go to your bank and get a check from the FDIC. To do that, you will need two forms of identification with your signature (a driver's license, passport, Social Security card, voter registration, or even a credit card) as well as any original documents for your accounts—a CD certificate, your last checking statement, or your savings-account passbook. If the account is a joint account and both account holders' signatures must appear on checks or withdrawal slips, then both must show up to claim the money. If only one signature is needed to make withdrawals or write checks, then only one person has to come to the bank to claim the money.

If you are an out-of-state depositor or can't get to the bank for some other reason, you can file your claim by mail. To claim more than $50 in deposits, you must send a *notarized* insurance claim form to the claim agent in charge of the closed bank. The FDIC can provide you with the form and the name and address of the claim agent. The FDIC usually takes a *minimum* of ten days to process these mail claims, so, counting time in the mail both ways, you may not have access to your money for two weeks or longer.

By the time the bank reopens to pay off depositors, the FDIC will already have come up with a list of what each person is owed. So you should be prepared to challenge their assessment—and document your own—if their figures and yours don't agree. Before they'll give you a check for your money, you must sign a statement that says you agree with their balance. If you disagree with what the FDIC says it owes you, you should be able to accept the amount they offer and then file a claims dispute for the rest. The FDIC representative at the bank can tell you how to file this claim, or you can call the FDIC's Consumer Affairs Department at 800-424-5488 or write to 550 17th Street N.W., Washington, D.C. 20429.

If you have uninsured money in the bank—for example, $50,000 of a $150,000 CD—you will receive a Receiver's Certificate for that amount. A Receiver's Certificate is basically a fancy way of saying you have a claim, along with other creditors, against the bank's assets when the bank is liquidated. The prospects for full payment of a Receiver's Certificate are slim, and getting even a small portion of your money can drag out for several years.

In the case of a failed savings-and-loan association or savings bank, the Resolution Trust Corporation handles the closing. The procedures are similar to those used by the FDIC, although Resolution Trust has been so deluged by closings and other details of dealing with the S&L meltdown that there's a much greater possibility of delays ranging from several days to several weeks before you get your money. In other words, even though you will eventually get your cash, you might have to endure a harrowing period of several weeks during which you don't have access to your money and your cash earns no interest, as was the case with John Calandro and his clients at Resource Savings in Texas.

ALL DEPOSITORS ARE NOT CREATED EQUAL: The Cases of Harlem's Freedom National and Boston's Bank of New England

Which of these three methods the FDIC or RTC chooses—and whether all the deposits in a bank or only insured deposits will be covered—depends to a large extent on which bank you're talking about. Quite simply, all banks—and therefore all depositors—are not created equal when it comes to government bailouts. In some banks, *all* depositors are fully protected, whether their accounts are insured or not. In others, only the insured depositors get full protection. So the U.S. government plays favorites when it comes to bailing out banks and protecting customers. This perfectly legal policy of letting some depositors lose money and protecting others from loss was illustrated last year in the very different ways the FDIC handled the failures of Freedom National Bank in Harlem and Bank of New England in Boston.

When Freedom National Bank, a small Harlem bank originally launched by a group of investors including former baseball player Jackie Robinson, failed in November 1990 after years of severe financial problems, the FDIC decided to liquidate the bank and adhere strictly to the $100,000 deposit insurance limit. The FDIC initially refused to pay off some $15 million in uninsured deposits, much of which was held in accounts owned by charities. As a result, organizations such as the United Negro College Fund and the National Urban League faced huge potential losses. Under intense political pressure, the FDIC eventually agreed to cover 50 cents on the dollar on many uninsured deposits.

But when the $22-billion behemoth Bank of New England in Boston failed just two months later, the FDIC not only stepped in to back insured deposits, but promised to make good on almost $17 billion in *uninsured* deposits as well. The Bank of New England bailout will eventually cost the FDIC some $2.3 billion, making it the third most costly bailout in U.S. banking history (so far).

Hmm. Uninsured depositors in small Harlem bank face losses. Uninsured depositors in big Boston bank suffer a Maalox moment, but then are fully protected. Understandably, several politicians and consumer groups immediately jumped all over the FDIC, claiming the agency was grossly unfair. There were even hints that the agency might be guilty of racial discrimination. But these allegations only muddle an already complicated issue. Many people readily concede the basic inequity of what occurred. "It's clearly unfair to shaft people at Freedom National and tell them they're only protected to fifty cents on the dollar while other uninsured depositors are fully protected," Robert Litan, a former bank regulator and now a senior fellow at the Brookings Institution, told an audience at a banking-reform conference in Washington, D.C., in the spring of 1991. After all, why should your deposit-insurance coverage be different just because you happen to do business with a smaller bank? Rules should be rules, and applying the same rules differently to different people *is* unfair.

But allegations of racial discrimination miss the point. The FDIC *did discriminate* against Freedom National. Not because it was a black-owned bank in poor Harlem, however, but because it is *small*. And the fact is that the U.S. has had a long-standing policy of making sure that depositors in big banks don't suffer big losses when that bank fails. This policy is known as TBTF or "too big to fail" and the reason it came about was to prevent a major crisis of confidence in our banking system. Large banks often depend on uninsured deposits—that is, deposits in checking accounts, CDs, and other accounts in excess of $100,000—for the bulk of their money. These deposits come from large companies, individuals, the U.S. government, cities and towns, and other banks. The theory goes that if a big bank failed and uninsured depositors 26 suffered major losses, it could trigger a domino effect that would send our banking system into a tailspin. Companies with deposits in the failing bank might be unable to pay creditors or make their payroll. Other banks with deposits in the failing bank might be pushed into bankruptcy too. The bad publicity and hysteria generated by such a calamity could lead to major runs on banks that would worsen the problem and possibly lead to a meltdown not just of the banking system but of our entire financial system, much like what happened in the 1930s. In other words, the failure of one large bank, if allowed to rage out of control, could lead to carnage on Wall Street and eventually become a nightmare on Main Street in cities and towns across the country. To prevent such an apocalypse, the FDIC is given the authority to protect uninsured depositors in cases where *not* doing so could jeopardize the economy overall or the economy of a particular region.

All right, so you see the sense of protecting big banks. But why, you may ask, don't we extend this largess to *all* depositors, regardless of the size of the bank? There are several reasons. One is that the total liabilities for deposit insurance would be too great. Now, the FDIC backs about $2 *trillion* in deposits. Adding uninsured deposits would increase the FDIC's total liabilities by 45 percent, bringing the total to almost $3 trillion. At a time when the financial system is already shaky, the idea is to cut back on potential liabilities, not add to them. Another reason our government doesn't just back all deposits is that it could create another S&L-like horror show. If bankers knew that all their deposits were insured no questions asked, they would take more risks with that money because the government, not the banks, would have to absorb losses. (Many people point out that this implicit promise by the government to protect big banks is exactly why most big banks are in such horrible shape today.) So the idea is that we limit the number of times all depositors, insured and uninsured, will be protected to those instances where our entire financial system or the economy of an entire region could be seriously hurt if uninsured depositors suffered losses.

All this is a long way of saying that the treatment you get and the risks you face as a depositor may depend not just on deposit-insurance regulations but on *the size of the bank you do business with.* Obviously you get more protection if the FDIC considers your bank "too big to fail" than if your accounts are in some small-fry institution that the FDIC is willing to liquidate. The question is: What size does a bank have to be before the FDIC considers it too big to fail? No one really knows—and the FDIC isn't saying because if it did, smart depositors might move their money to these banks with the assurance that all their money was absolutely safe even if the bank, as many big banks are today, was in absolutely horrible shape. As a result, some of the most poorly run banks would attract the most deposits. In chapter 4, we'll discuss whether you should look to the "too big to fail" doctrine as an extra layer of safety when choosing a bank (the short answer is no!). For now, though, let's move on to how our already precarious banking system is facing yet another, and perhaps its greatest, shock—a new round of government regulation.

WHY BANKING REFORM MAY PUT YOU AT
GREATER RISK

As if things weren't scary enough out there, you've got one more wild card to factor in when gauging the safety of the money you've stashed in bank accounts. And that is that Congress and the Bush administration have decided to fix things. Hold on to your checkbook. After all, Congress and the Reagan administration were the ones whose "cleanup" of the S&L problem in the early 1980s eventually led to the $1 trillion S&L bailout we face today—and will pay for over the next forty years. What, me jaded?

To be fair, we should give Congress a little credit here. At least they're only a few years late turning their attention to the banking crisis instead of almost a decade late as with the S&Ls. But early, on time, or, as usual, fashionably late, the big question is what will Congress do and what immediate and long-term consequences will their actions have? It goes without saying, of course, that anytime 535 members of Congress get involved in an issue, it's going to be decided against a backdrop of competing special interests, political posturing, and intentions ranging from selfless to selfish. In the case of banking reform, the chances of politics prevailing over reason are especially high. For one thing, in the House of Representatives alone there are a slew of committees and subcommittees with overlapping jurisdiction, which always causes trouble. And in the Senate, a large number of senators on the Banking Committee are up for reelection in 1992. Which means they face a quandary. If they actually pass comprehensive banking-reform legislation, there's a serious chance it will be unpopular with the voters. That's a political no-no. But if they don't do anything and the banking crisis gets worse, they'll be criticized for sitting idly by as banks disintegrate. That's a no-no too.

28   The bottom line is that several of the banking-reform initiatives that were being debated in Congress through the summer and fall of 1991

could put your money at even greater risk. Two aspects of banking reform may directly affect the safety of money you keep in a bank: namely, changes in deposit insurance and the move to give banks leeway to expand into businesses from which they are now largely excluded.

Deposit-insurance reform: Concerned that federal deposit-insurance protection has expanded beyond its original mandate of protecting the savings of small depositors, in 1991 the Treasury Department proposed to limit the coverage to $100,000 per person per bank, plus another $100,000 per person per bank for retirement accounts. Under present law, you can have well above $100,000 of insurance in a single bank, provided you understand the often-complicated deposit-insurance regulations. (These rules will be explained in chapter 3.) The Treasury Department also wanted to totally eliminate deposit-insurance coverage on CDs sold through brokers. Understandably, many bank customers cringe at the prospect of such cutbacks, which can have the effect of *increasing* the vulnerability of bank accounts and CDs at a time when the banking system is the most fragile it's been since the Depression. As it adjourned for its 1991 summer vacation Congress appeared unwilling to go along with these specific cutbacks. Still, there is always the possibility some reduction in deposit insurance might make it through at a later date, much the way the home-mortgage deduction has been chipped at by Congress over the years.

Wider bank powers: This part of the proposal defies the imagination. Only inside the Capital Beltway could someone propose something like this in public without fear of being committed to the nearest insane asylum. The gist of the "wider powers" proposals boils down to this: Since banks are having trouble making a profit these days, why not let them expand into areas like the securities, insurance, and real-estate business? The proposals would also allow industrial companies (GM or Ford, say) to own banks.

Never mind the fact that we already tried deregulation along similar lines with thrift institutions in the early 1980s, and we know where that got us. S&Ls got into a bunch of businesses they knew nothing about— junk bonds, commercial lending, real-estate investing—and wound up having to be rescued again, this time with a taxpayer bailout that, according to Veribanc, could run as much as $1 billion. That expensive 29 history lesson alone should be sufficient warning.

But even if you forget history—as the bureaucrats and politicians in Washington seem to have done—any reasonable person would wonder about the wisdom of letting banks get into the securities, insurance, and real-estate industries. Think of it this way. Banks are ailing, so our solution is to let them diversify into the securities industry, which lost $162 million before taxes in 1990 and saw its equity shrink by some $4 *billion*; the insurance industry, which is going through its own recent shake-out of failing companies with First Executive and other large insurance companies going down the tubes; and the real-estate industry, which is in the midst of a slump that could conceivably stretch into the twenty-first century. Why don't they just give banks licenses to manufacture buggy whips to give them a full complement of dead or dying industries?

The risk to you is twofold. First, if banks do get into these areas it will increase the chance that they'll want to sell you things like stocks, bonds, real-estate limited partnerships, and mutual funds. These may be fine investments on their own, but they are not federally insured, a fact that many bank customers may not understand since they're used to getting federally insured CDs and other accounts at banks.

The other risk is that as banks get into these chancy businesses they may very well fail, much as the S&Ls did. That means your deposits are at risk if not fully insured. Even if they are insured you may lose access to them while the regulators pick up the pieces of the failed bank. And if enough banks that go into these new ventures become insolvent, there's a chance that you, as a U.S. taxpayer, might face another S&L-style multibillion-dollar bailout.

Given the current crisis in the banking system and the additional risks banking reform may pose, it's more important than ever to make sure your money is fully protected by deposit insurance. The next chapter will take care of that by explaining everything you need to know about deposit-insurance regulations in this era of banking reform and by helping you adopt a strategy that will protect you even if Congress scales back deposit-insurance coverage. Of course, you're even better off if you never have to test the deposit-insurance system. And the way to do that is by sticking to safe, solid banks that are the least likely to fail. You'll learn how to do that in chapter 4, which also contains state-by-state lists of the strongest banks and S&Ls in the U.S.

3

EVERYTHING YOU NEED TO KNOW ABOUT DEPOSIT INSURANCE

Is the FDIC Insurance Fund Broke? (The Short Answer Is Yes.)

IN 1933, in an uncommon display of good sense, Congress set up the Federal Deposit Insurance Corporation. The new agency's mission was simple: Restore faith in a U.S. banking system that was being ravaged by an avalanche of bank failures in the wake of the 1929 Wall Street crash and the subsequent Great Depression. The FDIC achieved this goal by setting up a deposit-insurance fund—paid for by premiums from the banks themselves—which guaranteed the safety of bank deposits. To give the guarantee some weight, the promise was backed not just by the money in the FDIC fund but by the full faith and credit of the U.S. Treasury—in other words, your tax dollars. Initially only deposits of $2,500 or less were insured, although that gradually grew to the present ceiling of $100,000 (as we'll see in this chapter, you can actually get more than $100,000 of coverage by opening different categories of accounts). For more than half a century this relatively simple setup has worked. FDIC insurance has acted as a safety net to catch bank customers and protect their savings if their bank crashes to the ground.

But in the aftermath of the banks' bunco-game lending mentality of the financially dissolute eighties, that net has become so severely frayed that the failure of one major bank could tear it to shreds. As a result, many bank depositors are beginning to question whether the

FDIC has the resources to actually make good on its guarantees of deposit safety. In fact, there are at least two good reasons to question the FDIC fund's stability. One is the current rash of failures— over a thousand since 1985—that has drained the fund's reserves. By law, the FDIC fund is supposed to have $1.25 for every $100 of insured deposits in the banking system. This is considered an adequate cushion to pay depositors in failed banks and, at the same time, keep the fund solvent to pay off depositors in future failures. But, at the end of 1990, according to the FDIC's own figures, its bank insurance fund had only forty-two cents for each $100 of insured deposits or only *one-third* of the legal minimum.

But, as is often the case with government agencies, the official statistics don't tell the real story. And in the case of the FDIC, its own figures actually *overstate* the fund's health. Which leads us to the second good reason to doubt the solvency of the FDIC bank-insurance fund, namely, that the reports banks file with regulators and that the FDIC uses to project possible losses tend to underestimate the banks' problems and potential losses. Simply put, the banks have been more successful in taking advantage of accounting gimmicks to disguise their woes than they have been at making prudent loans. To get a better picture of the FDIC bank-insurance fund's true health, the General Accounting Office took an in-depth look at the financial condition of 368 troubled banks. In a report released in April 1991, the GAO concluded that if the probable losses from these banks were taken into account, the FDIC fund's balance in 1990 would be more like twenty-six cents for every $100 of insured deposits, or only *one-fifth* of the legally required minimum, well below the FDIC's forty-two-cent estimate. The GAO then went on to make a more chilling prediction: "By next year, unless the fund is rebuilt, it will almost certainly be insolvent as more troubled banks fail." The GAO figured that by the end of 1991, the FDIC fund could actually be $5 billion in the red.

Meanwhile, Veribanc, Inc., a private research company that assigns safety ratings to banks, says the FDIC fund was actually insolvent as of the end of 1990. According to Veribanc, if banks wrote off all their bad loans and sold all their repossessed real estate at the true market value, the resulting failures as of the end of 1990 would have cost the FDIC roughly $11.6 billion, putting the fund anywhere from $4 to $8 billion in the hole.

So who do you trust? The FDIC, which says the fund is wobbly but everything is still under control? The GAO, which claims the fund is down, but not out, though probably will be within a year if something isn't done to save it? Or a private research firm like Veribanc, which says the fund has actually been bankrupt since the end of 1990, it's just that nobody wants to admit it?

If history is any guide, the *bleakest* assessment of the FDIC fund's health is probably the most accurate. As more and more people began taking a closer look at the banking industry's problems, even the FDIC's assessments of the bank-insurance fund became less and less rosy. By mid-June FDIC chairman William Seidman was increasing his estimate of losses for the fund in 1991 and 1992 from $14 billion to $23 billion—a revision of more than 50 percent. In fact, what's going on with the FDIC fund today is eerily reminiscent of the debates that raged about the health of the savings-and-loan insurance fund in the mid-1980s. At that time, the S&L insurance fund supposedly was in the black with $5 billion in reserves. In reality, though, the S&Ls were in such horrible shape that when they started failing, that $5 billion dried up faster than a mud puddle in August. Worse yet, the *illusion* of a $5 billion reserve allowed regulators to ignore the growing S&L problem, which, in turn, snow-balled into a $1 trillion fiasco. Now, the banks aren't anywhere near the walking-dead status of the S&Ls in the mid-1980s. But if nothing is done to bolster FDIC reserves, the fund will be broke by the end of 1991 or shortly thereafter.

Unfortunately many of the proposals to strengthen the FDIC fund have an S&L-like "let's deal with it later" quality. The most popular involves increasing the fund's current $5 billion line of credit to any-where from $30 to $70 billion. The rationale for this is that even if the fund goes broke it can borrow from the U.S. Treasury or the Federal Reserve to pay off depositors in failed banks. But several people have problems with what it calls the "borrow as you go" approach. The GAO, for one, sees an expanded line of credit as little more than a big loan cosigned by you, the U.S. taxpayer. Once the money is lent, it's a small step to having taxpayers pick up the tab. In addition, the easy availability of borrowed money might tempt regulators to postpone dealing with the growing problem of bank failures, resulting in an even larger bailout in the future—in other words, a replay of the S&L "delay and pay, pay, pay" scenario. When you get right down to it, claiming that a bigger line of credit strengthens the fund is a bit like saying you can make Donald Trump more solvent by giving him big- 33 ger bank loans.

IF THE FDIC FUND FAILS IS YOUR CASH STILL
SAFE? (The Short Answer is Yes, but . . .)

Of course, the way Congress decides to deal with the deteriorating FDIC insurance fund could easily affect your finances over the long term even if your bank never fails. The reason: if a "borrow as you go" policy wins out, it increases the risk of a taxpayer bailout, and you know whose pocket money comes out of if that happens. But what about the short term? What happens if—make that when—the FDIC fund goes broke? Will it still make good on its promise to back insured deposits? Or will it find some way to weasel out of that obligation?

This much is sure: Should the FDIC fund run dry, *one way or another the U.S. government will honor its commitment to protect insured depositors.* Deposit insurance is one of the cornerstones of the nation's financial system. If the government walked away from its promise to back insured deposits with its full faith and credit, that cornerstone would crumble and bring down the rest of the system with it. So whether it means borrowing money from a line of credit from the Treasury or the Federal Reserve or some other source (the government is very good at borrowing), or having banks kick in extra deposit-insurance premiums to help pay off depositors, or an emergency appropriation from Congress (Congress is very good at appropriating money), the money will be found and insured deposits will be covered.

And in fact, we've already had an instance of a deposit-insurance fund running dry, yet still paying off depositors. The S&L crisis so depleted the S&Ls' former insurance fund, the old Federal Savings and Loan Insurance Corporation, that the fund had to be disbanded and its obligations assumed by a new fund, the Savings Association Insurance Fund, which is now under the jurisdiction of the FDIC (The savings-insurance fund, SAIF, is run by the FDIC but kept completely separate from the bank-insurance fund or BIF). Even now, the SAIF fund is still broke. That's right, there's not a penny in reserves to handle failing S&Ls. Instead, the government agency that closes down bankrupt thrift institutions and pays off depositors in those failed S&Ls relies mostly on appropriations from Congress for its cash.

Unfortunately this doesn't mean you have nothing to worry about if the FDIC fund's reserves evaporate. Sure, the government will come up with the money and honor its commitment, but *how quickly* will it come up with the money and in *what way* will it honor its commitment?

Already it often takes depositors in failed and liquidated S&Ls far longer to get their money than depositors in banks. It's not uncommon to have to wait several weeks to get your cash back from a failed thrift. If the FDIC fund goes the way of the S&L fund, it's possible that depositors in failed banks might see similar delays. That's not the end of the world, of course, but not being able to get to the cash in your savings or checking account for several weeks can wreak havoc in your daily life. Bank failures or no, landlords want their rent and banks want their mortgage payments.

Veribanc's Warren Heller also believes it's possible that, if the FDIC became hard pressed for money, the agency might enforce its rules and regulations more strictly. "In fact they've already tightened up considerably," says Heller. He notes that prior to 1982 it was rare that the FDIC didn't cover all depositors—insured and uninsured—in a bank failure. Today, unless a bank is so large that its failure is considered harmful to a region or the financial system overall, the FDIC is much more likely to give uninsured depositors a haircut—that is, pay off only the insured portion of their deposits or some fraction of the uninsured portion. The FDIC could also become more nitpicking in enforcing deposit-insurance regulations. Under this scenario, if the FDIC finds you guilty of a technical violation—forgetting to sign an account signature card or some such—the agency might consider your account uninsured and refuse to pay up.

And while Heller has no doubts that the federal government will ultimately pay insured depositors, he envisions the possibility that the government could decide to pay in some form other than cash. "I could imagine them paying depositors in savings bonds, for instance," says Heller. In other words, if money gets tight, the government might look for ways to stall giving you actual cash.

So what have we got? We know that the S&L insurance fund is already broke and that the FDIC fund probably will be if it isn't already. And we know that it is at least possible that the FDIC might begin to look for wriggling room when forced to pay off depositors in bankrupt banks. Given this combination of fact and possibility, it is more important today than ever before to make sure that you do not run afoul of deposit-insurance regulations. This already challenging task has become even more confusing because the U.S. Treasury and the Congress have decided to toy with deposit insurance and possibly change the rules. Since deposit insurance is the most important single thing standing between your savings and a possible loss in the event of a bank failure, it is imperative that you understand the rules and strictly abide by them.

35

(The rules for deposits in banks also apply to those in S&Ls and savings banks.) So to assure that your accounts in a bank or thrift are fully covered, let's first go over the deposit-insurance rules as of the summer of 1991 and then examine ways you can protect yourself against some of the recent moves to *cut back* on deposit-insurance coverage.

DEPOSIT-INSURANCE RULES AND REGULATIONS—AND HOW TO AVOID LETHAL TRAPS THAT MAY LEAVE YOUR MONEY UNINSURED

Remember back in high-school algebra class when you'd get those word-problem brain teasers? "If a 16-wheeler tractor-trailer left Pittsburgh at 4 A.M. doing 74 miles an hour traveling west and you left Peoria, Illinois, at midnight in your Honda Civic traveling east at 66 miles an hour, in what city would you have a head-on collision and what brand of accordion would the Honda Civic look like?" Well, figuring out the intricacies of FDIC deposit-insurance regulations requires a similar sort of mental agility. Deciphering the logic behind the regulations alternately requires the discriminating mind of a financial accountant, the keen insight of a legal scholar, and, most difficult, the ability to plod through and make sense of pages of dull bureaucratic language.

But there is one blessing in the complex maze of deposit-insurance regulations—namely, that you only run into complications once you have more than $100,000 in any single institution. So as long as you're below that $100,000 threshold, you needn't worry too much about deposit-insurance rules. Don't be so quick, however, to put yourself in the "I don't have anywhere near a hundred grand so I don't have to worry" category. There are a number of ways a bank account can swell to $100,000 or more in a hurry. Selling a house, inheriting money from a rich relative you never liked but now adore, getting a large distribution from your company retirement plan, unloading your old baseball-card collection, hitting the Pick-Six at Belmont Park racetrack—these are just a few of the ways you may find yourself in the position of pushing the $100,000 barrier in bank deposits. (Don't skip the rest of this chapter or the next just because you don't have $100,000 now or don't believe you ever will. Even if you have well below $100,000 in any one bank, there are still ways you can get tripped up. You may lose access to your cash for as much as several weeks. Or, worse yet, you may think your small savings are insured when in fact they are in an *unin-*

36

sured account or even possibly an *uninsured bank.* I'll explain the traps that even depositors with less than $100,000 may face both at the end of this chapter and in chapter 4.)

Before we get down to the nitty-gritty rules of deposit insurance, let's quickly review the basics. Essentially you get $100,000 of insurance coverage *per person* in *each* bank or thrift in *each* of several different "legal ownership" categories of accounts. Among the different categories in which you get $100,000 of insurance are individual accounts, joint accounts, retirement accounts, and various forms of trust accounts. Under this setup, there are two ways to increase your deposit-insurance coverage beyond the basic $100,000. One is to open accounts in several ownership categories (explained in detail below). The other is to simply open accounts at other banks. If you have $100,000 in accounts at the First National Bank and another $100,000 at the Second National Trust, all $200,000 is covered. Spreading your accounts among different branches of the *same* bank, however, *does not* increase your coverage. So if you have a $60,000 CD at the downtown headquarters of the First National Bank and another $50,000 CD at one of its suburban branches, you have $10,000 that is not insured. One more caveat: If you have accounts in two banks that merge, for six months the accounts are insured as if they were still in separate banks. After that, the insurance limits for a single bank apply. (Exceptions: CDs that mature more than six months after the merger are insured separately until maturity. In some cases, CDs that mature within six months of the merger may be reviewed and still qualify for separate insurance.

Before we get into the specifics of different categories of accounts, there's another important point you must remember—namely, that the $100,000 ceiling applies to principal *and interest.* So if you have a $100,000 CD paying 7 percent interest each year, at the end of one year, the CD is worth $107,000—which puts you over the insurance ceiling to the tune of $7,000. When you open accounts, make sure you give yourself enough leeway to assure your interest payments won't carry you over the insurance limit. For example, you might keep a maximum of $90,000 in any account. That way it would take more than a year's interest at 10 percent to put you over the limit. You could also direct the bank to pay you interest monthly instead of allowing it to accrue, or build up, in the account. For example, if you have a $100,000 CD paying 6 percent or $6,000 a year, you could have the bank send you the $500 in interest each month or, for that matter, have them deposit it in an account in another bank. This method, however, doesn't entirely eliminate your risk of loss. For example, if the bank with your $100,000 CD paying 6 percent fails on the fifteenth of the month, there would be one-half month's interest, or $250, which you have not been paid. That would bring your account total to $100,250—and you would be out $250. For maximum safety, therefore, don't go beyond that $90,000 self-imposed ceiling.

Probably the biggest misconception about deposit insurance is that you get $100,000 in insurance *per account.* Wrong. If you have a checking account with $10,000 in it, a savings account with $50,000, and a CD with $50,000 all in the same bank, then you have a total of $110,000 in deposits of which $10,000 is not insured. It *is* possible, though, to increase your coverage beyond $100,000 by opening accounts in several different ownership categories. That way you get $100,000 in coverage for *each* category. Here's a rundown of the ownership categories you're most likely to use and the regulations pertaining to each:

Individual Accounts: This category includes the kind of accounts you would usually have in your own name, such as a checking account, savings account, certificate of deposit, and money-market deposit account. (This is the bank version of the money-market accounts issued by mutual funds. Nonbank money-market funds, which have no federal insurance, are discussed separately in chapters 6, 7, and 8.) The $100,000 insurance ceiling applies to the combined balances of *all* accounts in this category that you have in a single bank. So if you have $10,000 in a checking account, $50,000 in a savings account, $50,000 in a CD and $20,000 in a money-market deposit account, your balance in this category is $130,000, which leaves $30,000 uninsured (any interest you're earning would put you further over the limit). Two things to remember here. The $100,000 limit is per individual. If your spouse, for example, also has a checking and savings account in his or her name, that is covered separately. Each of you gets $100,000 of coverage, provided the accounts are held individually. (Joint accounts are another category, which is discussed below.) This coverage is also *per bank*. In other words, you can get $100,000 of coverage on individual accounts in each bank where you have accounts. So if you're lucky enough to have $500,000 in CDs in your name spread equally among five banks, all are insured.

38 **Trap to avoid:**   To milk more coverage out of this category, some depositors try rearranging their names or Social Security numbers to

make it appear the accounts are owned by different persons. *Don't do it!* When a bank or thrift fails, payouts are made on the basis of who actually owns the money in the account. So when the regulators find out that the $50,000 checking account held by Ian Michael Smart and the $50,000 CD held by I. Michael Smart and the $50,000 savings account held by I.M. Smart are all owned by the same person, Mr. Smart will feel pretty dumb—especially when he's informed that $50,000 of his savings are uninsured.

Joint Accounts: In addition to the $100,000 of coverage on individual accounts, you also get $100,000 of deposit insurance on jointly held accounts. You can have several accounts in this category; for example, joint accounts with your spouse, former spouse, friends, relatives, worst enemies—virtually anyone. If you have several joint accounts, your interests in *all* the accounts are added together and insured up to $100,000. So if you have three joint accounts—one with your uncle Manny, another with Uncle Moe, and one with Uncle Jack—and each account has $80,000 in it, then you have a $40,000 interest in three accounts, which brings you to $120,000 in this category. So $20,000 of your money is uninsured.

By the way, no single joint account gets more than $100,000 in insurance. So if you and Uncle Manny have $120,000 in a joint account, each of you *does not* qualify for $60,000 of insurance. Instead, regulators lop the $20,000 in excess of the $100,000 ceiling off the account, and then give you and Uncle Manny $50,000 of coverage each. Again, if you and Uncle Manny get cute and set up one account with your name first and another with Manny's first, the FDIC will combine them together and consider them one account subject to the $100,000 ceiling.

Most people would love to have enough money to worry about exceeding the $100,000 insurance ceiling in this category. If you are fortunate enough to be in that position, it's a good idea to go over these rules very carefully with a bank officer before opening up any joint account.

Trap to avoid: This is probably one of the easiest categories to screw up in and *inadvertently* exceed the deposit-insurance limit. One common error is setting up a joint account that isn't a true joint account. For example, a joint account may not be fully insured if all the owners do not have equal rights to the funds. Say, you and a friend set up a joint account with $50,000 in it, but your friend never gets around to filling out the signature card. If the bank fails, regulators can claim that it's not a true joint account. The balance in that account will be considered your individual money for deposit-insurance purposes and be added to the balances in your individual accounts. If you already have $60,000 in the same bank in individual accounts—checking, savings, etc.—the $50,000 will bring your total to $110,000 in the individual category, leaving $10,000 uninsured.

IRA, Keogh, and Other Retirement Accounts: The money you save for retirement in an Individual Retirement Account or a Keogh Plan (a special type of plan available to the self-employed and those who work for self-employed people) also qualifies for separate deposit-insurance coverage. You get $100,000 coverage for the combined balances of all IRA accounts in one bank. If you have $60,000 in one IRA and $50,000 in another IRA at the same bank, you are $10,000 over the limit. If you have a Keogh account, you get an additional $100,000 coverage over and above the coverage for your IRA accounts. So if you have $100,000 in an IRA, plus $100,000 in a Keogh account, both are fully insured.

Employers sometimes keep pension plan or profit-sharing plan money in a bank. You get an additional $100,000 coverage for such employer-run plans provided the deposit records specifically disclose the employer's fiduciary relationship—that is, that this is a bona fide profit-sharing or pension plan. If you have pension money deposited in different pension plans of the same employer in the same bank, the account balances are added together and insured up to the $100,000 maximum. (Employer-sponsored pension money in banks is one area where the Treasury Department and others are looking to cut back on deposit-insurance coverage. See the section in this chapter called "How The Bureaucrats Would Like to Lower Your Deposit-Insurance Coverage" for more details.)

Trap to avoid: Many people today who switch jobs or retire get a lump-sum payment from their company pension plan. Often these payments can total well over $100,000. To preserve the tax-favored status of this money, people often put this lump sum into what is called an IRA Rollover account. Remember, though, that you get $100,000 in coverage for all IRA accounts combined. If you get a lump-sum payment from your company pension, 401(k), or other retirement plan and you want to roll it over into an IRA, split up the money among enough banks so that you don't have more than $100,000 in any one institution (Actually, since IRAs are usually long-term investments, this is a good time to keep your balance below $100,000 so the interest you earn won't put you over the $100,000 limit).

Trust Accounts: A trust is a way for an individual to transfer ownership of funds to someone else, a trustee, so that those funds will be used by the trustee to benefit a third person, the beneficiary. For example, you, being a generous, kind, loving person, might want to help out a deadbeat relative from your spouse's side of the family. But you know that if you just give this deadbeat a lump sum of cash outright, the money won't make it till the next day. So, instead, you can set up a trust account with many restrictions on how that person could dip into the money. The rules in this area are exceedingly complex; they make advanced calculus seem like simple arithmetic. For one thing, coverage varies depending on whether the trust is revocable (the person who set it up can revoke it) or irrevocable (the person who established it can't revoke it). Generally, in an irrevocable trust, each beneficiary is insured up to $100,000. With revocable trusts, however, the $100,000 coverage only applies for beneficiaries who are a spouse, child, or grandchild of the person establishing the trust. Since each qualified beneficiary gets $100,000 of coverage, a trust account can have more than $100,000 in it and be fully insured. A trust with three qualified beneficiaries, for example, could be fully insured up to $300,000. There are scores of exclusions, documentation requirements, and fine legal points in this area that can trip you up. As a result, if you have enough money to consider establishing trust accounts, you should probably first contact a financial planner or attorney to assure both that that trust is correctly set up and that it meets deposit-insurance rules.

Trap to avoid: The easiest error to make in this category is lack of proper documentation establishing the identity of the beneficiary— naming "my grandchildren" as beneficiaries, for example, as opposed to giving their actual names. If the interest of each beneficiary is not properly documented, the FDIC may limit the coverage to $100,000 for the entire account, rather than $100,000 for each beneficiary.

Testamentary Accounts: A testamentary account is a type of revocable trust that specifies that the money in an account will go to a named beneficiary when the owner of the account dies. These are sometimes called "payable on death" accounts. So, for example, if you want to be sure that the $50,000 in your savings account goes to your spouse, you could set up the savings account as a testamentary account naming your spouse as the beneficiary. Each beneficiary in a testamentary account qualifies for $100,000 of deposit insurance *provided the beneficiary is a spouse, child, or grandchild* of the owner of the account. The documentation requirements for testamentary accounts can be tricky. If you want to set up one of these accounts, go over the rules with an officer of the bank or an attorney or financial planner familiar with various types of trust accounts.

Trap to avoid: The easiest way to run afoul of the insurance rules on a testamentary or "payable on death" account is to open one for someone other than a spouse, child, or grandchild. For example, if you set up a $50,000 account stipulating that the money be paid upon your death to your good friend Bob, that account does not qualify for insurance in the testamentary category. Were the bank to fail, the $50,000 in that account would be added to the balances in your individual accounts. So if you already had $75,000 in a CD at the same bank, you would be $25,000 over the insurance limit.

Other categories of accounts: There are a few other types of accounts that qualify for $100,000 of deposit-insurance coverage. For example, funds in accounts held by an executor or administrator of an estate as well as business accounts may qualify for coverage of up to $100,000. Again, to be sure these types of accounts are indeed fully covered—the coverage can often overlap with individually held accounts and put you over the $100,000 limit—consult an officer of the bank or an attorney or financial planner.

Trap to avoid: While business accounts are insured up to a maximum of $100,000, there is a hitch for accounts held by sole proprietorships. The funds in the business accounts of a sole proprietorship are considered the same as if the owner held the money in an account in his or her name. So, let's say, you keep $25,000 in the checking account of your sole proprietorship and also have a $50,000 CD and $50,000 in a savings account in your name. For deposit-insurance purposes, the FDIC adds up all the money and insures it to the $100,000 limit in the individual account category. Which means $25,000 is uninsured.

42

*   *   *

Of course, no single discussion of the labyrinthine maze of regulations will cover every depositor's particular circumstances. For a more detailed look at the rules on deposit insurance for different types of accounts, get a copy of *Your Insured Deposit*, a booklet published by the FDIC that gives numerous examples of how deposit insurance works and potential traps. If your local bank doesn't have a copy of this booklet, you can get one by writing the FDIC Office of Consumer Affairs, 550 17th Street N.W., Washington, D.C. 20429. Despite the relatively generous deposit-insurance rules, people routinely screw up or simply don't pay enough attention to make sure they are getting maximum protection under the rules. "In almost every failed bank where we have a depositor payoff," says Claude Rollin, counsel for the FDIC, "we have depositors who lose money. Some don't understand the regulations and others just assume everything is covered." *Never* make that assumption. Before making any deposit that will put your deposit balance at any single bank over $100,000, you should speak to an officer of the bank to make absolutely sure *all* your deposits are fully covered. If you have multiple accounts whose combined balances total more than $100,000, and if you have any doubts at all as to whether all your money is insured, *move some of it to another bank.* There's no reason to subject yourself to the risk of misunderstanding the regulations and leaving some of your money uninsured when you can just as easily spread your money around and keep less than $100,000 in any one bank—and therefore be fully insured.

HOW THE BUREAUCRATS WOULD LIKE TO LOWER YOUR DEPOSIT-INSURANCE COVERAGE

In February 1991, with an onslaught of bank failures pushing the FDIC's bank-deposit insurance fund toward insolvency, the U.S. Treasury Department unveiled proposals to overhaul the deposit insurance offered by banks, S&Ls, and credit unions. The Treasury's proposals would do two things—one good and one not so good. First, the new regulations would eliminate many of the mind-bending rules and make deposit insurance much easier for the nonbureaucratic mind to understand. That's good. But the new regulations would also reduce the amount of insurance coverage you can get at federally insured banks and S&Ls. Whether that's good is debatable. And for most people that debate is probably academic, since the change may not affect the level 43 of insurance they already get. But if you have multiple accounts in a bank and the combined balances add up to more than $100,000, these new regulations, if passed into law, could have serious implications for your financial health.

Let's focus on the changes that could have a direct effect on the safety of your savings—the new deposit-insurance limits. First, we'll look at the possible changes and then look at how you should protect yourself in the event these changes or something similar to them become law. If enacted, the proposals would:

Cut back deposit insurance to $100,000 for all accounts in one bank—plus an additional $100,000 for retirement accounts: Instead of the current system under which you can spread several hundred thousand dollars' worth of insured accounts among different ownership categories, the guys at Treasury recommended limiting deposit insurance to $100,000 per individual for all accounts at one bank or S&L. In addition to that limit, you would get $100,000 in total coverage for all your retirement accounts—such as IRAs and Keoghs—at one institution. As you see, it's a much more simple and streamlined version of deposit insurance than the monstrosity bristling with caveats and exceptions I explained earlier. No special provisions for testamentary or trust accounts, none for joint accounts. It basically boils down to $200,000 in coverage per person per bank—$100,000 for retirement accounts and $100,000 for all other accounts.

Remember, these limits are *per bank*, so you would *still be able to extend your deposit-insurance coverage by opening accounts at other banks!* Initially the Treasury Department floated the idea of eventually making this $100,000-plus-$100,000 for retirement limit apply system-wide—that is, to all your accounts at all federally insured institutions. In other words, you would have $100,000 limit for the combined balances in *all* your regular accounts and $100,000 for *all* your retirement accounts wherever you kept them. Under this plan, you would not be able to increase insurance coverage by opening accounts at other banks and S&Ls. But, thankfully for those with more than $100,000 in savings accounts, this harsh limit appears to have as much chance of succeeding as Kitty Kelley has of being invited to Nancy Reagan's next birthday party.

Eliminate deposit insurance on deposits sold by brokers and
44 **other salesmen:** Many brokerage firms, ranging from giants like Merrill Lynch to small regional and local firms, sell CDs to their customers, much the same as they sell stocks or bonds. Similarly, some

financial planners sell CDs. Often, these CDs pay a higher rate of interest than the CDs you buy at a bank, which makes them an easy sell. As long as these broker-sold CDs were issued by a federally insured bank or S&L, the CDs have qualified for federal insurance. Because many people believe that high-yielding broker-sold CDs helped push many S&Ls into bankruptcy—and therefore cost U.S. taxpayers big bucks—the Treasury Department as well as many people in Congress would like to *eliminate* deposit insurance on the CDs brokers sell.

Restrict so-called pass-through insurance for pension funds and, possibly, other company retirement plans: Often, company pension plans invest some of their money in bank CDs. Under current law, each person in the pension plan can qualify for $100,000 of deposit insurance. So if you work in a company with one hundred people in your pension plan, each CD your company owns at each bank would be fully insured up to $10 million (one hundred employees times $100,000 coverage for each employee). This is called "pass-through" insurance because the deposit insurance, in effect, passes from the bank through the pension plan to the employees in the plan. But many people in the Treasury Department and Congress believe that the original founders of bank deposit insurance never intended it to be used to protect pension funds. They say this practice expands the liabilities of the bank insurance fund by billions of dollars—and therefore makes taxpayers more vulnerable to a potential bailout. As a result, the Treasury Department as well as some legislators would like to restrict this coverage to a simple $100,000 per pension account instead of $100,000 for every person in the pension plan.

As soon as the Treasury Department released its telephone-book-thick report detailing these and other bank-reform proposals, a huge hue and cry went up about the wisdom of the deposit-insurance reforms. Some people sensibly pointed out that deposit insurance had gotten out of hand and that U.S. taxpayers were on the hook in ways never imagined when the system was first developed in the 1930s. Other people also sensibly noted that with banks failing at the rate of roughly one every two days and people's confidence in the financial system at a low ebb, maybe now wasn't a great time to tinker with the insurance. By the time Congress took its summer recess in August 1991, deposit insurance and bank reform in general had become such touchy issues that the poor congressmen and congresswomen were still testing the winds to find out which side blew fairest. So how do you arrange your affairs to make sure you're protected if they stop talking and do something? Let's take a look at a couple of possibilities.

Even if Congress passes a bank-reform bill in its second 1991 session or later, the chances are pretty good that it won't include a major revision of deposit insurance, especially since Congress's own investigative agency, the General Accounting Office, has warned that now is a bad time to fool around with deposit-insurance limits.

Another possibility is that deposit insurance will be reduced in some way. As of late summer 1991, the chances of cutting back deposit insurance to the Treasury's $100,000 for all retirement accounts combined plus $100,000 for all other accounts at any one bank seemed slim. Apart from the difficulty of selling such a reduction in deposit insurance to the public—i.e., voters—Congress was much more preoccupied with the issues of how to recapitalize the depleted FDIC fund and whether to allow banks to expand into new businesses. Most Congress watchers, therefore, predicted that legislators would concentrate their attention on these issues rather than a political hot potato like watering down deposit insurance.

Two politically palatable cutbacks could be made, however—namely, doing away with the pass-through insurance for pension plans and eliminating insurance on broker-sold CDs. If the pass-through coverage for pensions is eliminated, it would not affect your IRA or Keogh money or any of the individual accounts you keep in a bank. It could, however, affect money your company pension plan invests for you in a bank. To find out whether any of your pension money is vulnerable, check with the benefits department at your company. Someone there should be able to tell you whether any of your pension plan's assets are kept in bank accounts or CDs and, if so, whether that money is covered by federal deposit insurance. Since you don't have a direct say in how this money is invested, the most you can do is let the company know that you expect them to invest your money prudently and, if they put it into banks, tell them you expect them to put it into sound banks.

As for CDs and other deposits sold by brokers and financial planners, there's a good chance insurance coverage on at least some such CDs will be eliminated. Lobbyists for the brokerage industry will fight hard to keep the insurance coverage, but this is another politically easy cut to make—which means Congress is likely to make it. If they don't eliminate deposit insurance for such CDs entirely, they may eliminate it for CDs sold by banks that are in financial trouble. This is a potential danger area for many savers because many brokerage firms peddle CDs

46

on a regular basis. The advice here is simple: No matter how attractive the rate, you should not buy a CD from a broker, financial planner, or any other salesman, unless it is *federally insured*. It is just too risky for a conservative saver. A broker may try to entice you by saying the bank is sound or by saying that all the bank's other deposits are insured, but don't let that sway you. For money you can't afford to lose, you want *federal* insurance. If the broker tries to convince you that the CD is covered by another type of insurance called SIPC (Securities Investor Protection Corporation), then you really know the broker is trying to snowball you. SIPC is *not* federal insurance and it only partially insures cash and securities in brokerage accounts against the failure of the *brokerage* firm. If a broker sells you a CD that is not federally insured and the bank fails, SIPC will not pay you one cent. In short, you should not buy any CD from a broker or any other middleman if there is the slightest chance that it is not federally insured.

HOW TO PROTECT YOURSELF IF THEY CUT BACK ON DEPOSIT INSURANCE

Even if Congress hasn't made substantive changes in deposit insurance by now, it doesn't mean your deposit-insurance protection can't be cut back in the future. As a result, you should carefully monitor any changes in the regulations concerning deposit insurance. That shouldn't be hard to do since newspapers and magazines will jump all over the smallest tidbit of news concerning this important topic. In the meantime, though, there are a few steps safety-conscious savers can take— and should take—to cover themselves whether the deposit-insurance rules are overhauled or left alone. In fact, you will make your savings safer by arranging your bank accounts as if deposit-insurance coverage *were* being cut back along the lines proposed by the Treasury Department.

Unless there's some incredibly compelling reason to keep more than $100,000 in multiple accounts at the same bank—and I can't think of one—*don't keep more than $100,000 in any one bank or S&L*. It's that simple—$100,000 per person per bank. If you're lucky enough to have a stash in excess of $100,000, *spread it around*. This way, you're covered under the old rules and under the Treasury Department's proposal to limit insurance to $100,000-plus-$100,000-for-retirement accounts per bank per person. You're also likely to be covered under any new scheme Congress is likely to adopt now or in the future. In the *extremely* unlikely event they enact a $100,000-plus-$100,000-for-retirement accounts limit systemwide—that is, you couldn't get more than the $100,000-plus-$100,000 protection no matter how many banks you used—then no fancy titling of accounts or shifting your money to additional banks will save you anyway. If that happens, you'll have to examine the other safe options discussed in this book, such as sticking to solid banks that are least likely to fail and putting your money in super-safe money-market funds or highly rated insurance companies.

But even without the threat of deposit-insurance reform hanging over your head and even if you have well below $100,000 in your accounts, it's smart to diversify your savings among several banks. And that's because . . .

YOU CAN ACTUALLY LOSE IN AN INSURED ACCOUNT

That's right. Even the shield of federal deposit insurance has a few small chinks in it that can cost you money and wreak a considerable emotional toll. Of course, you're still better off with the insurance than without it—but it's important to know just what its limitations are and what to expect should you have to rely on the FDIC. Let's quickly go over a few ways you can lose even in an insured account—and look at ways to minimize the loss or hassle:

You can lose access to your money for several days to several weeks: Ideally the FDIC closes a failed bank on a Friday and has already found another financially secure bank to take over the failed bank's deposits. In that case, you probably will only lose access to your money during the weekend, something you'll probably find out when the ATM won't give you any cash.

But if the FDIC can't find a healthy bank to take over the failed institution, it may have to pay off just insured depositors. In that case, even if your accounts are fully insured, you could lose access to your money while the FDIC—or, in the case of a failed S&L, the Resolution Trust Corporation—sorts out how much each insured depositor is paid. Exactly how long that takes depends on a number of factors, including how good the records are at the bank and whether you're able to produce acceptable documentation to substantiate your claim. At best you may only be separated from your money for a day or two. But it is 48 possible you might have to wait several weeks, as financial planner John Calandro and his clients did in the case of Resource Savings in Texas. During that time you will not be paid any interest on your money. In addition, you will be unable to use the checking account in the failed bank and the checks you wrote will bounce. The ATM machine won't dispense cash. Your money is effectively in prison until released by the FDIC or RTC. As a result, you will probably suffer severe disruptions in your financial affairs and may even have to borrow money to tide you over until the regulators sort out the mess and pay you off.

The best way to reduce the risk and hassle of not being able to get at your money is by not limiting all your accounts to one bank. Even if you have just a small savings account at one other bank, at least you have a reserve to dip into in the event your main bank goes bust and your cash is tied up.

The interest rate on your money can be lowered—or eliminated entirely: If the FDIC convinces another bank to take the deposits of a failed institution, your deposits are effectively switched over to the new bank. That bank then can and probably will lower whatever rate of interest you were getting on CDs and checking, savings, and money-market deposit accounts. So even if your 9 percent CD still had two years to run, the new bank can lower the interest rate on it. The new bank must notify you of the lowered interest rate and you then have a two-week window to withdraw your money without penalty. If you don't remove your cash, your deposits will then earn whatever rate of interest the new bank offers. If you don't respond at all to the bank's notice, the bank can even put your money in a non-interest-bearing account until you do respond.

If your bank fails and your money is switched to a new bank, you should quickly compare the rate of interest the new bank is paying with what other banks in your area are offering. You can do this by looking in the financial section of your local newspaper or by calling several banks in your area. If you believe the new bank's rate isn't high enough, then close your account *within the two-week grace period* and move your money to another bank. If you procrastinate beyond the two-week grace period, you can end up paying a withdrawal penalty for moving your cash.

Loans and lines of credit may be canceled, frozen, or called for immediate payment: The treatment you get as a borrower after a bank fails depends on a number of factors such as whether or not the loan is current or delinquent, whether your bank has been taken over by a healthy institution after failing, and what rights your loan contracts give the acquiring institution. Most loans have what are known 49 as "acceleration clauses." Under such a clause, the lender usually has the right to demand immediate full repayment from you if you default or fall behind in loan payments. (Fine print in the contracts of home-equity lines of credit made before November 1989 may allow the lender to call the loan at any time. Federal law prohibits such provisions in contracts made after that date.) But banks often exercise discretion in exercising acceleration clauses, on the theory that they stand a better chance of getting paid by working out a reasonable payment schedule with the borrower than by simply demanding immediate payment. But when regulators or a new bank take over a failed bank, understanding and compassion get swept aside. If you're delinquent on the loan, gird yourself for them to demand immediate payment.

You can still run into problems, though, even if you're not behind on a loan. Let's say you have a $50,000 home-equity line of credit or any type of revolving line of credit against which you've borrowed $25,000. If your bank fails, the regulators or the new bank that acquires your failed bank may be able to freeze that line, which means you won't be able to draw on the $25,000 of remaining credit. And if you have, say, a $50,000 line against which you haven't borrowed a dime, the regulators or the new bank may be able to simply cancel it. This can cause big problems if you've been counting on money from a line of credit to pay for large expenses such as medical bills or a child's education. You can avoid a demand for immediate payment by keeping your loan payments current and by checking your loan documents to see under what conditions it gives the lender the right to call the loan. And if the availability of credit is crucial to you—perhaps to run a business or to meet large expenses—consider developing borrowing relationships with more than one bank. That way, if one goes down, you can fall back on the other.

The FDIC can and will apply your insured-bank-account money to overdue loans: This is probably one of the least known of the FDIC's powers. Let's say that you have $50,000 in a CD account at the same bank where you have a home-equity loan for $50,000. If that bank fails, your $50,000 CD is completely insured. But, if you also happened to be two months behind on the payments on your home-equity loan at the time the bank failed, you may get a nasty little surprise—namely, the FDIC may use your $50,000 CD to pay off your loan. When the FDIC takes over a failed bank, its mission is to reduce the bank's losses
as much as possible. One way of doing that is getting payment on delinquent loans by exercising its right to call in a delinquent loan. Under

federal law, the FDIC has the power to take a depositor's insured deposits and apply them to any outstanding delinquent loan balance. And FDIC usually exercises that power. "Generally when a depositor has money in the bank and a loan is in default," says Rollin, "we will take that money whenever we can get it."

I certainly don't want to suggest ways for people behind in their loans to evade payment. Nonetheless, it is true that if you are behind in your loans at a bank that fails, but you keep your savings accounts at a separate bank, the FDIC does not have the power to automatically dip into deposit accounts at a different institution to bring your loan at a failed bank current.

By the way, having a loan and deposit accounts at a bank can also work to your advantage when a bank is failed and liquidated. For example, if you have $150,000 in one CD in your name and your bank fails and depositors must be paid off because a healthy bank won't take the bank over, $50,000 is uninsured. But if you also happen to have a loan at the same bank—for example, a $50,000 home-equity loan—most states will allow you to apply the uninsured funds to the loan, in this case repaying the loan in full. Of course, this isn't as good as getting your entire $150,000 back. But it's a lot better than *not* getting the $50,000 or, at best, waiting several years in the hope that you'll recoup some of your $50,000 after the bank's assets are sold and the money is divided up among depositors and creditors.

Deposit insurance, like everything else in life, isn't perfect. But when used correctly, it can protect you from the most devastating financial setback—that is, the outright loss of your entire savings. Still, given the possibility that you may suffer minor losses and experience hassles and emotional trauma in the wake of a bank failure, you are far better off avoiding shaky banks altogether and, instead, sticking to the ones least likely to fall apart. Before I tell you how to do just that in the next chapter, let's go over one final caveat—namely, the fact that not all banks, nor all accounts within banks, are covered by federal deposit insurance.

BEWARE: NOT ALL BANKS—OR ACCOUNTS— ARE INSURED

While almost all banks and savings-and-loan associations are covered by federal deposit insurance, there are some financial institutions out there that may not be. More than a dozen states, for example, allow credit unions and, in some cases, banks to operate with private, rather than federal, insurance. It was the failure of one of these private insurers—the Rhode Island Share and Deposit Indemnity Corporation—that triggered a banking crisis that affected the accounts of roughly 30 percent of the population of the state of Rhode Island in 1991. (For more on this crisis and how Rhode Islanders will be digging out of this mess for years to come, see chapter 5.) And there are also a handful of uninsured banks and other banklike institutions doing business with customers who may not even be aware of the risks they are taking. Some of these noninsured institutions operate under dubious legal status. Others simply escape the often lax gaze of state and federal regulators, as was the case with the Latin Investment Corporation, a quasi-bank in Washington, D.C., that catered mostly to Salvadorean immigrants and went bankrupt in 1990. Even though Latin Investment Corporation—"el banquito" to its mostly non-English-speaking customers—only paid a Scrooge-like 3 percent on savings, it managed to attract an estimated $6 million to $13 million in deposits from immigrants who were largely ignorant of the U.S. banking system. Unfortunately, since Latin Investment Corporation had neither a bank charter nor federal insurance when it failed, its depositors are unlikely to see all, if any, of their money again.

There are also a number of scam artists who set up an office, give it a name that has the ring of authenticity—Prudential Bank, Ltd., or Metropolitan Security Bank, for instance—and then collect deposits by advertising in local papers or by passing themselves off as financial advisers who are marketing CDs. One such rogue bank in Oklahoma City even traded off the venerable J.P. Morgan's reputation, calling itself the Morgan Guaranty Bank, N.A. To avoid getting tripped up in any such schemes, you should always be wary of doing business with new financial institutions of any kind. If a bank or savings-and-loan association claims to have federal insurance, but you still have doubts, check with the Federal Deposit Insurance Corp. (FDIC, Consumer Affairs Department, 550 17th Street N.W., Washington, D.C. 20429). If it doesn't claim to be federally insured, you shouldn't be banking there anyway.

In addition to quasi-banks and the scamsters, there are also a few banks that operate legally without insurance. You're unlikely to run across these institutions, such as white-shoe Brown Brothers Harriman bank, because they are private firms that do business mostly with corporations or very wealthy individuals. Let's put it this way: if this is the first time you've heard of Brown Brothers, it's not likely they'll want you as a customer anyway. But there are also a few uninsured banks scattered around the country that made it through the Depression unscathed and were exempted from deposit-insurance regulations. But don't assume that a bank is safe just because it has been around a long time—or even weathered the Depression. Century-old banks can, and do, fail.

When you're dealing with that portion of your money that you've earmarked for complete safety, when you can't afford to take any chances and you want the security of a bank deposit, *there is absolutely no good reason for going to an uninsured bank.* Don't put your money in any bank, no matter how tantalizing an interest rate it's paying, unless you see either the FDIC sticker or, in the case of savings-and-loan associations, the SAIF sticker (Savings Association Insurance Fund).

Finally, never assume that just because you bought a savings instrument or investment at a bank that it is automatically insured. While bank deposits—savings accounts, checking accounts, and CDs—are federally insured, there is a whole other panoply of products that banks peddle that are not covered at all by the FDIC's deposit-insurance umbrella. A recent report by the General Accounting Office listed fourteen uninsured products that are currently being sold at banks. Those investment products are: fixed and variable annuities, bank holding-company obligations; certificates of deposit of more than $100,000; commercial paper, common or preferred stock; corporate bonds; mutual funds; public limited partnerships; repurchase agreements; subordinated debt (this is what Mabel Dixon and the other victims bought at Germania Bank in St. Louis); Treasury bills, notes and bonds; unit investment trusts; U.S. government agency obligations; and zero-coupon bonds. The city of Denver even offered $3 million in municipal bonds yielding more than 7 percent through the branches of a local bank, calling the bonds Denver Mini-bonds. Although municipal bonds usually come in denominations of $5,000—more than most bank customers are likely to pay—the Mini-bonds were offered at a face value of $333.33 each, or three for a thousand bucks. The obvious question: Would people who picked up a three-pack of Mini-bonds at the bank realize that not only is this investment not federally insured, but that the market value of a bond *drops* when interest rates rise? If they had to unload their Minis in an emergency, they could face a loss.

What's more, banks have been pushing these uninsured products much, much more aggressively the past few years and will continue to do so in the future. The basic reason: the banks, as well as the people selling you such products, can earn high commissions on many of these products. At more and more banks these days, the salaries of everyone from the teller to the customer-service representative to the branch manager depend on how many of these types of products the bank can sell you, much like a new-car salesman may try to push high-cost options like power sunroofs, tape decks, and leather bucket seats. The banks even have a name for this sales effort. They call it "cross-selling." Which means when you come in to open up a savings account or a CD, they're also going to try to "cross-sell" you an annuity or a mutual fund or some other kind of investment. While some of the investments listed above might be perfectly fine, it's important you don't confuse them with insured bank deposits. Buying a stock or a mutual fund at a bank involves the exact same risks as buying one from a brokerage house, namely, that the price of that stock or mutual fund can go down as well as up. If the price goes down and you sell, your loss is in no way covered by federal insurance. The same goes for one of the hottest products banks are pushing today: fixed annuities. You have to be especially careful of these since they work much like CDs. You invest a certain amount of money—usually $5,000 or more—and your investment earns a fixed interest rate for a specific period of time, usually one to five years, much the same as a CD. In fact, annuities often pay slightly higher rates than CDs and have the added advantage of deferring taxes. You don't pay taxes on the interest until you withdraw that money. But there are important differences. If you pull your money out of an annuity before age $59\frac{1}{2}$, you not only pay taxes on the earnings, but you pay a 10 percent penalty. And annuities are not covered by federal insurance. Even though a banker might sell you the annuity, it is actually issued by an insurance company. So the safety of your savings is entirely dependent on the health of the insurance company, a somewhat frightening prospect today considering the collapse of major insurers such as Mutual Benefit Life, Executive Life, Fidelity Bankers Life, and First Capital Life. (For more on how to evaluate the risks in insurance companies and choose safe ones, see chapters 9 and 10.)

So if your intent is to put your savings into a safe, insured account, don't let some commission-hungry bank salesman steer you into an uninsured investment. If you stick to insured bank deposits and follow the strategies outlined in this chapter, you should be safe. But to be doubly sure you don't get sucked into the banking crisis, you should stick to strong, well-capitalized, safe banks. The next chapter will tell you what you need to know to do that.

HOW TO CHOOSE THE
SAFEST BANKS

Caution: This Bank May Be Hazardous
to Your Financial Health

WITH banks dropping faster than Third World dictators and the FDIC insurance fund careening toward self-destruction, it would be great if there were some simple way of weeding out the lousy banks from the stalwarts. Maybe a regulation requiring weak banks and S&Ls to post a notice in their windows along the lines of the warning on a pack of cigarettes. "Caution: This bank is in sorry, sorry shape. Doing business here could be detrimental to your financial health." With such a warning, you could easily steer clear of shaky banks and avoid the trauma of going through a bank or S&L failure and the financial havoc that can accompany it. And, who knows, if banks knew that they might be forced to prominently post such a sign, maybe they wouldn't be as quick to make risky and imprudent loans to the Trumps, the corporate takeover artists, the junkmeisters, and other financial profligates of the world.

Well, it'll never happen. One reason is that someone would have to come up with a set of guidelines to dictate when a bank would have to hang such a poster in its window. Though hardly an insurmountable obstacle, getting the various agencies that regulate banks and S&Ls to agree on uniform standards could take years, decades, eons. But there's another, more compelling reason—namely, that the *last* thing that the banking industry and federal regulators want you to know is that a bank is weak and could ultimately fail. Don't believe me? Then just try to get the names of the banks on the FDIC's problem bank list. As of the end of June 1991, this list of financially troubled banks—that is, banks with an above-average likelihood of failing because they are short on capital or long on bad loans or other problems—contained the names of some 1,044 banks with a total of $400 billion in assets. Call the FDIC and ask for the names of those banks, however, and you will be politely told that the FDIC does not make this information public. "We don't even provide it to Congress," says David Barr, an FDIC spokesman. Why, you may legitimately ask, wouldn't the regulatory agencies charged with protecting your interests share such valuable information with you? Simple. They know that if *you* knew that a bank was perilously close to failure, you would probably pull your money out and walk down the street to another bank that wasn't on that list. And if that happened, the loss of customers might just tip that bank over the edge into insolvency, which means the regulators might have to seize it and spend money from the bank insurance fund to reimburse depositors.

So, from a public-policy viewpoint, withholding information about problem banks makes some sense. Regulators don't want to do anything that might push a bank that's in intensive care into the morgue. Therefore, the banking industry and the regulators take a "Don't Worry, Be Happy" line with the public. Don't worry. You needn't concern yourself with your bank's financial condition. Be happy. Your deposits are federally insured.

But, for you as an individual concerned about the safety of your overall personal finances, the song is a bit off key. True, as long as your money is insured, the FDIC prevents you from suffering a loss. But, as we've seen in chapters 1 and 2, the current regulations for federal insurance bristle with exceptions and possible pitfalls. And even if your deposits are completely insured, there's the possibility you might lose access to your money, or have a loan canceled or called in for immediate payment. In short, unless you're a glutton for financial upheaval or have a secret fetish for dealing with large impersonal government bureaucracies like the FDIC or RTC, you probably want to take every reasonable step you can to avoid getting sucked into the banking crisis. "Why would you want to deal with an institution that might not be there when you really need it," says Paul Bauer, president of the Bauer Group, a research company in Coral Gables, Florida, that assigns safety ratings to banks, S&Ls, and credit unions. "If a bank goes under it can screw up your whole life. Why take the chance when you can deal with solid, well-capitalized institutions that should be around to make good on their commitments?"

For those safety-conscious savers who think Bauer is right—you're better off watching the banking crisis from the sanctuary of a safe and solid bank—this chapter will tell you how to identify the healthiest banks and S&Ls. You will learn to do that in two ways. First I'll explain how you can perform a do-it-yourself diagnostic checkup on a bank or S&L by examining a few easy-to-calculate financial ratios. But, since even these relatively simple tests may be considered too much work for some people, you may prefer the second way of homing in on sturdy banks and S&Ls—by going directly to private research companies that specialize in monitoring the safety of the nation's financial institutions. The names and phone numbers of those companies, as well as a list of top-rated banks and S&Ls in every state, appears at the end of this chapter.

But before we get into ways of taking the pulse of your bank, let's take a quick look at the "Too Big to Fail" or TBTF theory of safety, which claims that, if you stick to very large banks, you don't have to worry about their financial condition because the government just isn't going to let them go under. TBTF has a certain elemental appeal because it frees you from having to do much legwork when choosing a bank. Just choose a big one, and theoretically you're safe. But choosing a bank that is too big to fail may be harder than it seems and, besides, it's questionable whether you should rely on TBTF at all these days.

CAN YOU RELY ON TOO BIG TO FAIL?

Basically the argument for the TBTF school of safety goes like this: Since the failure of a very large institution might shake the foundations of our financial system, the FDIC has the option of bailing out big banks by protecting uninsured as well as insured depositors. This is essentially what the FDIC did when Continental Illinois National Bank, with $33.6 billion in assets, became the largest U.S. bank ever to fail (so far, anyway) back in 1984. The FDIC repeated this policy with at least four other banks since 1985, most recently in January 1991 with the $22 billion-in-assets Bank of New England.

But it would be foolish for you to assume that a big bank is automatically safer than a small one. For one thing, there's the problem of telling which banks will be protected by the TBTF policy. Just how large does a bank have to be before it is considered too big to let go? Is the policy limited only to so-called money-center banks, the behemoths like Citibank, Chase, and the recently merged Chemical-Manufacturers Hanover? The truth is nobody really knows. Though some banking experts figure a bank must have at least $10 billion in assets to be covered by TBTF (which means that only about the fifty largest banks in the U.S. would qualify), the fact is that there is no specific threshold at which a bank qualifies for such protection. And no bank qualifies automatically. Though the Bank of New England was bailed out under the TBTF doctrine, some banking experts believe the FDIC might have just let the bank fail if the U.S. weren't in a recession at the time and if the economy in the Northeast weren't in such horrible shape. "What they're really looking at more than asset size is how much the institution is woven into the U.S. financial system and global financial markets," says Robert Swanton, a vice president in the bank-rating division of Standard & Poor's. "And what kind of catastrophe could result if the bank went under." Swanton notes, for example, that when the relatively small National Bank of Washington (only $1.6 billion in assets, hardly a heavyweight in the banking world) failed in August 1990, all depositors, insured and uninsured, were covered by the FDIC. The reason: a large number of foreign banks had uninsured deposits with the bank and the FDIC didn't want to undermine foreign banks' faith in the U.S. banking system.

Even if you did know which banks the federal regulators consider too big to fail today, there's another reason not to bank on too big to fail—namely, that federal regulators, in an attempt to protect the already devastated bank-insurance fund from more heavy losses, seem to be moving away from this policy altogether. During the banking-reform debate in Congress in 1991, for example, the House Banking Committee voted to limit sharply the FDIC's ability to reimburse uninsured depositors after 1994. "I believe pressure will mount to abandon too big to fail," says Dan Brumbaugh, a former bank regulator and outspoken critic of the TBTF policy. "I would not have uninsured deposits in a money-center bank."

Finally, even if your bank is big and important enough to merit protection under TBTF, that policy doesn't necessarily protect you from *all* the hassles of being a customer of a failing bank. Usually, the FDIC will arrange a takeover of the failing bank and insure all deposits. Thus, even if you had uninsured money in the bank (something you would *never* have, of course, after reading chapters 1 through 3), your deposits would be protected. But your interest rate on your deposits could be slashed, loans could be called in, lines of credit could be frozen or canceled. The money in your accounts would be safe, but your personal finances could be a wreck.

The bottom line: As long as you follow the deposit-insurance guidelines discussed in the previous chapter, your money should ultimately be safe no matter what federally insured bank or S&L you're in. But if even the thought of going through the emotional and financial upheaval of a bank failure is anathema to you, then forget about too big to fail and, instead, seek out the banks whose safety comes not from a bureaucratic doctrine, but from good management and a strong financial statement.

CHECKING YOUR BANK'S VITAL SIGNS

Fortunately you don't have to have an MBA in finance to take the financial pulse of your bank. By examining a few financial ratios and statistics that even people who suffer from math anxiety can easily calculate, you can assess the financial soundness of your bank—and decide whether you want to keep your savings there. Warren Heller, research director at Veribanc, one of several companies that assign safety ratings to banks, has devised a simple do-it-yourself checkup that looks at the three most important factors relating to bank safety: the amount of capital the bank has, how much it is weighed down by problem loans, and whether or not it is making a profit. If the bank passes these three tests, Heller estimates that its chances of failing are less than 1 in 3,000. To run this diagnostic series of tests, you will have to gather some financial information on your bank. When we get into the actual tests, I'll tell you exactly what you need and where to get it. Other than that, all you need is about fifteen to thirty minutes of time to go over the financial data, a pencil and pad to jot down a few numbers, and, unless you're an incredible whiz at long division, a calculator. The calculations you'll be doing are simple—subtracting a few numbers, dividing others to come up with percentages—so any calculator will do.

THE EQUITY TEST

The single most important indicator of the soundness of a bank and its ability to survive is the amount of equity it has. Equity, also sometimes called *capital* or *surplus* or *net worth*, is the amount of money a bank or S&L has left over when all its liabilities, such as consumer deposits and CDs, are subtracted from its assets, mostly business loans and securities. In other words, if you take everything that a bank owns—its assets—and then subtract everything it owes—its liabilities—what you have left is equity. If there is no equity, then the bank is insolvent. Equity is important to a bank—or to any business, for that matter—because it represents a cushion the bank can fall back on to absorb losses from bad loans or other unprofitable ventures. The more equity a bank has, the better it can weather recessions and other times when business is bad. If the bank has only a tiny bit of equity, it's possible that losses incurred over the period of a year or even a shorter period of time might be enough to sink it.

The benchmark that bank regulators and financial analysts use to determine whether a bank has enough equity is the *equity ratio*, also known as the bank's *capital ratio*. This ratio, expressed as a percentage of assets, is calculated by dividing the bank's equity by its assets. To get the figures you need to calculate the equity or capital ratio for your bank, ask for a copy of the institution's most recent statement of condition or its annual, semiannual, or quarterly report. You shouldn't have trouble getting this information for most publicly held banks—that is, those banks whose stock trades on a national or regional stock exchange. Usually a call to the shareholder relations department of the bank will get you what you need. If a bank is privately held, however, it may be reluctant to provide detailed information—especially if it's having problems. In that case, you're probably better off simply ordering a report from one of the bank-rating companies discussed below.

Assuming you can get one or all of these reports, look for the bank's balance sheet. This presents a list of the bank's assets on one side and, on the other, a list of the bank's liabilities and equity. The figure you want is *total assets*. Jot down this figure on a piece of paper. Next, look for the bank's equity. This may be called *equity, total equity, shareholder's equity*, or even *net worth* or *surplus*. Once you have this figure, there's an easy way to make sure it's right. Simply take the total asset number you jotted down earlier and subtract the total liabilities figure that's listed on the balance sheet. The result should match the figure you're using for equity. Now take the equity figure and divide it by total assets. Thus, for example, if a bank has $100 million in assets and $5 million in equity, you would divide $5 million by $100 million to come up with an equity ratio of 5 percent.

To pass the equity test, your bank must have an equity ratio of *at least* 5 percent. That's a fair cutoff point since the average capital ratio for all banks is roughly 6.5 percent. To be considered strong, a bank should have a capital ratio of 6 percent to 7.5 percent and to be considered exceptionally strong, a bank should have a ratio of higher than 7.5 percent. A bank with an equity ratio below 5 percent would have to be considered weak. And if the equity ratio is 3 percent or less, the bank is very weak. If your bank has an equity ratio of 3 percent or less that doesn't mean it will fail, but it does mean that it has a cushion that is below average for the banking industry and that it is more vulnerable to failure than better capitalized banks. By the way, if you subtract liabilities from assets and get a *negative* number, that means your bank has no equity and is insolvent. If it's still operating, it's probably only because overburdened federal regulators haven't gotten around to closing it. Unless you want to get caught up in the hassles of a closing, you should withdraw your money and head for another bank as soon as possible.

THE PROBLEM LOAN TEST

One of the main reasons some seemingly well capitalized banks fail is that their equity is wiped out by losses from loan defaults. One way to tell how well insulated your bank is from possible future defaults is to compare the amount of problem loans the bank has to the bank's loan-loss reserves—that is, money the bank sets aside out of its earnings to cover potential loan losses. If the bank hasn't set aside a large enough reserve, losses could quickly eat up its equity cushion, possibly causing the bank to fail.

To do this test, get either the bank's annual report or its quarterly call report. First, scan the report for the headings that are usually used to describe problem loans. The three most common categories are "past due," "nonaccrual," and "nonperforming" loans. Add up the numbers in all these categories and write it down. Next, look for the loan-loss reserve balance. This amount is usually listed under the heading "loan loss reserves" or "balance of reserve for loan losses."

If the loan-loss reserves are greater than the total value of all problem loans, that means your bank has set aside enough money to handle foreseeable loan losses. Your bank passes this test and you can go on to test number 3.

But if problem loans *exceed* loan-loss reserves, it means that, if all problem loans went bad in the near future, your bank wouldn't have enough reserves to cover the losses. In other words, your bank does 61 not have a large enough margin of safety to handle potential losses. To gauge how big a problem future loan losses might be, you've got to do a few more calculations. Deduct the loan-loss reserves from the total amount of problem loans. Let's call the result "excess problem loans." For example, if your bank had loan-loss reserves of $5 million and total problem loans of $8 million, that would give you excess problem loans of $3 million. Subtract excess problem loans from the equity figure you used in test one. This will give you a figure we'll call "discounted equity." So, for example, if your bank had equity of $5 million and you subtracted $3 million in excess problem loans, that would give you discounted equity of $2 million. Now, divide discounted equity by total assets. This will tell you what kind of capital or equity cushion your bank has after taking bad loans into account. If this figure is less than 4 percent, your bank fails this test. Of course, if you get a *negative* number when you subtract excess problem loans from equity, you don't even have to calculate the equity ratio. Your bank automatically fails this test because a negative result means that if all problem loans go bad they will completely wipe out your bank's equity cushion.

THE PROFITABILITY TEST

This third and final test looks at whether your bank is making money and, if not, how quickly it's losing it. A bank's profitability is an important gauge of its financial health for the simple reason that if losses are large enough and go on for long enough, they will eventually erode the bank's equity and push the institution into insolvency.

For this part of the checkup you must look at the bank's income statement. The income statement sometimes goes by other names, including profit-and-loss statement, income and expenses, statement of operations, and income report. Go to the bottom of the statement and look for the figure next to Net Income. If that figure is positive, your bank is profitable and it passes this test.

If the net income figure is negative (in which case, it may appear in parentheses or be labeled a Net Loss), then your bank suffered a loss and you have to go a bit further to see if it can still pass the profitability test. Divide the loss by the number of months covered by the income statement. If you're using an annual report, that period is twelve months. If you're using a semiannual report, use six months, and if you have a quarterly report, divide the loss by three months. This will give you the average monthly loss rate. So, for example, if your bank's annual report shows a $12 million loss, the loss rate is $1 million a month. Next, divide the equity figure you used in test one by the average monthly loss rate. This will tell you how many months the bank can go on losing money at that monthly rate before it runs out of equity. Thus, a bank with $5 million in equity and a $1 million monthly loss rate would deplete its equity in five months. If losses at your bank are enough to deplete its equity in less than twelve months, it fails this test.

A truly safe bank or S&L should pass all these tests quite easily. If your bank fails one of these tests, you should certainly reevaluate your relationship with it—and double-check to make sure every cent you have in that bank is federally insured. If your bank fails two of these tests—especially if it flunks the profitability test—you should probably start shopping around for a stronger bank. And if your bank can't pass muster on any one of these tests, run, don't walk, to a safer bank.

COMPANIES THAT WILL RATE A BANK'S SAFETY FOR YOU

Understandably, some people would rather undergo root-canal work than spend time sifting through a bank's financial statements. If you are one of those people—or you would like to see if a professional bank analyst agrees with your assessment of your bank's condition—you may want to check out three companies that assign safety ratings to banks and S&Ls. To derive these ratings, all of these companies use the financial information that banks and S&Ls are required by law to file with federal regulators each quarter. There's another good reason to consult with these companies. While the three tests I've just described can provide a quick look at the overall health of your bank, companies that specialize in rating the soundness of financial institutions can engage in a far more detailed analysis of a bank's safety than most individuals can or would want to. For example, in addition to discounting equity for problem loans, these companies can adjust equity according to the riskiness of a bank's assets. Thus, a bank that makes riskier business loans would need more capital to get a high safety rating than a bank that stuck to home mortgages. Similarly, these organizations can factor into their ratings such criteria as the bank's liquidity—how quickly the bank can convert assets to cash if need be—and trends in the bank's net earnings. Furthermore, these companies can tell you how the safety 63 of your bank compares to banks in general or other banks in your state.

That way, if you do decide to get out of your present bank, you'll also have the names of some strong banks with which you'll feel more comfortable doing business.

The Bauer Group, in Coral Gables, Florida, gives 12,250 banks a safety rating that ranges from five stars (the safest) to zero stars (banks that are insolvent and, possibly, already taken over by regulators). Bauer also assigns safety ratings to 2,503 S&Ls, using the same ranking system. Based on data as of the end of March 1991 (the latest available as this book went to press), 3,559 banks (29 percent of all those rated) and 877 S&Ls (35 percent of all rated) got Bauer's top five-star rating. (The introduction to the tables at the end of this chapter explains the criteria a bank or S&L has to meet to merit five stars.) If you want to assess the condition of your bank—or one you're considering doing business with—you can order a detailed six-page analysis of a single institution, which includes its rating, for $35. For $75, Bauer will provide a report that gives financial data and the safety ratings for all banks in your state. These reports are also available for S&Ls. For these reports and information on others that are also available, call 305-441-2062 or write the Bauer Group, P.O. Drawer 145510, Coral Gables, FL 33114-5510.

Veribanc, Inc., a company in Wakefield, Massachusetts, also monitors the safety of banks and S&Ls, assigning safety ratings to 12,699 banks and 2,513 S&Ls. Veribanc has devised a rating system that uses a combination of one to three stars and a color code of green, yellow, and red. Under Veribanc's system, the highest-rated bank or S&L would be green and have three stars. Based on end of March 1991 data, 9,429 banks and 1,258 S&Ls received Veribanc's highest rating—green and three stars. You can get an instant rating for any bank or S&L over the phone for $10 ($3 for each additional rating). Veribanc also provides a short report on a specific bank or S&L for $25. You can also get ratings and key financial ratios for all banks or S&Ls in your state for $110. In addition, Veribanc has compiled a list of what it calls Blue Ribbon banks. The 1,526 banks in this group must achieve a green three-star rating and meet fifteen additional criteria, including stringent standards for equity, liquidity, profitability, delinquent loans. For $35, Veribanc will give you its Blue Ribbon report, which lists all the Blue Ribbon banks in your region of the country. For these services call 800-442-2657 or write Veribanc, Inc., P.O. Box 461, Wakefield, MA 01880.

A third company, Sheshunoff Information Services in Austin, Texas, also evaluates the safety of banks and S&Ls on the basis of their equity ratio, asset quality, earnings, and liquidity. Sheshunoff grades 12,323 banks on a numerical scale of 0 to 99. To get Sheshunoff's highest rating of A+, a bank must score 90 to 99, and to get an A rating a bank must score between 70 and 89. About 30 percent of the banks rated get either an A or A+. Sheshunoff uses the same 0-to-99 rating system to rate 2,992 S&Ls, but does not assign the S&Ls a letter grade. For $25, you can get a six-page report that includes a bank or S&L's rating as well as pertinent financial information on the institution. Sheshunoff also sells a report for $50 that gives the ratings and financial data on every bank or S&L in a particular state. To order these reports or to get information on other services, call 800-456-2340 or write Sheshunoff Information Services, Capitol Station, P.O. Box 13203, Austin, TX 78711-9969.

THE SAFEST BANKS AND S&LS

With more than twelve thousand banks now operating in the U.S., it would be unwieldy to give the safety ratings for all in this book. But to give you a sampling of some of the banks across the country that did warrant the highest rating from at least one of the bank-rating companies, I asked the Bauer Group to provide the names of the five largest banks and thrift institutions (S&Ls and savings banks) in each state that got Bauer's top five-star rating. Those two lists of the strongest banks and S&Ls in each state appear at the end of this chapter.

Keep in mind, however, that the top-rated banks and S&Ls listed in this book are not the *only* ones that meet rigorous standards for safety. These are the *largest* banks to get one rating company's *highest* rating. It is possible that your bank also receives an above-average rating for safety from the Bauer Group, Veribanc, Sheshunoff, or all three. So don't yank your money out of the bank you're currently doing business with just because it doesn't appear on this list.

Remember, too, that just because a bank gets a top rating from Bauer, Veribanc, Sheshunoff, or, for that matter, any other ratings company, doesn't guarantee the bank can't fail. For one thing, all these companies rely on information the banks themselves file with federal regulators. If that information disguises the true health of the bank—for example, if the bank understates its problem loans to regulators—the strength indicated by the rating may be illusory and the bank could fail. 65 In general, though, these companies have very good track records and the chances of a bank or S&L failing while it has their top rating are extremely low. So while a high rating doesn't offer an iron-clad guarantee, it does offer an extra margin of safety.

Finally you must remember that the financial condition of a bank or any financial institution isn't static. A bank's condition can deteriorate and its rating may be lowered. For the highest level of safety, you may want to initially check your bank's ratings with more than one of the ratings companies—to guard against the chances that one company just blew it on its rating—and then check back with at least one ratings company every quarter to make sure your bank has maintained its high rating. You should also remain alert to other signs that your bank might be in trouble. For example, if you're always reading negative stories in the newspaper about your bank's problems with bad loans or troubles with regulatory agencies or management shake-ups, you should keep particularly close tabs on its rating. And no matter how highly rated a bank or S&L is, you should always make sure your money is fully covered by deposit insurance.

Before we get to the lists of the strongest financial institutions in each state, I want to make a few quick points about S&Ls.

ARE THERE ANY SAFE S&LS OUT THERE?

The trials and tribulations of the S&L industry are too well known and have been written about in sufficiently gory detail for us to waste much time or space recapitulating the sad saga here. Suffice it to say that— from the antics of S&L sleazster Charles Keating and his attempts to buy the influence of five U.S. senators with campaign contributions to the stocking of S&L boards of directors with such unqualified nincompoops as Neil "My Father's the President" Bush—it was one of the sorriest episodes in U.S. financial history. It's hard to find any white hats in this fiasco. S&L officers and directors were inept, corrupt, or, often, both. The regulators who weren't asleep at the switch were actively helping push the industry into bankruptcy at taxpayer expense. As for congressional oversight—the very concept was a joke in the 1980s. This is a situation where twenty-twenty hindsight wasn't needed to see what was going on. The whole industry was deteriorating right there for the industry, the regulators, and Congress to see. But no one wanted to blow the whistle. The predictable result: relatively few of the people who caused this most expensive of financial catastrophes are paying for their role in it, while people like you and me who had very little to do with the incompetents and scamsters are facing a bill that could total anywhere from $500 billion to $1 trillion over the next forty years.

What you may not realize, however, is that not all S&Ls are financially comatose and ready to move on to the Great Liquidator in the Sky. Some are actually solvent, thriving institutions. These are the S&Ls that, by and large, didn't see junk bonds as their salvation, didn't jump blindly into bad real-estate deals, didn't invest in mushroom farms and most certainly didn't have officers who pillaged the S&L to line their own pockets. No, the healthy S&Ls that are still around are the ones that stuck to the dull, plodding, predictable businesses that they knew best—lending money for home mortgages and investing in government-backed bonds. Of course, if you're a conservative, safety-conscious saver, these are exactly the types of S&Ls you want to do business with, the S&Ls that dared to be dull. You will find the state-by-state listing of the sturdiest S&Ls immediately following the list of the strongest banks.

T A B L E   4 · 1

The Safest Banks in the United States

The following banks are not the only top-rated banks in each of the United States and Puerto Rico. Rather, they are the largest banks in each to earn the highest five-star ranking from the Bauer Group, a company in Coral Gables, Florida, which assigns safety ratings to banks, S&Ls, and credit unions. To earn the Bauer Group's top rating, a bank must meet a number of stringent criteria, including a capital ratio of at least 9 percent. In calculating that ultraconservative cushion, 50 percent of loan delinquencies greater than ninety days which exceed loan-loss reserves are not counted toward capital. Similarly, repossessed assets are not only marked down to market value, but the Bauer Group assesses a 25 percent charge against those assets and deducts that amount from capital as well. For those states that did not have five five-star banks, the Bauer Group provided the names of banks with Bauer's next-highest rating, four stars. To warrant four stars a bank must meet a still strict minimum capital ratio of 6 percent. Four-star banks are designated by an asterisk. For more on how to get rankings from bank-rating organizations and how to get a more comprehensive list of ratings on the banks in your state, see pages 63–65.

Name	City	Assets ($ in millions)	Capital ratio†	Telephone
ALABAMA				
First National Bank of Jasper	Jasper	$ 343.2	9.5%	205-221-3121
Peoples Bank & Trust Co.	Selma	217.4	10.2	205-875-1000
First National Bank	Scottsboro	142.2	14.1	205-259-6000
United Security Bank	Thomasville	136.2	9.5	205-636-5424
Bank of Prattville	Prattville	112.5	10.8	205-365-5951
ALASKA				
National Bank of Alaska	Anchorage	1,957.3	10.2	907-276-1132
First National Bank of Anchorage	Anchorage	1,178.6	16.9	907-276-6300
Key Bank of Alaska*	Anchorage	715.2	6.9	907-562-6100
First Bank*	Ketchikan	179.8	8.6	907-225-6101
Denali State Bank	Fairbanks	62.4	11.8	907-456-1400
ARKANSAS				
State First National Bank	Texarkana	381.4	9.6	214-792-7166
Bank of Bentonville	Bentonville	278.8	9.1	501-273-3331
First National Bank of El Dorado	El Dorado	271.8	9.0	501-862-6683
First National Bank of Springdale	Springdale	271.2	10.6	501-751-3400
First National Bank of Magnolia	Magnolia	202.7	9.1	501-234-1234
ARIZONA				
Firstar Metro Bank and Trust*	Phoenix	91.1	6.5	602-256-7994
Community Bank of Arizona	Wickenburg	65.3	10.2	602-684-7881
Rio Salado Bank*	Tempe	62.8	7.3	602-345-8800
Southern Arizona Bank*	Yuma	58.1	6.8	602-784-7505
Western Security Bank*	Scottsdale	19.5	10.5	602-866-2220

Name	City	Assets ($ in millions)	Capital ratio†	Telephone
CALIFORNIA				
Farmers & Merchants Bank of Long Beach	Long Beach	$1,416.9	16.0%	213-437-0011
Mechanics Bank of Richmond	Richmond	647.4	11.3	415-620-1600
Exchange Bank	Santa Rosa	552.4	11.2	707-545-6220
Farmers & Merchants Bank	Lodi	519.1	9.1	209-334-1101
Savings Bank of Mendocino City	Ukiah	281.5	9.3	707-462-6613
COLORADO				
United Bank Greeley, NA	Greeley	197.9	11.5	303-352-1651
Mountain States Bank	Denver	156.5	11.4	303-388-3641
Colorado State Bank	Denver	132.8	12.0	303-861-2111
First National Bank in Loveland	Loveland	130.3	9.7	303-667-3443
Farmers State Bank	Fort Morgan	94.6	15.4	303-867-5661
CONNECTICUT				
Village Bank & Trust	Ridgefield	108.9	9.7	203-438-9551
Citizens National Bank	Putnam	68.9	13.3	203-928-7921
Bank of South Windsor	South Windsor	49.1	10.7	203-644-4177
Prime Bank	Orange	26.0	16.7	203-799-1299
Fleet National Bank of Connecticut	Hartford	5.3	99.2	203-520-3400

Name	City	Assets ($ in millions)	Capital ratio†	Telephone
DELAWARE				
American Express Centurion*	Newark	$9,273.3	6.0%	302-454-2500
Manufacturers Hanover Bank	Wilmington	1,501.3	16.2	302-428-3300
Baltimore Trust Co.	Selbyville	206.9	11.8	302-436-8236
First National Bank of Wyoming	Wyoming	75.5	16.4	302-697-2666
County Bank	Rehoboth Beach	21.8	20.9	302-226-9800
DISTRICT OF COLUMBIA				
Signet Bank*	Washington	480.9	6.8	202-331-5600
Citizens Bank Washington*	Washington	202.8	8.6	202-626-0100
Industrial Bank of Washington*	Washington	138.2	7.4	202-722-2000
National Capital Bank of Washington	Washington	98.6	18.3	202-546-8000
Security Trust Company	Washington	15.3	59.0	202-624-4158
FLORIDA				
Peoples Bank of Lakeland	Lakeland	551.9	10.9	813-687-6500
United National Bank	Miami	455.8	9.4	305-374-3933
First National Bank of South Miami	South Miami	244.3	9.7	305-667-5511
Sun Commercial Bank	Panama City	224.8	9.7	904-785-3416
Coconut Grove Bank	Miami	220.7	14.0	305-858-6666
GEORGIA				
Brand Banking Co.	Lawrenceville	196.6	11.0	404-963-9225
Trust Co. Bank of Rockdale	Conyers	190.2	10.1	404-483-7242
Bank of Canton	Canton	164.9	10.2	404-479-1931
Southeastern Bank	Folkston	159.3	11.6	912-496-7345
Etowah Bank	Canton	143.4	10.1	404-479-8761

Name	City	Assets ($ in millions)	Capital ratio†	Telephone
HAWAII				
First Hawaiian Bank*	Honolulu	$5,023.3	6.3%	808-525-7000
Central Pacific Bank	Honolulu	1,068.0	6.8	808-544-0500
First Interstate Bank Hawaii*	Honolulu	875.4	7.9	808-525-8200
GECC Financial Corp.*	Honolulu	753.8	10.6	808-527-8200
City Bank*	Honolulu	618.7	7.0	808-546-2411
IDAHO				
West One Bank Idaho*	Boise	3,486.4	6.2	208-383-7000
Bank of Commerce	Idaho Falls	185.3	11.8	208-523-2020
Farmers National Bank of Buhl	Buhl	73.2	10.8	208-543-4331
Security State Bank of Mud Lake	Mud Lake	16.7	9.3	208-663-4440
Twin River National Bank	Lewiston	15.4	12.4	208-743-2565
ILLINOIS				
Hickory Point Bank and Trust Co.	Decatur	651.8	11.9	217-877-1236
Mid City National Bank of Chicago	Chicago	369.3	9.2	312-421-7600
Peoples Bank	Bloomington	325.4	9.4	309-828-5211
Manufacturers Bank	Chicago	323.1	10.2	312-278-4040
Magna Millikin Bank	Decatur	295.2	9.5	217-429-4253
INDIANA				
Merchants National Bank of Muncie	Muncie	476.6	9.2	317-747-1500
Mercantile National Bank of Indiana	Hammond	411.3	10.7	219-932-8220
National City Bank of Evansville	Evansville	338.2	9.8	812-425-6261
Bank One	Bloomington	317.9	9.8	812-339-1131
Merchants National Bank Terre Haute	Terre Haute	291.5	9.2	812-234-5571

Name	City	Assets ($ in millions)	Capital ratio†	Telephone
IOWA				
Davenport Bank & Trust Co.	Davenport	$1,833.6	12.4%	319-383-3211
West Des Moines State Bank	West Des Moines	288.5	10.7	515-225-2300
First National Bank	Ames	222.6	9.0	515-232-5561
Central State Bank	Muscatine	217.7	13.7	319-263-3131
Clinton National Bank	Clinton	202.7	9.2	319-243-1243
KANSAS				
Industrial State Bank	Kansas City	187.4	9.4	913-831-2000
Union National Bank & Trust Co. of Manhattan	Manhattan	150.8	11.1	913-537-1234
Citizens Bank & Trust Co.	Manhattan	115.9	9.5	913-776-9400
Walnut Valley State Bank	Eldorado	97.5	11.0	316-321-1250
Douglas County Bank	Lawrence	97.4	12.6	913-843-7474
KENTUCKY				
Mid American Bank & Trust Co.	Louisville	983.9	10.3	502-589-3351
Citizens Bank & Trust Co.	Paducah	464.3	9.2	502-444-6321
Farmers Bank & Capital Trust	Frankfort	393.5	10.9	502-227-1600
Citizens State Bank	Owensboro	238.1	9.1	502-926-2020
Bank of Murray	Murray	224.3	11.2	502-753-1893
LOUISIANA				
Calcasieu Marine National Bank	Lake Charles	834.2	10.7	318-439-4541
First National Bank of Lake Charles	Lake Charles	301.1	10.4	318-477-7630
Concordia Bank & Trust Co.	Vidalia	245.8	12.0	318-336-5259
Saint Landry Bank & Trust Co.	Opelousas	225.3	10.1	318-942-7516
Metairie Bank & Trust Co.	Metairie	194.2	21.4	504-834-6330

Name	City	Assets ($ in millions)	Capital ratio†	Telephone
MAINE				
Key Bank of Maine*	Augusta	$1,922.6	6.8%	207-623-4721
Camden National Bank*	Camden	287.7	8.1	207-236-8821
Bar Harbor Banking & Trust*	Bar Harbor	194.9	9.4	207-288-3314
First National Bank of Damariscotta*	Damariscotta	162.3	7.1	207-563-3195
Union Trust Company of Ellsworth	Ellsworth	161.9	9.5	207-667-2504
MARYLAND				
Citizens National Bank	Laurel	406.5	9.9	301-725-3100
First United National Bank & Trust	Oakland	314.7	9.7	301-334-9471
First National Bank of St. Mary's	Leonardtown	193.6	10.2	301-475-8081
Carrollton Bank of Baltimore	Baltimore	187.8	11.0	301-837-9800
Calvin B. Taylor Banking Co.	Berlin	176.4	13.0	301-641-1700
MASSACHUSETTS				
Enterprise Bank & Trust Co.	Lowell	139.2	10.1%	508-459-9000
National Grand Bank of Marblehead	Marblehead	126.8	10.2	617-631-6000
Northmark Bank	North Andover	122.8	9.2	508-686-9100
Broadway National Bank of Chelsea	Chelsea	110.2	9.6	617-884-2650
Liberty Bank & Trust Co.	Boston	33.8	13.3	617-742-4700
MICHIGAN				
Liberty State Bank & Trust	Hamtramck	1,211.9	9.2	313-871-9400
Monroe Bank & Trust	Monroe	519.5	10.2	313-241-3431
Chemical Bank & Trust Co.	Midland	481.1	9.4	517-631-9200
City Bank & Trust Co.	Jackson	389.6	11.8	517-877-2711
Peoples State Bank	Hamtramck	141.1	17.0	313-875-2000

Name	City	Assets ($ in millions)	Capital ratio†	Telephone
MINNESOTA				
First National Bank of Bemidji	Bemidji	$ 173.8	10.4%	218-751-2430
Golden Valley Bank	Golden Valley	167.0	9.8	612-541-1300
First Western Bank St. Louis	St. Louis Park	147.8	9.9	612-935-5145
Winona National & Savings Bank	Winona	125.6	17.0	507-454-4320
Grand Rapids State Bank	Grand Rapids	120.7	9.9	218-326-9414
MISSISSIPPI				
National Bank of Commerce of Mississippi	Starkville	436.3	9.0	601-323-1341
Peoples Bank of Biloxi	Biloxi	259.2	13.3	601-435-5511
First Columbus National Bank	Columbus	187.1	10.9	601-328-7932
Peoples Bank	Ripley	153.7	9.5	601-837-8191
Bank of New Albany	New Albany	151.1	11.1	601-534-8171
MISSOURI				
Exchange National Bank of Jefferson	Jefferson City	251.8	11.1	314-636-2151
Third National Bank of Sedalia	Sedalia	207.8	9.6	816-827-3333
Cass Bank and Trust Company	St. Louis	207.0	10.3	314-621-9400
Bank of Washington	Washington	185.8	13.0	314-239-7831
Saint Johns Bank & Trust Co.	St. Johns	183.5	9.7	314-428-1000
MONTANA				
Farmers State Bank	Conrad	73.9	24.0	406-278-5514
Valley Bank of Kalispell	Kalispell	71.2	10.9	406-755-7123
First State Bank of Malta	Malta	60.7	14.5	406-654-2340
Farmers State Bank	Victor	56.6	10.6	406-642-3431
Yellowstone Bank	Laurel	56.4	12.4	406-628-7951

Name	City	Assets ($ in millions)	Capital ratio†	Telephone
NEBRASKA				
Packers Bank & Trust Company	Omaha	$ 115.0	9.0%	402-731-4900
McCook National Bank	McCook	97.2	14.5	308-345-4240
Jones National Bank & Trust	Seward	91.0	11.7	402-643-3602
Washington County Bank	Blair	88.2	10.5	402-426-2111
First National Bank of Fairbury	Fairbury	87.9	10.5	402-266-5931
NEVADA				
Valley Bank of Nevada*	Las Vegas	2,862.6	6.5	702-386-1000
Nevada State Bank*	Las Vegas	311.7	8.7	702-383-4111
Fallon National Bank	Fallon	27.4	10.5	702-423-7081
First National Bank of Ely	Ely	27.1	39.1	702-289-4441
Nevada Community Bank	Las Vegas	12.5	42.3	702-368-1969
NEW HAMPSHIRE				
Monadnock Bank*	Jaffrey	155.0	7.5	603-532-7788
North Conway Bank*	North Conway	141.5	9.4	603-356-5466
New London Trust Company*	New London	130.6	7.3	603-526-2535
Pemigewasset National Bank of Plymouth*	Plymouth	103.8	8.0	603-536-2733
Community Bank & Trust Company	Wolfeboro	27.2	11.2	603-569-8400
NEW JERSEY				
Newton Trust Company	Newton	150.7	9.9	201-383-2400
Community Bank of Bergen County	Maywood	118.8	11.9	201-843-2300
Brunswick Bank & Trust Company	Manalapan	70.8	17.0	201-431-3000
The Dreyfus Consumer Bank	Paramus	65.3	11.5	201-678-5220
Sussex County State Bank	Franklin	64.5	9.8	201-827-2404

Name	City	Assets ($ in millions)	Capital ratio†	Telephone
NEW MEXICO				
Western Commerce Bank	Carlsbad	$ 116.0	9.7%	505-887-6686
Portales National Bank	Portales	66.6	9.6	505-356-6601
First New Mexico Bank	Deming	61.4	9.3	505-546-2691
Valley National Bank	Espanola	55.5	10.0	505-753-2136
Ranchers State Bank	Belen	50.2	13.7	505-864-4487
NEW YORK				
Merchants Bank of New York	New York	631.2	11.1	212-669-6600
Suffolk County National Bank of Riverhead	Riverhead	500.5	9.5	516-727-2700
Sumitomo Trust & Banking Co. USA	New York	493.1	16.2	212-326-0500
Sterling National Bank & Trust Co.	New York	474.6	17.3	212-826-2200
Mitsubishi Bank and Trust Co.	New York	460.7	10.3	212-363-9270
NORTH CAROLINA				
Security Bank & Trust Co.	Salisbury	356.8	12.5	704-633-7800
Bank of Granite	Granite Falls	325.6	11.8	704-396-3141
Lexington State Bank	Lexington	305.7	11.4	704-246-6500
First Charter National Bank	Concord	240.1	10.8	704-786-3300
Fidelity Bank	Fuquay-Varina	239.5	10.3	919-552-2242

Name	City	Assets ($ in millions)	Capital ratio†	Telephone
NORTH DAKOTA				
Valley Bank & Trust Company	Grand Forks	$ 118.0	10.4%	701-772-5551
First National Bank & Trust Co. of Williston	Williston	114.3	10.6	701-572-2113
First National Bank & Trust Co. of Bottineau	Bottineau	89.0	9.7	701-228-2236
Liberty National Bank & Trust	Dickinson	75.9	12.3	701-227-0881
Community National Bank of Grand Forks	Grand Forks	59.0	9.2	701-746-6401
OHIO				
Security National Bank & Trust	Springfield	411.6	9.6	513-324-6800
First National Bank of Zanesville	Zanesville	283.5	11.0	614-452-8444
Fifth Third Bank of Southern Ohio	Hillsboro	267.2	11.1	513-393-4204
Wayne County National Bank of Wooster	Wooster	237.0	10.1	216-264-1222
Delaware County Bank	Delaware	219.8	9.2	614-363-1133
OKLAHOMA				
First National Bank & Trust Co.	McAlester	337.8	10.3	918-426-0211
First National Bank of Midwest City	Midwest City	178.0	9.1	405-732-4571
Security National Bank & Trust Co.	Norman	176.9	9.1	405-321-7170
First National Bank in Durant	Durant	127.9	9.0	405-924-4242
First National Bank of Altus	Altus	115.4	11.0	918-267-3645

Name	City	Assets ($ in millions)	Capital ratio†	Telephone
OREGON				
Pioneer Trust Bank	Salem	$ 108.0	12.7%	503-363-3136
National Security Bank	Newport	99.4	10.7	503-265-9444
Valley of the Rogue	Rogue River	93.0	9.9	503-582-3216
Douglas National Bank	Roseburg	76.9	9.4	503-440-2600
Pacific Continental Bank	Eugene	42.6	10.6	503-686-8685
PENNSYLVANIA				
Bank of Pennsylvania	Reading	818.9	9.3	215-378-3600
Farmers First Bank	Lititz	675.3	11.5	717-626-4721
Third National Bank & Trust	Scranton	407.3	9.3	717-358-8230
Citizens & Northern Bank	Ralston	405.1	9.2	717-724-3411
Farmers Trust Company	Carlisle	341.1	9.5	717-243-3212
PUERTO RICO				
Banco Central Corp.*	San Juan	1,726.6	8.4	809-725-4627
Scotiabank de Puerto Rico*	San Juan	615.4	10.6	809-725-3939
Royal Bank de Puerto Rico*	San Juan	549.6	7.5	809-753-2000
Banco Commercial de Mayaguez*	Mayaguez	510.1	6.8	809-832-3717
First Community Trust Company	San Juan	37.8	39.4	809-753-7080
RHODE ISLAND				
Home Loan & Investment Assoc.*	Providence	267.0	8.4	401-272-5100
Domestic Safe Deposit Company*	Cranston	87.6	7.6	401-943-1600
First Bank & Trust Co.*	Providence	66.3	7.7	401-421-3600
Centreville National Bank of Warwick	West Warwick	33.7	17.8	401-821-9100
Island Trust Company	Newport	19.2	29.7	401-847-3452

78

Name	City	Assets ($ in millions)	Capital ratio†	Telephone
SOUTH CAROLINA				
M. S. Bailey & Son	Clinton	$ 102.3	9.3%	803-833-1910
Farmers & Merchants Bank	Holly Hill	91.5	10.5	803-496-3430
First National Bank of Holly Hill	Holly Hill	86.2	11.5	803-496-5011
Arthur State Bank	Union	84.5	13.3	803-427-1213
Enterprise Bank of South Carolina	Ehrhardt	83.1	12.6	803-267-3191
SOUTH DAKOTA				
First Dakota National Bank	Yankton	147.3	9.3	605-665-7432
Pioneer Bank & Trust Co.	Belle Fourche	141.5	10.8	605-892-2536
Farmers & Merchants Bank	Huron	140.3	11.3	605-352-6444
Valley National Bank	Sioux Falls	101.6	10.5	605-336-3740
Farmers State Bank	Winner	93.8	9.6	605-842-1313
TENNESSEE				
Valley Fidelity Bank & Trust Co.	Knoxville	562.1	9.1	615-521-3000
Pioneer Bank	Chattanooga	409.3	10.2	615-265-2551
First Farmers & Merchants National Bank	Columbia	298.0	9.8	615-388-3145
Greene County Bank	Greeneville	217.9	11.8	615-639-5111
Barretville Bank & Trust Co.	Barretville	197.0	19.1	901-829-4211
TEXAS				
American State Bank	Lubbock	525.4	9.5	806-763-7061
North Dallas Bank & Trust Co.	Dallas	331.3	11.3	214-387-1300
First State Bank & Trust Co.	Mission	296.9	12.2	512-585-4801
First Bank & Trust Co.	Groves	242.8	13.5	409-963-1141
First National Bank in Big Spring	Big Spring	228.6	12.1	915-267-5513

Name	City	Assets ($ in millions)	Capital ratio†	Telephone
UTAH				
Central Bank & Trust Co.	Springville	$ 118.6	11.2%	801-375-1000
Barnes Banking Co.	Kaysville	100.8	14.6	801-376-3424
Bank of American Fork	American Fork	100.6	12.0	801-756-7681
Utah Bank & Trust Co.	Bountiful	73.7	11.9	801-292-6211
Community First Bank	Clearfield	66.9	14.8	801-773-8600
VERMONT				
First Vermont Bank & Trust Co.*	Brattleboro	648.8	7.2	802-254-8711
Merchants Bank*	Burlington	578.4	8.6	802-658-3400
Howard Bank*	Burlington	522.6	8.4	802-658-1010
Granite Savings Bank & Trust	Barre	132.1	9.6	802-479-3313
Citizens Savings Bank & Trust	St. Johnsbury	66.1	9.0	802-748-3131
VIRGINIA				
American National Bank & Trust Co.	Danville	219.8	10.8	804-792-5111
Union Bank & Trust Co.	Bowling Green	199.3	10.0	804-633-5031
George Mason Bank	Fairfax	197.3	9.6	703-352-1100
Second National Bank	Culpeper	182.1	10.1	703-825-4800
Bank of Southside Virginia	Carson	169.7	12.2	804-246-5211
WASHINGTON				
First Independent Bank	Vancouver	409.5	13.4	206-699-4242
Cashmere Valley Bank	Cashmere	195.1	9.3	509-782-1501
Yakima Valley Bank	Yakima	108.4	9.3	509-453-1515
Enterprise Bank of Bellevue	Bellevue	68.6	13.2	206-454-7070
Whidbey Island Bank	Coupeville	62.4	10.1	206-678-4555

Name	City	Assets ($ in millions)	Capital ratio†	Telephone
WEST VIRGINIA				
Wheeling Dollar Bank	Wheeling	$ 294.1	11.7%	304-234-9000
Union National Bank of Clarksburg	Clarksburg	265.9	9.5	304-624-3400
Bank of Raleigh	Beckley	244.5	10.5	304-255-7000
Security National Bank & Trust	Wheeling	220.9	14.5	304-233-0600
Raleigh County National Bank	Beckley	220.5	13.3	304-256-7262
WISCONSIN				
First National Bank of Kenosha	Kenosha	379.9	10.0	414-658-2331
Tri City National Bank	Oak Creek	265.8	9.8	414-761-1610
Park Bank	Milwaukee	205.1	9.4	414-223-3000
Bank of Sturgeon Bay	Sturgeon Bay	186.5	10.5	414-743-5551
Bank of Burlington	Burlington	145.8	9.5	414-763-9141
WYOMING				
Key Bank Wyoming	Jackson	201.5	9.0	307-733-4884
Rock Springs National Bank	Rock Springs	199.4	13.3	307-362-8801
Key Bank Wyoming	Rock Springs	164.1	10.6	307-362-7840
North Side State Bank	Rock Springs	93.6	12.4	307-362-5601
Rawlins National Bank	Rawlins	82.8	10.4	307-324-2203

SOURCE: The Bauer Group, Coral Gables, Florida; data as of 3/31/91.

* This is a four-star institution.

† This is the capital ratio before deductions for bad loans or repossesed assets. Bad loans and repossessed assets have been factored into the capital ratio when assigning ratings.

The Safest Thrift Institutions in the United States

The following thrifts—savings-and-loan associations and savings banks—are not the only top-rated thrifts in each state and Puerto Rico. Rather, they are the largest thrifts in each to get the top, five-star ranking from the Bauer Group, a company in Coral Gables, Florida, that assigns safety ratings to banks, thrifts, and credit unions. To earn the Bauer Group's top rating, a thrift must meet a number of stringent criteria, including a capital ratio of at least 6 percent. In calculating that ultraconservative cushion, 50 percent of loan delinquencies greater than ninety days that exceed loan-loss reserves are not counted toward capital. Similarly, repossessed assets are not only marked down to market value, but the Bauer Group assess a 25 percent charge against those assets and deducts that amount from capital as well. In cases where a state did not have five five-star thrifts, the Bauer Group provided the names of the largest four-star thrifts. To merit a four-star rating a thrift must meet a still strict minimum capital ratio of 4.5 percent. (Four-star thrifts are designated by an asterisk.) For more on how to get rankings from rating organizations and how to get a more comprehensive list of ratings on the thrifts in your state, see pages 63–65.

Name	City	Assets ($ in millions)	Capital ratio† (percentage)
ALABAMA			
First Federal Savings Bank	Decatur	$ 230.9	10.1%
First Federal of Alabama	Jasper	188.7	6.3
First Federal Savings and Loan	Bessemer	97.8	12.5
Cullman Savings and Loan Assoc.	Cullman	82.5	13.0
Home Federal Savings Bank	Lafayette	81.9	9.7
ALASKA			
Mount McKinley Savings Bank	Fairbanks	101.0	10.2
ARIZONA			
First Arizona Savings & Loan*	Glendale	69.8	5.0

Name	City	Assets ($ in millions)	Capital ratio† (percentage)
ARKANSAS			
First Federal Savings & Loan*	Texarkana	$ 129.9	6.4%
First Federal Savings & Loan	Camden	105.2	7.9
Benton Savings & Loan Assoc.*	Benton	97.9	6.1
Security Savings Bank	Conway	72.3	6.4
Heritage Federal Savings & Loan	Monticello	35.1	6.5
CALIFORNIA			
Citibank, Federal Savings Bank	San Francisco	12,835.5	13.1
Eurekabank	San Carlos	1,901.6	6.5
Heart Federal Savings & Loan	Auburn	932.4	7.1
California Savings & Loan Assoc.	San Francisco	492.6	10.3
Quaker City Federal Savings & Loan	Whittier	392.8	8.6
COLORADO			
San Luis Valley Federal Savings & Loan Assoc. of Alamosa	Alamosa	76.7	10.9
Morgan County Federal Savings & Loan Assoc. of Fort Morgan	Fort Morgan	43.6	12.8
Colorado Savings Bank	Englewood	41.4	11.1
Rocky Ford Federal Savings & Loan	Rocky Ford	20.5	6.9
Del Norte Federal Savings & Loan	Del Norte	11.0	10.4
CONNECTICUT			
New Haven Savings Bank	New Haven	1,744.9	8.9
American Savings Bank	New Britain	955.8	11.7
First Federal Savings & Loan	Waterbury	701.2	7.3
First Federal Savings & Loan	East Hartford	481.0	8.2
American Bank of Connecticut	Waterbury	342.9	9.3
DELAWARE			
Artisans Savings Bank	Wilmington	294.7	7.1
Ninth Ward Savings & Loan*	Wilmington	87.6	4.7
DISTRICT OF COLUMBIA			
Citybank, Federal Savings Bank	Washington	1,152.0	23.0

Name	City	Assets ($ in millions)	Capital ratio† (percentage)
FLORIDA			
Citibank Federal Savings Bank	Miami	$ 2,426.7	13.6%
First Federal Savings & Loan	Fort Myers	989.7	8.1
Home Savings Bank	Hollywood	972.4	7.2
First Federal Savings Bank of Charlotte County	Punta Gorda	358.9	11.7
First Federal Savings & Loan Assoc. of Lake County	Leesburg	243.0	7.5
GEORGIA			
Gwinnet Federal Bank	Lawrenceville	276.6	12.4
First Federal Savings Bank of La Grange	La Grange	173.4	9.1
Thomas County Federal Savings & Loan	Thomasville	124.1	9.8
Charter Federal Savings & Loan	West Point	119.5	8.5
First Federal Savings & Loan	Valdosta	107.1	8.4
HAWAII			
First Federal Savings & Loan Assoc. of America	Honolulu	979.5	11.4
Pioneer Federal Savings Bank	Honolulu	564.8	8.7
IDAHO			
First Federal Savings & Loan Assoc. of Twin Falls*	Twin Falls	200.1	4.9
First Federal Bank of Idaho*	Lewiston	88.7	6.8
ILLINOIS			
Bell Federal Savings & Loan	Chicago	1,897.4	8.1
Northwestern Savings & Loan	Chicago	1,308.1	11.3
Liberty Bank for Savings	Chicago	484.0	12.0
Liberty Federal Savings & Loan of Chicago	Chicago	434.5	8.0
Calumet Federal Savings & Loan	Chicago	407.9	8.5
INDIANA			
Indiana Federal Savings & Loan	Valparaiso	573.7	9.4
Ameriana Savings Bank	Newcastle	279.5	12.5
Peoples Bank	Munster	218.2	8.4
Peoples Federal Savings Bank of DeKalb County	Auburn	217.4	13.8
First Bank of Lafayette	Lafayette	215.6	10.5

Name	City	Assets ($ in millions)	Capital ratio† (percentage)
IOWA			
First Federal Savings Bank of Iowa	Davenport	$ 320.5	8.5%
First Federal Savings & Loan Assoc. of Storm Lake	Storm Lake	201.4	6.8
Hawkeye Federal Savings Bank	Boone	94.6	6.9
First Federal Savings & Loan of Lincoln—Iowa	Council Bluffs	94.0	35.8
Webster City Federal Savings Bank	Webster City	91.3	9.3
KANSAS			
Capitol Federal Savings & Loan	Topeka	3,540.1	8.9
Inter-State Federal Savings & Loan Assoc. of Kansas City	Kansas City	251.4	8.8
Landmark Federal Savings Assoc.	Dodge City	164.2	6.4
Mutual Savings Assoc.	Leavenworth	153.6	7.9
Citizens Savings & Loan Assoc.	Leavenworth	149.1	6.6
KENTUCKY			
Sunrise Bank For Savings	Fort Mitchell	277.4	6.5
Kentucky Enterprise Federal Savings & Loan	Newport	275.6	6.9
First Federal Savings & Loan	Bowling Green	241.7	8.4
First Federal Savings Bank of Elizabethtown	Elizabethtown	210.7	15.4
Lexington Federal Savings Bank	Lexington	182.6	12.9
LOUISIANA			
Eureka Homestead Society	New Orleans	99.6	7.5
Guaranty Savings & Homestead Assoc.	New Orleans	83.4	22.1
Union Savings and Loan Assoc.	New Orleans	74.7	18.7
State-Investors Savings & Loan	Metairie	69.2	6.9
Hibernia Homestead & Savings Assoc.	New Orleans	48.5	16.3
MAINE			
Bangor Savings Bank	Bangor	597.1	9.0
Gorham Savings Bank	Gorham	201.6	8.8
Norway Savings Bank	Norway	200.2	10.3
Skowhegan Savings Bank	Skowhegan	196.0	9.5
Franklin Savings Bank	Farmington	192.9	8.8

Name	City	Assets ($ in millions)	Capital ratio† (percentage)
MARYLAND			
Maryland Federal Savings & Loan	Hyattsville	$ 756.2	7.1%
Custom Savings Bank	Pikesville	318.0	9.6
Rosedale Federal Savings & Loan	Baltimore	279.9	10.6
Reisterstown Federal Savings Bank	Reisterstown	225.1	9.4
Leeds Federal Savings & Loan	Baltimore	202.7	8.7
MASSACHUSETTS			
South Boston Savings Bank	Boston	1,543.0	6.9
New Bedford Institution for Savings	New Bedford	1,259.2	14.7
Peoples Savings Bank	Worcester	910.6	7.4
Salem Five Cents Savings Bank	Salem	612.5	8.3
Sterling Bank	Waltham	564.5	8.5
MICHIGAN			
Capitol Federal Savings Bank	Lansing	520.2	6.5
Citizens Federal Savings Bank	Port Huron	395.6	6.3
Ottawa Savings Bank	Holland	254.5	7.5
First Federal Savings & Loan Assoc. of Lenawee County	Adrian	227.7	15.9
Eaton Federal Savings Bank	Charlotte	122.8	9.3
MINNESOTA			
Home Federal Savings Bank	Spring Valley	363.1	6.9
First State Federal Savings & Loan	Hutchinson	127.8	9.2
Redwood Falls Federal Savings & Loan	Redwood Falls	36.4	10.1
Lake City Federal Savings & Loan	Lake City	31.2	10.7
Jackson Federal Savings & Loan	Jackson	27.9	10.0
MISSISSIPPI			
First Federal Savings & Loan	Pascagoula	157.8	6.6
Community Federal Savings & Loan	Tupelo	121.3	10.0
Home Federal Savings & Loan	Meridian	79.4	8.9
Inter-City Federal Savings Bank	Louisville	27.2	9.9
Cleveland Federal Savings Bank	Cleveland	21.9	8.4

Name	City	Assets ($ in millions)	Capital ratio† (percentage)
MISSOURI			
United Savings & Loan Assoc.	Lebanon	$ 430.4	6.6
Guaranty Federal Savings & Loan Assoc. of Springfield	Springfield	156.2	6.9
First Savings Bank	Mt. Vernon	147.9	6.6
The Cameron Savings & Loan Assoc.	Cameron	128.1	10.4
Ozarks Federal Savings & Loan	Farmington	125.8	6.8
MONTANA			
Security Federal Savings Bank	Billings	252.0	9.2
First Federal Savings Bank of Montana	Kalispell	175.4	11.7
United Savings Bank	Great Falls	94.1	20.9
Empire Federal Savings & Loan	Livingston	69.6	14.9
Pioneer Federal Savings & Loan	Deer Lodge	45.7	8.2
NEBRASKA			
Firstier Savings Bank	Omaha	132.3	6.2
The Equitable Bank & Loan Assoc. of Grand Island	Grand Island	90.5	7.2
Security Federal Savings	Lincoln	40.2	6.6
Tecumseh Building & Loan Assoc.	Tecumseh	33.0	8.8
The Madison County Building & Loan Assoc.	Madison	29.8	11.8
NEVADA			
American Federal Savings Bank*	Reno	591.0	6.0
NEW HAMPSHIRE			
Cheshire County Savings Bank	Keene	413.1	9.4
Portsmouth Savings Bank	Portsmouth	278.2	14.2
Mascoma Savings Bank	Lebanon	248.9	8.5
Laconia Savings Bank	Laconia	231.2	13.0
Merrimack County Savings Bank	Concord	170.8	8.8

Name	City	Assets ($ in millions)	Capital ratio† (percentage)
NEW JERSEY			
Hudson City Savings Bank	Paramus	$3,602.2	7.8%
Investors Savings & Loan Assoc.	Millburn	1,750.8	6.2
Provident Savings Bank	Jersey City	1,510.1	6.6
Bankers Savings	Perth Amboy	1,315.9	7.4
Morris Savings Bank	Morristown	1,041.1	7.8
NEW MEXICO			
First Federal Savings Bank	Roswell	142.4	9.0
Alamagordo Federal Savings & Loan*	Alamagordo	116.1	9.5
Century Federal Savings & Loan	Santa Fe	111.2	7.9
Gallup Federal Savings & Loan	Gallup	40.1	12.1
NEW YORK			
Manhattan Savings Bank	New York	5,877.1	8.8
Greenpoint Savings Bank	Brooklyn	5,295.5	11.9
The Long Island Savings Bank	Syosset	2,721.3	8.2
Albany Savings Bank	Albany	2,136.3	7.1
Independence Savings Bank	Brooklyn	1,589.5	8.2
NORTH CAROLINA			
Home Federal Savings & Loan	Charlotte	603.5	7.7
Piedmont Federal Savings & Loan	Winston-Salem	517.7	12.2
Gate City Federal Savings & Loan	Greensboro	465.5	8.7
First Federal Savings Bank	Winston-Salem	381.1	12.3
Security Federal Savings Bank	Durham	284.4	9.5
NORTH DAKOTA			
Heritage Federal Savings Bank	Cando	15.1	5.1
OHIO			
Third Federal Savings & Loan Assoc.	Cleveland	3,133.6	9.4
Hunter Savings Assoc.	Cincinnati	991.0	7.6
Home Savings & Loan	Youngstown	905.2	7.7
First Federal Savings & Loan	Youngstown	431.3	10.3
First Federal Savings & Loan	Warren	408.6	7.0

Name	City	Assets ($ in millions)	Capital ratio† (percentage)
OKLAHOMA			
Fidelity Federal Savings & Loan	Claremore	$ 81.4	10.0%
Home Federal Savings & Loan Assoc. of Ada	Ada	80.9	6.6
The Globe Savings Bank*	Harrah	63.5	11.9
Osage Federal Savings & Loan Assoc. of Pawhuska	Pawhuska	45.4	6.5
First Commercial Bank*	Lawton	40.7	5.4
OREGON			
Klamath First Federal Savings & Loan Assoc.	Klamath Falls	323.7	9.8
First Security Bank of Oregon*	Salem	230.0	10.0
First Federal Savings & Loan*	McMinnville	129.3	5.2
Evergreen Federal Savings & Loan	Grants Pass	124.2	6.3
PENNSYLVANIA			
Germantown Savings Bank	Bala-Cynwyd	1,401.4	7.1
Franklin First Federal Savings	Wilkes-Barre	917.2	9.8
United Federal Savings Bank	State College	602.7	10.4
Keystone Savings Assoc.	Bethlehem	427.5	7.5
Prime Savings Bank	Philadelphia	340.8	10.0
PUERTO RICO			
Oriental Federal Savings Bank	Humacao	303.9	7.1
R & G Federal Savings Bank*	Guaynabo	96.5	5.4
Catano Federal Savings Bank*	Catano	15.7	5.8
RHODE ISLAND			
Citizens Savings Bank	Providence	2,759.1	7.3
Savings Bank of Newport	Newport	334.6	7.8
Centreville Savings Bank	West Warwick	271.2	16.9
SOUTH CAROLINA			
First Federal Savings & Loan	Anderson	311.4	6.9
United Savings Bank	Greenwood	287.0	9.8
First Federal Savings & Loan	Spartanburg	260.2	8.5
Oconee Savings & Loan Assoc.	Seneca	192.8	8.6
Heritage Federal Savings & Loan	Laurens	180.1	7.6

Name	City	Assets ($ in millions)	Capital ratio† (percentage)
SOUTH DAKOTA			
First Federal Savings Bank	Watertown	$ 145.3	8.7%
Brookings Savings & Loan Assoc.*	Brookings	68.6	5.2
TENNESSEE			
Home Federal Savings & Loan Assoc. of Upper East Tennessee	Johnson City	799.8	12.2
First Federal Savings & Loan	Chattanooga	623.8	10.3
Security Trust Federal Savings & Loan Assoc.	Knoxville	227.2	7.2
Elizabethton Federal Savings Bank	Elizabethton	146.8	10.2
First Federal Savings Bank	Clarksville	143.4	6.5
TEXAS			
Colonial Savings & Loan	Fort Worth	462.2	8.5
San Antonio Federal Savings Bank	Weslaco	285.7	20.8
Orange Savings & Loan Assoc.	Orange	149.0	6.8
First Federal Savings & Loan	Tyler	116.6	8.4
Mineola Federal Savings & Loan	Mineola	78.9	8.2
UTAH			
Firstfed America Bank	Logan	39.8	12.3
VERMONT			
Northfield Savings Bank*	Northfield	300.5	7.1
Passumpsic Savings Bank	St. Johnsbury	198.2	8.3
Bennington Co-Op Savings & Loan Assoc., Inc.	Bennington	68.7	6.7
Wells River Savings Bank*	Wells River	65.1	6.1
Brattleboro Savings & Loan*	Brattleboro	35.1	6.3
VIRGINIA			
Pioneer Federal Savings Bank	Hopewell	497.3	8.4
Fredericksburg Savings & Loan	Fredericksburg	447.3	9.3
Franklin Federal Savings & Loan	Richmond	343.7	10.0
Co-Operative Savings Bank	Lynchburg	205.6	8.2
Community Federal Savings Bank	Staunton	122.6	10.1

Name	City	Assets ($ in millions)	Capital ratio† (percentage)
WASHINGTON			
Washington Federal Savings & Loan Assoc.	Seattle	$ 2,622.0	11.9%
University Savings Bank	Seattle	984.1	6.4
Pioneer Savings Bank	Lynwood	767.3	11.8
Yakima Federal Savings & Loan	Yakima	519.7	10.7
First Federal Savings Bank of Washington	Walla Walla	336.8	6.9
WEST VIRGINIA			
Huntington Federal Savings & Loan	Huntington	244.0	9.8
Fed One Savings Bank	Wheeling	225.3	6.9
First Empire Federal Savings & Loan Assoc.	Charleston	188.0	10.9
Hancock County Federal Savings & Loan Assoc.	Chester	155.3	8.3
Point Pleasant Federal Savings & Loan Assoc.	Point Pleasant	49.5	13.0
WISCONSIN			
Security Bank State Savings Bank	Milwaukee	2,175.2	12.1
Mutual Savings Bank of Wisconsin	Milwaukee	1,174.4	9.1
St. Francis Federal Savings Bank	St. Francis	664.4	7.8
Advantage Bank State Savings Bank	Kenosha	379.2	9.2
Wauwatosa Savings & Loan	Wauwatosa	368.4	11.5
WYOMING			
First Federal Savings Bank	Sheridan	92.0	15.2
Tri-County Federal Savings & Loan Assoc.	Torrington	55.1	9.8
Buffalo Federal Savings & Loan	Buffalo	32.8	13.1
Security First Savings & Loan	Cheyenne	28.0	6.5

SOURCE: The Bauer Group, Coral Gables, Florida; data as of 3/31/91.

* This is a four-star institution.

† This is the capital ratio before deductions for bad loans and repossessed assets. Bad loans and repossessed assets have been factored into the capital ratio assigning ratings. 91

≋ 5 ≋

HOW SAFE IS YOUR CREDIT UNION?

The Rhode Island Scare

OVERALL, credit unions are in pretty good financial shape. In many ways, as you'll see later in this chapter, you may actually be better off doing business with a federally insured credit union than with a federally insured bank. Still, like banks and S&Ls, credit unions have also had some problems. And nowhere have the problems been more severe than in Rhode Island, where the failure of several large credit unions led to a reexamination of the safety of credit unions nationwide. Before we get into specific strategies you can use to make sure the money you keep in credit unions is completely safe, let's take a look at the Rhode Island credit-union scare and see what lessons can be drawn from it.

It didn't take long for hundreds of thousands of people in Rhode Island to realize 1991 was going to be anything but a Happy New Year. Just two hours after his New Year's Day swearing-in ceremony, Rhode Island's new governor, Bruce G. Sundlun, suddenly shut down forty-five credit unions and small banks in the state, hoping to prevent a run on the institutions after some of the sleaziest financial dealings outside of S&L-dom led to the collapse of their private insurance organization, the Rhode Island Share and Deposit Indemnity Corporation (RISDIC). The governor's move effectively prevented some 300,000 Rhode Islanders—30 percent of the state's population—from getting their hands on more than $1 billion in deposits frozen in their accounts. "I had $10,000 in accounts in the Davisville credit union," says one Rhode Island resident who prefers to remain anonymous. "It doesn't sound like much, but it is my life's savings." Yet wondering when—make that *if*—this person would ever see his money again wasn't all he had to worry about in those first few days of the New Year. He had a more pressing immediate concern: he was broke. Like many others, this credit union member had his paycheck directly deposited to his checking account. And his entire salary for the month of January had just been deposited in the Davisville Credit Union before it was shut down. "I was left with $30 to my name," he says. "Everything else was tied up in my credit-union accounts."

As word of the seizure spread, hundreds of panicked, mostly lower- and middle-income working people descended on their credit unions, hoping to get all, some, *any* of their cash out. But they were too late. State troopers, wearing leather storm coats and those Smokey the Bear hats, had already moved in to prevent disgruntled depositors from taking their vengeance when they found they couldn't take their money. What the mostly elderly depositors didn't know then, however, was that, while they were being assured that rumors about a shutdown were false and that their savings were completely safe, some of the bigwigs who had access to inside information were busily pulling their own money out. According to the *Providence Journal*, Rhode Island Central Credit Union president John Lanfredi withdrew some $300,000 in December, the month before Governor Sundlun shut down the credit unions. Gee, what a lucky break for him.

After the initial shock of the closings, the panic subsided a bit as the trusting residents of Rhode Island figured their state government, including the brand-new governor, would surely sort out the mess within a few days—or at least give people access to their cash in the meantime. But that's when the real disappointment set in. While a few of the banks and credit unions managed to switch to federal insurance and reopen within a few days and others within a few weeks, twelve institutions—two banks and ten mostly large credit unions—were still closed as of mid-May. Which means that a full *five* months after the governor declared a bank holiday on January 1, an estimated two hundred thousand or so depositors—that's 165 account holders for every square mile in this smallest state in the union—were still unable to get much, if any, of the savings whose safety was supposedly guaranteed by an institution created and overseen by the state of Rhode Island. To add further injury, *not a cent* in interest was being paid on captive depositors' money. The state eventually did give depositors some of the money in their accounts—a paltry $500 or so on some savings accounts and an even more miserly $250 on some checking accounts. But aside from these ridiculously small sums, if you wanted your cash, you had to prove financial hardship. Even then the procedures were cumbersome and, to some people's minds, demeaning. "I was given a one-time allotment of $300 for food for my family," says the man whose money was frozen in his Davisville Credit Union accounts. "To get money to pay medical bills, I had to submit a letter from a doctor. I had to show them my oil bill to get cash to pay it. I had to present all this documentation at the local Social Security office. Not to get government money, but to get money out of *my own savings account.* I consider that an outrage."

Eventually the state created a new organization—the Depositors Economic Protection Organization, or DEPCO—to assume RISDIC's liabilities and pay off depositors. But many people considered this organization just another outrage, and soon people in Rhode Island were referring to DEPCO as DEATH CO. Under a string of partial payments proposed by DEPCO, some credit-union depositors might not get all their savings back for three years or more. Naturally, no interest would be paid during that time, so depositors could effectively lose another 10 percent or so of their money to inflation. Then the final kick in the shins. Because the credit unions and RISDIC had been allowed to deteriorate so badly under the vigilant gaze of Rhode Island's legislature, the DEPCO bailout could wind up costing state residents as much as $500 million. That gave Rhode Islanders the dubious distinction of paying for *two* bailouts. Like everyone else, Rhode Island taxpayers were already shouldering their share of the S&L bailout, a cost that, including interest and other direct costs, could run to $1 trillion or $10,592 for each household in the U.S. Now they are being asked to pony up an additional $1,300 for each household in the state to pay for DEATH CO.'s $500 million tab. If the FDIC requires a taxpayer bailout too, then lucky Rhode Islanders will be bailing out three government agencies simultaneously. If that happens, the Rhode Island legislature might just as well dissolve DEPCO since, after picking up the check for three bailouts, Rhode Island residents probably won't have any savings left for DEPCO to protect anyway.

94   So, what hundreds of thousands of Rhode Islanders woke up to on New Year's Day 1991 was the state's worst financial hangover since the

Great Depression, a mini-S&L scam, New England style. Not only are savings at risk, but people found themselves unable to draw on loans and lines of credit they depended on. Many small businesses were devastated, some forced into bankruptcy. The emotional toll has also been staggering, according to Jack Kayrouz, a small-business owner who, faced with the state's inertia about resolving the mess, founded a consumer interest group called Citizens for Depositors' Rights to address the problem. "Sixty to seventy percent of these depositors are elderly—people who worked forty or fifty years to accumulate their savings," says Kayrouz. "We've turned them into beggars. We've even had some people commit suicide."

As was usually the case during the egocentric eighties, it wasn't rabble-rousing revelry by credit-union members that led to this hangover. They weren't partying on bloated interest rates or asking the credit-union management to make risky loans. No, this debacle was brought on by inept and sometimes corrupt credit-union managers, by a state-chartered private deposit-insurance organization that misled depositors about its safety, by state regulators doing an unbelievably horrible job of policing these institutions, and by legislators who were supposed to be protecting the interest of Rhode Island residents, but were instead ignoring their constituents' concerns or even catering to other interests. Legislators were also more than a little cozy with the people they were supposed to be overseeing. In one instance, the chairman of a Rhode Island House of Representatives committee that considered—and let die—legislation to switch from RISDIC to a federal insurance agency was married to a director of a RISDIC-insured credit union.

The saddest part of this tragicomedy of errors and corruption was that it all could have been prevented. Although the failure in 1990 of the tiny Heritage Loan and Investment Company and the disappearance of Heritage's president amid allegations of embezzlement and mob connections triggered RISDIC's collapse, the fact is that many politicians and elected officials in the state knew years earlier that RISDIC was headed for collapse. An investigation of RISDIC's condition ordered in 1985 by then state attorney general Arlene Violet found rampant evidence of "large risky, improperly documented loans . . . unduly concentrated loans to officers, directors, and other 'insiders,' " and, perhaps most troubling, a "misrepresentation carefully drawn to create the impression that RISDIC has what no state-sponsored private insurer has, namely, access to the Federal Treasury." In other words, 95

Rhode Islanders were misled by an agency chartered by their own state. These and other warnings were ignored and RISDIC and its member institutions were allowed to career toward insolvency over the next five years. Echoing the feeling of many other depositors who had trusted RISDIC, trusted the regulators, trusted the legislature, and trusted the governor, Jack Kayrouz says, "I feel we've been betrayed by the State of Rhode Island and the federal government. We've been treated like second-class citizens."

BEWARE PRIVATELY INSURED CREDIT UNIONS

Though an extreme case, the experience of Rhode Island's credit unions shows that, since you can't completely trust the regulators, it's up to you to make sure the credit union where you have your savings or checking account or even a car loan, home mortgage, or home equity line of credit is truly safe. Once you determine that, you must occasionally monitor the financial health of your credit union to make sure it hasn't gotten careless and become more precarious. This way you can help prevent yourself from getting sucked into the black hole created when an institution fails, namely, possible loss of your money if your deposits exceed insurance ceilings, loss of access to your savings for several weeks even if your deposits are totally insured and, if you happen to be behind in your loan payments when your credit union disintegrates, the possibility that your loan may be called—that is, you may be required to come up with payment in full, immediately.

Of course, the Rhode Island mess was especially complicated by the fact that the credit unions' members were relying not on the U.S. government but *private* deposit insurance. Even though RISDIC was chartered by the state and gave the impression of having federal and state backing, it had neither. Fortunately, most credit unions—just over 90 percent of the fourteen and a half thousand out there—*are* federally insured. These institutions are regulated by the National Credit Union Administration, a federal agency, and backed by the National Credit Union Share Insurance Fund (NCUSIF), which is in turn backed by the full faith and credit of the U.S. government. So while you can lose access to your money if a federally insured credit union fails, you won't lose your deposit, so long as you meet the federal insurance requirements (we'll go over these in detail shortly).

96   But credit unions in nineteen or so states still operate with private insurance. And, indeed, somewhere around fourteen hundred credit

unions in the U.S. are still privately insured. To put it as bluntly as possible, if you are truly concerned about the safety of your savings your first line of defense is to *avoid privately insured institutions* and instead do business only with credit unions covered by the National Credit Union Administration's Share Insurance Fund. *Look for that NCUA sticker before depositing a dime.* Some proponents of private insurance may claim that privately insured institutions are safer because, knowing there's no federal promise to fall back on, they are more cautious. Or that some private insurers have as large a safety cushion as the federal insurance fund, the NCUSIF. And some people who favor private insurance point out that private insurers protect deposits up to $500,000—a much higher level than NCUSIF. It really doesn't matter how much of this is truth and half truth. The fact is that the record of private insurance agencies is stinko, period. In 1985, private insurers in Maryland and Ohio failed, precipitating a banking crisis in those states. Ditto Rhode Island's RISDIC. And as for the private insurers' "we insure deposits up to $500,000" line, don't give it a moment's consideration. That was a selling point in Rhode Island with RISDIC, which couldn't even make good on $10,000 deposits, let alone $500,000. Remember, anyone can promise to insure anything they want. Backing up that promise with cold cash is another thing. The only foolproof deposit-insurance systems around are the ones backed by the full faith and credit of the United States Treasury. And even then you've got to make sure you meet the insurance qualifications and don't fall through one of the many cracks in the system. Eventually you may not even have the choice of going to a privately insured credit union. That's because the number of privately insured credit unions is going down as at least ten states are in the process of requiring credit unions to switch to federal insurance or nudging them in that direction. That doesn't mean a privately insured credit union will actually get federal insurance. Some credit unions will be turned down if they're not healthy enough. In the meantime, since there are still privately insured institutions out there, avoid them. Your savings will be far, far safer if you limit yourself to credit unions that have full-fledged *federal* backing.

Now, the mere fact that a credit union is federally insured doesn't mean that it can't fail. After all, federally insured banks and S&Ls have proven thousands of times that they're no Bart Simpson underachievers when it comes to insolvency. They can fail with the best of them. And though credit unions certainly haven't been dropping as quickly as banks and thrifts, more than a few have flopped or come pretty darn close in

97

recent years. In 1990, according the National Credit Union Share Insurance Fund report, about 125 credit unions failed or were receiving assistance to prevent them from failing, while another 678 credit unions were in trouble because of such problems as bad loans and inadequate capital levels. In one of the more memorable, and ironic, collapses in 1990, the credit union of the Federal Home Loan Bank Board—the government agency that used to regulate the S&L industry—went broke and had to be merged into another institution. Apparently the credit union did as fine a job overseeing its own affairs as its members did regulating the S&Ls. While this number of failures is hardly enough to raise a general alarm about the safety of credit unions, there are certainly enough problems so that conservative savers will want to make sure their own credit unions are in the solid and secure category and not one of those troubled institutions staggering toward insolvency.

WHY CREDIT UNIONS MAY BE SAFER THAN BANKS

Fortunately, on that score, there are plenty of perfectly solid, safe credit unions to choose from. And, in fact, though this may be far from a ringing endorsement these days, in some ways credit unions are actually safer than banks. Credit unions generally have a capital cushion as good as, if not better than, that of the banks—which means they have an equivalent or better margin of safety if something goes wrong, for instance, if borrowers default on their loans or the economy turns sour and profits go down. As with a bank, the best barometer of that safety margin—or comfort cushion, if you will—is a credit union's capital ratio. This expresses the credit union's capital, also known as its equity or net worth, as a percentage of assets and tells you how large a cushion the credit union has to cover losses. The higher that ratio or percentage, the bigger the cushion and, in general, the safer depositors are. Overall, according to the National Credit Union Administration, federally insured credit unions at the end of 1990 had a capital ratio of 7.6 percent, a bit higher than the capital ratio for banks. You should realize that the credit union's capital ratio is slightly overstated because of an accounting gimmick. When banks pay their deposit-insurance premium to the FDIC, that premium is deducted from their revenue and, therefore, lowers their profits and their capital ratio. This makes sense, since the bank no longer owns that money—the insurance fund does. Federally insured credit unions use a different system. They are required to turn over 1 percent of all their deposits to the federal deposit-insurance fund. So a credit union with $100 million in deposits would turn over $1 million to the fund. But even though the fund has the money, credit unions are allowed to count this 1 percent of deposits as part of their capital. This is clearly a bit of double counting, but even allowing for that, credit unions overall are extremely well capitalized.

Besides their comfortable capital cushion, the credit unions' insurance fund—the NCUSIF—is much more fiscally fit than the FDIC's bank-insurance fund. At the end of 1990, the NCUSIF had over $2 billion in reserves or roughly $1.25 for each $100 in insured deposits. In a July 1991 report on credit-union safety, the General Accounting Office recommended raising this $1.25 reserves-to-deposits ratio closer to $1.30 for an extra measure of safety. But the GAO did not sound any alarm about the security of the credit-union insurance fund and, indeed, even noted that it's quite fit compared to the bank-insurance fund, which is scraping along at its lowest level since it was founded more than fifty years ago. (GAO also asked that credit unions file financial reports more frequently—quarterly rather than semiannually—and give more detail about the quality of the credit union's management and assets.) Both funds have federal backing, of course, but the credit-union deposit-insurance fund has relatively far more in reserves to draw on to pay off depositors when failures do occur. The FDIC would ultimately pay off insured depositors, but if a few big banks go under the FDIC might have to go begging to the U.S. Treasury for a loan to do it. And if things get bad enough, the FDIC could conceivably have to hit up everybody's favorite soft touch, the one who can always be relied on to bail government agencies out of the messes they should have avoided, the U.S. taxpayer.

Safety concerns aside, credit unions are actually a better deal than banks in a lot of other ways. Though they may not pay as high a rate on checking accounts, credit unions charge lower monthly fees for checking, on average, and almost three-quarters of credit-union checking customers pay no fee at all versus just over half of bank checking customers. Credit unions also often beat the banks' rates on auto loans, home mortgages, and home equity loans. One reason credit unions can often charge less than banks for comparable services is that they have a big tax advantage. Unlike banks, credit unions are not-for-profit organizations that are therefore exempt from federal and most state and local income taxes. The savings that result from this favorable tax treatment are passed on to credit-union members in the form of lower fees and loan rates and, sometimes, higher rates on savings. Bankers, who do pay income taxes, complain bitterly about this uneven playing field. And they're right. This does give credit unions an unfair edge. So, shed a tear or two, if you wish, for those kindhearted noble bankers plugging along valiantly even though the odds are stacked against them. But don't let your sympathy prevent you from taking advantage of credit unions' favored tax status. If you can get a better deal on a loan or a checking or savings account at a credit union—and you probably can—dry your eyes and grab it. If you still feel bad about the bankers' plight, take some of the money you save by doing business with a credit union instead of a bank and contribute it to the Charitable Fund for Old and Destitute Bankers. There is no such fund now, of course, but if things don't improve for the banks there will be.

But, you may be saying, all the advantages credit unions offer are nice, but I don't think I'm eligible to join one. I'm not a card-carrying member of Teamsters Trucker Union Local 261 and I don't belong to the Mystical Brotherhood of Elk and Moose Lodge Officers. Relax. Today, it's easier than ever to join a credit union, which is one reason membership has zoomed to some sixty-three million people. While many people still join a credit union through their employer, there are plenty of other avenues to membership. Often a social or religious organization may launch a credit union. And some credit unions are open to people who reside in a certain community. Others may be open to people who work in a particular shopping mall or industrial park. In Texas, there's even a credit union for gay men and women—the Dallas Gay Alliance Credit Union. If you're really interested in joining a credit union, chances are pretty good you'll be able to join one some way, somehow. To get details on joining a credit union in your area, call your state's credit union league (there's usually an office in your state capital) or call the Credit Union National Association (CUNA) at 800-356-9655. (This can get confusing, but CUNA is the credit union's trade association. NCUA, on the other hand, is the National Credit Union Administration, a federal agency.)

HOW CREDIT-UNION DEPOSIT INSURANCE WORKS

Of course, this higher level of safety offered by credit unions presumes you're dealing with a federally insured one *and* that your savings meet the federal insurance guidelines. Blow it on these two counts and all bets are off. It's easy to make sure a credit union meets the first test—that is, it has federal insurance. Just look for that NCUA sticker that shows the credit union's deposits are insured by the National Credit Union Share Insurance Fund. If a credit union is covered by federal insurance, this sticker should be prominently displayed.

Meeting the second test—that is, assuring your savings are actually covered by federal insurance—is a bit more difficult. And the fact that the U.S. Treasury and Congress are toying with that insurance as part of reforming the nation's bank-reform laws can make this task even more confusing—and raise the consequences of misunderstanding exactly what's insured. Since the issue of whether your deposits are actually insured will be the single most important one you face if your credit union ever capsizes, let's first take a look at how deposit insurance works under the present system. Once we've done that, we'll examine how it's likely to work in the after-bank-reform era.

The current rules covering deposit insurance in credit unions are virtually the same as those the FDIC imposes on bank deposits, which is to say they are hopelessly complex and require the mind of an accountant or Talmudic scholar to follow the twisting logic. But, then again, since the rules only get complicated once you have more than $100,000 in one credit union, you don't have to bother much about the labyrinthine maze of regulations if you have less than that amount in all your accounts combined. But, if you're not in that enviable position now, don't automatically assume you won't be. Credit union account balances can easily balloon over $100,000 a number of ways. You sell your house, you get a lump-sum payment from your pension plan, you inherit big bucks from a rich relative, a lot of things can happen.

Here's how the regulations for credit-union deposit insurance work. As with banks, you get $100,000 of insurance coverage *per person* in *each* credit union in *each* of several different categories of accounts. This means you can expand your insurance coverage by making deposits in several different credit unions and banks. Spreading your money among different branches of the same credit union *does not* increase your insurance coverage, however, since these are all considered to be deposits in one credit union. Remember, too, that *interest* payments count toward the insurance limit. So if you have a $100,000 CD paying 8 percent annual interest, at the end of a year, your CD is worth $108,000, leaving $8,000 uninsured. Give yourself enough leeway so interest payments won't put you over the insurance limit. One way is to keep, say, $90,000 at the maximum, so you would need more than a year's interest at 10 percent to put you over a hundred grand. Or, you can tell the credit union to send you your interest earnings each month or deposit them into an account at another bank or credit union.

The biggest mistake people make about deposit insurance—in both banks and credit unions—is assuming the coverage applies *per account.* It does not. If you set up three savings accounts in your name and put $50,000 in each for a total of $150,000 in one credit union, $50,000 of that money is uninsured. You can, however, have multiple accounts whose combined balances exceed $100,000 and yet be fully insured, provided you have accounts in different ownership categories. To make this all clear, let's explain the deposit-insurance coverage you get in the categories you're most likely to use. These categories and the rules applying to them are essentially the same as those outlined for banks in chapter 3.

Individual Accounts: This category includes the type of accounts you are most likely to own: checking (or share draft) accounts, savings (or savings share accounts), and certificates of deposits (share certificates). The coverage limit of $100,000 applies to the combined balance of *all* such accounts held in one person's name. So, if you have $60,000 in a CD, $40,000 in a savings account, and $5,000 in a checking account, you have $105,000 in this category, which leaves $5,000 uninsured. This insurance limit is for each individual. So if your wife, say, has checking, savings, and CD accounts in her own name, she gets her own $100,000 of coverage for her accounts. As long as your accounts and hers are held individually, the insurance limits are completely separate and do not detract from each other's coverage in any way. Don't try a ploy like rearranging your name or Social Security number in an attempt to expand your coverage in this category. When a credit union fails, payouts are determined on the basis of who actually owns the money in the account. So if you have changed a digit in your Social Security number or rearranged your name on different accounts, you still won't be reimbursed for anything beyond $100,000.

Joint Accounts: In addition to the coverage for individual accounts, you also qualify for $100,000 of deposit insurance in jointly held accounts. This might be, for example, a joint checking account in the name of both a husband and wife or, for that matter, two friends. In fact, you can have several joint accounts that qualify for insurance—for example, maybe you have joint accounts with your wife, a friend, an uncle, a mistress, whatever. Warning: It's very easy to get tripped up in this category. For a joint account to qualify for insurance, all people named to it must have equal rights to the account. So if you and your cousin set up a joint checking account, but your cousin doesn't have the same rights as you to make withdrawals from the account, regulators may say it's not a true joint account. In that case, the money in that account is deemed yours and added to the balances of any individual accounts you might own. Depending on how much you have in individual accounts, this could put you over the $100,000 insurance limit. It's a good idea to go over this very, very carefully with a credit-union officer to make sure you don't inadvertently exceed the insurance limits or fall into one of the many traps in this category.

IRA and Keogh accounts: The money you put aside in an Individual Retirement Account is insured up to $100,000. This protection only applies if your IRA or Keogh account is invested in insured bank accounts, such as CDs or savings and money-market accounts. If you have your IRA invested in stocks, bonds, or mutual funds that your credit union happens to sell, then your money is not covered by federal insurance. If you have more than one IRA account at the same credit union, the $100,000 ceiling applies to the combined balances. If you also happen to have a Keogh retirement savings plan (a special type of plan available to the self-employed and people who work for the self-employed), that, too, gets $100,000 coverage, separate from the IRA and any individual or joint-account coverage.

Testamentary and trust accounts: Testamentary accounts are those in which the proceeds go to a named beneficiary after the death of the person establishing the account. Thus, you could set up a testamentary savings account and name, say, a grandchild as the beneficiary of the account upon your death. You would usually retain complete control of the account during your life. If the beneficiary is a spouse, child, or grandchild of the owner of the account, the money in the account is covered for up to $100,000 for each beneficiary. So if you put $200,000 into a testamentary account for your two grandchildren, both would get $100,000 insurance and the entire account would be insured. But if you set up such an account for any other beneficiaries—your brother and sister, for example—they would not qualify for insurance and the $200,000 would be added to the balances of any individual accounts you own and the total applied against the $100,000 individual account limit. If you had $50,000 in individual accounts, that would give

103

you $250,000 in this category, leaving you with $150,000 in uninsured deposits.

A trust account is a method for transferring the ownership of funds from the owner of those funds to a trustee, who, in turn, uses the funds for the benefit of yet a third person, the beneficiary. The rules for trust accounts get complicated real fast. Generally, trust accounts are insured for up to $100,000 for each beneficiary who is also a member of the credit union. If you are putting substantial amounts of money in testamentary and trust accounts, you probably should not be going it alone or even just consulting a credit-union officer. You're better off dealing with a financial planner or attorney familiar with setting up trusts. That person should then also be able to help you sort out the deposit-insurance rules applying to these types of accounts.

There are a few other ownership categories—for example, accounts held by executors or administrators of an estate and accounts held by a corporation or partnership. Generally the $100,000 insurance coverage limit applies to these accounts as well and this $100,000 coverage is *in addition* to the insurance coverage you may be entitled to on any of the accounts in the five categories mentioned above.

Clearly there isn't enough space here and no reader would have the time, interest, or patience to go over every possible circumstance and combination of accounts to determine whether they are insured. To be sure that any account you establish is actually covered and that you are not exceeding the insurance limits or inadvertently opening an uninsured account, get a copy of the booklet *Your Insured Funds*, which is published by the NCUA and explains in some detail and with many examples exactly how the coverage works for various types of accounts. If your local credit union doesn't have this booklet, call the NCUA at 202-682-9650 or write for a copy to National Credit Union Administration, Washington, D.C. 20456. If, after reading the booklet, you're still not positively sure your money is covered, sit down with a credit-union officer and have him or her explain to you why your account is covered and ask the officer to point out the relevant section in *Your Insured Funds*. In the case of trust and testamentary accounts, you may also want to talk to a financial planner or attorney before opening an account. If you have any doubts at all as to whether your money in a specific account is fully covered because you have multiple accounts that put you over the $100,000 threshold, play it safe and *deposit the money in an account in another federally insured institution*. That can be another credit union (though not just another branch) or a secure bank. There's no reason to risk losing money because of inadequate deposit-insurance coverage when you can expand your coverage by simply keeping less than $100,000 in several federally insured institutions.

You should also be aware of a technical, but potentially important, difference between money on deposit with a credit union and money you deposit in a bank account. When you put money in a credit union, you are actually buying shares rather than making deposits (hence the name share draft or share certificate accounts). Although these shares aren't traded the way stock in a company might trade on the New York Stock Exchange, they are similar in another way to owning stock. Should your credit union fail, the NCUSIF would pay off all insured shares. But if you hold any *uninsured* shares, those shares would be viewed more like stocks than deposits and you would not be paid off until all other creditors were paid. So if your credit union failed and were liquidated, waiting in line behind other creditors would reduce your chances of getting back any money in uninsured shares. All the more reason to make sure your money is *fully insured* and that you find a credit union that won't fall apart.

WILL CREDIT-UNION DEPOSIT INSURANCE COVERAGE BE CUT BACK?

Just as they're trying to do with bank deposit insurance, the U.S. Treasury Department would like to cut back on the level of deposit insurance you can get at a single credit union (For details on moves to lower deposit insurance for bank accounts, see chapter 3.) Although the Treasury proposals related to credit unions also addressed some accounting issues and questions such as what federal agency would oversee the insurance fund, the proposals that can affect the safety of your savings are those relating to the new deposit-insurance limits. Essentially the guys at Treasury are proposing the same cutbacks that they've suggested for banks: $100,000 per individual for all accounts at one credit union, plus an additional $100,000 of coverage at each credit union for retirement accounts such as IRAs and Keoghs. So you would really have $200,000 in coverage per credit union. While this would cut back coverage in each institution, you could still expand your insurance protection by opening accounts at other federally insured banks, S&Ls, or credit unions.

As of midsummer 1991, it appeared unlikely that Congress would adopt the Treasury Department's $100,000-plus-$100,000 restriction. Still, there's always the chance that if deposit-insurance levels remain unchanged this time around, they could be lowered sometime in the future.

Fortunately there are a couple of simple and effective ways to protect your savings whether the current rules remain or Congress adopts new ones.

THE BEST STRATEGY TO KEEP YOUR CASH SAFE

The first thing you should do is keep abreast of any changes in the regulations concerning deposit insurance. You can do that by simply reading the financial section of the daily newspaper. If you see a news report about a change in deposit insurance and don't understand it, go to your credit union and have them explain what it means and exactly how it affects any and all accounts you have at that institution. In the meantime, though, you should also follow these two simple rules, which also apply to any money you have in banks:

Do not keep more than $100,000 at any single credit union: Even though you can get more than $100,000 of insurance by spreading accounts into various ownership categories, it simply does not pay for conservative investors to push the limits on deposit insurance. If you're fortunate enough to have more than $100,000 in savings, spread it among several credit unions and banks. Your money will be completely protected by deposit insurance under current law and will also be covered under any new regulations Congress is likely to adopt. It actually makes good sense to diversify your savings among several banks and credit unions even without the possibility of deposit-insurance reform. If your savings are stashed at just one credit union and it fails, *even if they're fully insured* you'll probably lose access to your money for at least a short time and possibly as long as six weeks. But if you've sprinkled your money around to several credit unions and banks, you can always draw on accounts at other institutions.

Stick to strong credit unions that are not likely to fail in the first place: Ultimately deposit insurance is like a life-insurance policy. Because you want your family to be secure after you're gone, you want to have a life-insurance policy with a nice big death benefit. But, considering the implications of collecting that benefit—i.e., you've got to die—you're not too eager to use it. Likewise, you want the protection of deposit insurance, but you'd prefer never have to go through the hassle of using it. Even if you have less than $100,000 in accounts and even if your money is completely insured, getting sucked into a credit-union failure can cause severe disruptions in your personal finances. (For details on the hassles you can experience when a federally insured institution fails, see the section in chapter 3 titled, "You Can Even Lose in an Insured Account.) The best way to avoid the emotional and financial trauma of going through a credit-union failure is to join only strong, well-capitalized, financially secure credit unions that are unlikely to fail.

EVALUATING THE FINANCIAL HEALTH OF A CREDIT UNION

For most people, assessing the financial condition of a credit union on their own is probably much like the challenge of building their own house—a difficult undertaking usually better left to people who do that sort of thing for a living. Still, just as being familiar with what constitutes sound construction can pay off when you're buying a home, so, too, can understanding the basics about gauging a credit union's health help you choose a credit union that's on solid financial footings. Here, then, are a few guidelines to determine whether you want to keep your savings at your present credit union or put your money into a credit union you're considering joining. If you prefer not to do the analysis yourself, the final section of this chapter gives the names of two organizations that can assess the financial condition of your credit union for you and provides a list of the strongest credit unions in each state.

As with banks, the single most important measure of a credit union's financial condition is its capital, or equity, ratio. This tells you how much of a cushion the credit union has to absorb losses from bad loans or unprofitable business. The capital ratio is expressed as a percentage and is calculated by adding together all the credit union's reserves plus retained earnings and then dividing this figure by total assets. You can usually get this information from the financial statement that must be posted each month in the office of each federally insured credit union. The statement includes financial information for the fiscal year to date. The capital ratio on average for all federally insured credit unions is 7.6 percent, so if your credit union's capital ratio is above this it's probably a bit stronger than average and a bit weaker if it falls below 7.6 percent. 107 In general, a capital ratio of 5 percent or more is considered adequate—

though still below average—and you should be very wary if the capital ratio is 3 percent or lower since that's the range where National Credit Union Administration examiners begin to worry.

Though it's difficult to truly gauge the quality of a credit union's investments, one area to look at is the amount of commercial or business loans the credit union makes. The reason: commercial loans account for far more loan losses than any other types of loans credit unions make. That's because most credit unions don't have the lending expertise necessary to make commercial loans (given the banks' record, their expertise appears shaky too). In fact, only a relative handful of credit unions even make commercial loans and even for those institutions business loans account for only a small part of all assets, about 3.7 percent on average. The financial statement posted in the credit union should list the amount of commercial loans outstanding. Although there's no dollar amount or percentage that should automatically trigger an alarm bell, the National Credit Union Administration has proposed a new regulation that would limit credit unions' commercial lending to the amount of capital they hold. So if a credit union had $50 million in assets and $5 million in total reserves—that's a capital ratio of 10 percent—it would not be allowed to have more than $5 million or 10 percent of its assets in business loans. If your credit union has more commercial loans outstanding than it does capital, you should probably check with one of the loan officers to find out exactly what kind of loans they are and whether or not payments are current on them. It's usually a particularly bad sign if a small credit union is making commercial loans out of state since a small institution may not have the resources to adequately monitor such loans. In the Rhode Island fiasco, one credit union's undoing came from making real-estate loans on condo projects in Florida. This was a clear case of coals to Newcastle. With New England's real-estate market already obliterated, the credit union didn't have to look any farther than its own backyard to make bad real-estate loans.

You should also check out the credit union's profitability. Look for the net income figure in the financial statement posted in the credit union. If that number is positive, at least the credit union is making money. If it's negative, it's losing money. This isn't a good sign, but what's more important than a mere loss is how quickly it's losing money. If the losses are occurring at a high enough monthly rate to wipe out the credit union's equity within a year or so, you are better off in a more profitable credit union. Finally, a federally insured credit union should be examined once a year by an NCUA examiner and its books should be audited annually by a supervisory committee appointed by the credit union's board. Although the credit union doesn't have to make the NCUA exam available to members, the credit union shouldn't have any qualms about telling you the date and results of the last exam. As a credit-union member, you can ask to see a summary report of the annual audit.

For most people these procedures understandably fall under the "too much work" category. Fortunately you can check out your credit union's financial status much more easily by going to one of the two companies that rate the financial strength of credit unions, as well as banks and S&Ls. Both organizations use financial information the credit unions must file semiannually with the National Credit Union Administration. The Bauer Group, in Coral Gables, Florida, assigns 9,105 credit unions a safety rating ranging from five stars (the safest) to zero stars (troubled and perhaps already taken over by regulators). For $75, the Bauer Group will provide a list of all five-star credit unions in the U.S. or, for the same price, you can get the safety ratings and important financial information on all the credit unions in your state. If you're more interested in assessing the condition of a particular credit union—one you belong to or are thinking of joining—you can order a detailed six-page analysis of the institution, which includes its rating, for $35. For these reports and information on others that are also available, call 305-441-2062 or write the Bauer Group, P.O. Drawer 145510, Coral Gables, FL 33114-5510. Veribanc, in Wakefield, Massachusetts, rates 13,753 credit unions and uses a combination of one to three stars and a green, yellow, and red color-coded safety-rating system. Green is the highest rating reserved for credit unions operating at a profit and with a capital ratio of at least 5 percent, while red credit unions are insolvent or operating with a capital ratio below 3 percent. Credit unions receive one to three stars, depending on how high they rank within their color code. You can get an instant rating for any credit union over the phone for $10 ($3 for each additional rating). Veribanc also provides a short report on a specific credit union for $25; or, you can get the ratings and key financial ratios for all credit unions in your state for $110. For these services call 800-442-2657 or write Veribanc, Inc., P.O. Box 461, Wakefield, MA 01880. If you have significant amounts of money in a credit union or you're at all worried about the health of your institution, it may pay to consult one or even both of these rating services. Keep in mind, however, that while these ratings organizations are diligent about the accuracy of their ratings, they do rely on information filed by the credit unions themselves with federal regulators. That means there's always the possibility that a credit union may intentionally or unintentionally file information that is wrong or makes the institution appear healthier than it is. To guard against this possibility, you should check periodically with the Bauer Group or Veribanc to make sure a credit union's rating has not been lowered.

THE STRONGEST CREDIT UNIONS IN THE U.S.

While it's not possible to list all top-rated credit unions (3,823 get Bauer's highest rating and 9,320 earn Veribanc's), I asked Paul Bauer at the Bauer Group to provide me with a list of the five largest five-star credit unions in each state. To earn this five-star rank, a credit union must meet a number of stringent criteria concerning asset quality and profitability and, most important, meet an extremely high capital-ratio standard of *at least* 9 percent. Passing this acid test makes these credit unions among the strongest, if not *the* strongest, in the U.S. The standards are so strict, in fact, that in one state, Alaska, only one credit union made the cut (four four-star credit unions, which are also very strong, have been added to round out the list). These ratings are revised at least semiannually. So before you open an account at any of these institutions, you should make sure the credit union still wears those prestigious five stars. For belt-and-suspenders safety, you can check a credit union's ratings with both Bauer and Veribanc and limit yourself to credit unions that earn both companies' highest rating.

T A B L E   5 · 1

The Safest Credit Unions in the United States

The following credit unions are not the only top-rated institutions in the United States and Puerto Rico. Rather, they are the largest five-star credit unions in each as ranked by the Bauer Group of Coral Gables, Florida, a company that assigns safety ratings to banks, S&Ls, and credit unions. To earn the Bauer Group's five-star ranking, a credit union must meet a number of stringent criteria, including a capital ratio of at least 9 percent. In calculating that ultraconservative cushion, 50 percent of loan delinquencies greater than ninety days that exceed loan-loss reserves are not counted toward capital. Similarly, repossessed assets are not only marked down to market value, but the Bauer Group assesses a 25 percent charge against those assets and deducts that amount from capital as well. To be especially sure of the financial strength of a credit union, you may also want to check its ranking with another ratings company such as Veribanc, Inc. For information on how to contact the Bauer Group and Veribanc and how to get a more comprehensive list of credit union ratings in your state, see page 109.

Name	City	Assets (in $ millions)	Capital ratio† (percentage)
ALABAMA			
APCO Employees	Birmingham	$ 237.6	9.3%
AOD	Bynum	57.6	9.2
Alabama State Employees	Montgomery	32.7	14.6
ACIPCO	Birmingham	32.1	14.2
Sloss	Birmingham	30.7	13.4
ALASKA			
Frontier Alaska State	Anchorage	69.4	6.5
Alaskan	Anchorage	56.6	7.1
Alps	Sitka	14.8	11.4
City of Fairbanks	Fairbanks	2.4	8.7
ARIZONA			
Tucson Telco	Tucson	20.7	10.7
Pinal County	Florence	19.8	9.6
Pyramid	Tucson	18.4	10.5
Southeastern Arizona	Douglas	8.9	15.1
Bashas' Associates	Scottsdale	7.5	11.0
ARKANSAS			
Little Rock AFB	Jacksonville	111.9	9.5
Crossett Paper Mills Employees	Crossett	47.8	10.0
Telcoe	Little Rock	38.1	14.1
Fairfield	Pine Bluff	34.5	17.9
Pine Bluff Cotton Belt	Pine Bluff	22.9	10.8
CALIFORNIA			
LMSC	Sunnyvale	808.2	10.9
Orange County Teachers	Santa Ana	732.7	14.0
Provident Central	Burlingame	557.0	9.1
McDonnell Douglas West	Torrance	378.6	10.3
Travis	Vacaville	367.2	10.6

111

Name	City	Assets (in $ millions)	Capital ratio† (percentage)
COLORADO			
Denver Public School Employees	Denver	$ 151.1	11.3%
Safeway Rocky Mountain	Denver	67.2	10.2
Gates	Denver	62.3	19.4
Municipal Credit Union of Denver	Denver	46.3	10.0
Colorado Central	Arvada	39.0	14.8
CONNECTICUT			
Sikorsky	Stratford	146.6	11.8
Briston Teachers	Briston	38.5	12.4
Bridgeport City Employees	Bridgeport	19.8	10.2
State Police Credit Union	Meriden	15.8	9.7
New London Telephone Employees	New London	13.9	12.1
DELAWARE			
Nylon Capitol	Seaford	67.1	11.9
Gemco Employees	Wilmington	26.5	10.1
DPL	Newark	19.0	9.6
Delaware State Employees	Dover	16.2	11.8
Diamond State Telco	New Castle	8.0	16.3
DISTRICT OF COLUMBIA			
Transportation	Washington	53.9	11.0
Transit Employees	Washington	45.6	15.6
PASB Who	Washington	42.1	13.2
AFL CIO Employees	Washington	38.8	10.6
Treasury Department	Washington	36.4	10.1
FLORIDA			
Eastern Financial	Miami	758.3	10.7
Tropical Telco	Miami	249.8	10.0
Tyndall	Panama City	227.9	10.6
Pen Air	Pensacola	214.8	9.1
Florida Aircraft	Lake Park	142.0	9.3

Name	City	Assets (in $ millions)	Capital ratio† (percentage)
GEORGIA			
Delta Employees	Atlanta	$ 611.7	9.6%
Robins Warner	Robins	294.6	12.7
Union Camp Savannah	Savannah	43.9	11.6
GP Brunswick	Brunswick	39.1	10.7
State Employees	Atlanta	28.3	10.0
HAWAII			
Hawaii State Employees	Honolulu	264.4	10.6
Oahu Educational Employees	Honolulu	215.7	9.3
Hawaiian Tel Employees	Honolulu	117.3	11.0
Kauai Community	Lihue	109.5	9.6
IDAHO			
Pocatello Simplot	Pocatello	11.1	13.6
F M C Employees	Pocatello	9.9	16.7
Simplot Employees	Caldwell	9.6	9.2
I N G	Boise	8.9	15.7
IDADIV Railway	Nampa	8.5	10.4
ILLINOIS			
Selfreliance Ukrainian	Chicago	116.7	9.4
Scott	Scott A. F. B.	111.4	9.3
Granite City Steel & Community Employees	Granite City	56.9	10.4
Illiana	Calumet City	51.9	9.2
United	Chicago	49.7	11.7
INDIANA			
Inland Employees	East Chicago	152.8	10.0
Independent	Anderson	72.6	11.3
Crane Employees	Crane	54.6	10.6
Solidarity	Kokomo	53.5	9.3
WGE	Muncie	46.0	10.8
IOWA			
Du Trac Community	Dubuque	118.4	11.0
Dupaco Community	Dubuque	94.9	9.6
Deere Community	Ottumwa	31.3	14.9
Citizens Community	Fort Dodge	22.4	10.1
Telco-Triad Community	Sioux City	21.8	11.7

Name	City	Assets (in $ millions)	Capital ratio† (percentage)
KANSAS			
Yellow Freight Employees	Shawnee Mission	$ 85.0	9.2%
Rubber Workers Local 307	Topeka	49.2	13.1
Cessna Employees	Wichita	30.8	9.1
Farmway	Beloit	26.5	15.1
Telephone Employees Credit Union	Wichita	25.4	9.9
KENTUCKY			
Commonwealth	Frankfort	167.5	14.0
Ashland Armco Employees	Ashland	36.0	17.1
B & W	Louisville	34.7	12.6
Paducah	Paducah	32.0	9.8
C Plant	Paducah	29.3	9.1
LOUISIANA			
LA Capitol	Baton Rouge	67.5	12.2
Baton Rouge Teachers	Baton Rouge	65.8	9.6
Exxon	Baton Rouge	51.8	11.5
Greater New Orleans	New Orleans	46.6	13.8
Kraftman	Bastrop	44.3	10.9
MAINE			
St. John's (Brunswick)	Brunswick	54.2	9.6
Oxford	Mexico	36.5	9.8
Fraser Employees	Madawaska	35.8	10.2
Otis Division	Jay	30.9	17.9
Eastmill	E. Millinocket	24.5	10.4
MARYLAND			
Municipal Employee C.U. of Baltimore	Baltimore	259.2	10.1
First Financial of Maryland	Lutherville	116.4	9.2
Baltimore County Employees	Towson	78.2	9.2
Giant Food	Greenbelt	39.5	20.4
Maryland Steelworkers	Baltimore	29.1	10.7
MASSACHUSETTS			
Pittsfield G.E. Employees'	Pittsfield	212.6	10.1
Southbridge	Southbridge	90.2	9.2
Boston Post Office Empl.	Boston	55.8	11.1
Massachusetts	Boston	52.2	10.7
Massachusetts Institute of Technology Employees	Cambridge	47.0	10.6

Name	City	Assets (in $ millions)	Capital ratio† (percentage)
MICHIGAN			
Dow Chemical Employees	Midland	$ 298.5	10.1%
Unisys	Troy	212.6	12.1
Detroit Municipal	Detroit	169.2	12.8
T & C	Pontiac	169.2	9.8
Communications Family	Saginaw	1,162.9	11.6
MINNESOTA			
Hiway	St. Paul	144.4	10.0
City and County Employees	St. Paul	117.4	11.3
Teacher	Minneapolis	111.1	9.1
Honeywell Employees	Minneapolis	95.0	10.8
Minneapolis Telco	Minneapolis	77.4	9.2
MISSISSIPPI			
Keesler	Biloxi	251.4	9.6
Ingalls Employees	Pascagoula	62.1	11.2
Mississippi Telco	Jackson	45.3	11.0
Old South	Natchez	17.2	12.1
Mississippi Postal Employees	Jackson	16.5	16.7
MISSOURI			
St. Louis Postal Employees	St. Louis	56.6	9.7
St. Louis Teachers	St. Louis	47.9	9.7
K.C. Police	Kansas City	45.8	9.2
Gateway Telco	St. Louis	37.8	11.5
Gateway Federal Employees	St. Louis	36.9	11.2
MONTANA			
Whitefish C.U. Association	Whitefish	68.6	15.9
State Capitol Employees	Helena	28.3	10.1
Montana Power Employees	Butte	10.9	9.8
B.N. Park	Whitefish	8.6	13.2
Mountain State	Billings	7.7	11.2
NEBRASKA			
Bell	Omaha	152.0	9.1
Metro Health Services	Omaha	38.6	9.5
Burlington Employees	Lincoln	29.6	9.6
F C E	Omaha	26.2	9.9
Allied Railroad Employees	Alliance	23.6	14.1

Name	City	Assets (in $ millions)	Capital ratio† (percentage)
NEVADA			
Nevada Community	Carson City	$ 62.2	9.6%
Sierra Pacific Employees	Reno	18.0	12.2
S P Sparks Employees	Sparks	11.7	12.8
Virgin Valley	Mesquite	8.4	12.9
Reno City Employees	Reno	7.1	9.8
NEW HAMPSHIRE			
Service	Portsmouth	242.7	13.4
United Brotherhood	Berlin	40.3	22.2
L'Ange Gardien	Berlin	17.2	10.4
Freudenberg-NOK Employees	Bristol	1.9	14.0
St. Joseph Hospital Employees	Nashua	1.7	12.5
NEW JERSEY			
The Atlantic	Kenilworth	101.7	9.3
SGC	Edison	40.3	10.5
Lusitania	Newark	37.9	13.5
Tri-Co	Morristown	37.0	13.0
Deepwater Industries	Deepwater	31.9	15.3
NEW MEXICO			
ZIA	Los Alamos	41.8	11.5
State Employees	Santa Fe	25.4	9.2
Rio Grande	Albuquerque	15.2	12.5
Hobbs Municipal Schools	Hobbs	15.1	12.4
Guadalupe	Sante Fe	12.9	10.4
NEW YORK			
Melrose	Woodside	285.2	20.7
Polish & Slavic	Brooklyn	248.1	11.5
Nassau Educators	Valley Stream	192.7	9.3
Self Reliance NY	New York	186.2	12.8
Progressive	Forest Hills	127.9	22.5
NORTH CAROLINA			
Carolinas Telco	Charlotte	163.5	13.6
Piedmont Aviation	Winston-Salem	71.8	11.2
Premier	Greensboro	66.2	15.6
Champion	Canton	45.2	10.9
Weyco Credit Union	Plymouth	38.3	10.2

Name	City	Assets (in $ millions)	Capital ratio† (percentage)
NORTH DAKOTA			
Community	New Rockford	$ 46.9	11.3%
United Savings	Fargo	10.9	9.6
Prairie	Minot	7.7	9.9
Fargo Public Schools	Fargo	6.2	10.7
Ray Cooperative	Ray	5.5	9.8
OHIO			
General Electric Evendale Employees	Cincinnati	212.0	10.5
Nationwide	Columbus	148.5	9.2
Telhio	Columbus	146.1	12.2
Gas Company Employees	Columbus	108.7	9.4
Mead Employees	Chillicothe	89.9	11.7
OKLAHOMA			
Communication	Oklahoma City	116.4	17.2
U.S. Employees Oklahoma City	Oklahoma City	48.4	12.1
Red Crown	Tulsa	42.6	9.7
NEO	Miami	27.8	10.2
Municipal Employees C.U. of Oklahoma City	Oklahoma City	27.2	9.4
OREGON			
Wood Products	Springfield	111.9	10.0
Forest Products	Klamath Falls	61.5	9.6
Portland Area Community Employees	Portland	54.4	9.7
Portland Postal Employees	Portland	49.9	13.5
Oregon Central	Portland	42.9	9.3
PENNSYLVANIA			
US Air	Coraopolis	272.5	9.3
Utilities Employees	Reading	145.9	13.1
Citadel	Thorndale	120.9	11.6
Harrisburg Belco	Harrisburg	71.6	9.8
USX	Pittsburgh	70.1	11.4
PUERTO RICO			
Caribe	Hato Rey	43.9	14.6
PR Telco Employees	San Juan	36.5	11.3
VAPR	San Juan	34.9	10.2
Fort Buchanan	Fort Buchanan	12.7	9.6
Ramey	Ramey	5.1	11.5

Name	City	Assets (in $ millions)	Capital ratio† (percentage)
RHODE ISLAND			
C. U. of Central Falls	Central Falls	$ 211.9	21.2%
Pawtucket	Pawtucket	122.1	23.5
The Peoples	Middletown	110.7	10.6
Dexter	Central Falls	64.6	11.3
Westerly Community	Westerly	62.3	14.8
SOUTH CAROLINA			
Charleston Naval Shipyard	Charleston	349.5	9.1
Springmaid	Lancaster	279.5	9.4
SPC Cooperative	Hartsville	60.6	12.4
May Plant	Lugoff	50.4	9.7
S.C. Telco	Greenville	43.1	10.3
SOUTH DAKOTA			
Sioux Falls Bell	Sioux Falls	11.9	9.4
Lead Miners	Lead	9.2	10.1
Rosebud	Winner	8.5	9.4
Dakotaland	Horon	7.7	14.7
Rushmore Electric	Rapid City	5.6	10.1
TENNESSEE			
AEDC	Tullahoma	249.7	10.4
Memphis Area Teachers'	Memphis	162.0	10.6
City of Memphis	Memphis	65.0	9.7
Chattanooga Area Schools	Chattanooga	48.2	11.4
Memphis Kimberly-Clark Employees	Memphis	42.5	11.4
TEXAS			
Randolph-Brooks	Universal City	443.9	9.9
Texas Dow Employees	Lake Jackson	274.1	9.1
Fort Worth	Fort Worth	192.3	10.6
Amoco	Texas City	144.6	9.6
Lackland	San Antonio	108.6	11.6
UTAH			
America First	Riverdale	616.2	10.5
Goldenwest	Ogden	106.3	10.4
Cyprus	Magna	77.5	10.1
Granite District Credit Union	Salt Lake City	62.7	9.3
Beehive Credit Union	Salt Lake City	34.0	9.6

Name	City	Assets (in $ millions)	Capital ratio† (percentage)
VERMONT			
Vermont State Employees	Montpelier	$ 82.5	12.3%
Vermont V A F Employees	White River Junction	7.0	13.0
Burlington City Employees	Burlington	2.8	11.5
Windsor County South	Springfield	1.6	24.3
Rutland CCTY Teach & Municipal Employees	Rutland	1.4	11.2
VIRGINIA			
Langley	Hampton	359.0	9.8
Newport News Shipbuilding Employees	Newport News	342.4	11.7
Apple	Fairfax	143.8	11.1
Waynesboro DuPont Employees	Waynesboro	131.1	9.2
Martinsville DuPont Employees	Martinsville	81.5	10.6
WASHINGTON			
Hapo	Richland	76.8	11.9
Whatcom Educational	Bellingham	73.6	13.4
Safeway	Bellevue	53.9	9.6
AGE	Seattle	52.3	12.0
Alaska Airlines Employees	Seattle	17.4	9.1
WEST VIRGINIA			
Steel Works Community	Weirton	106.1	12.8
Mobay Employees	Newmartinsville	58.9	9.3
People's	Institute	21.9	11.3
Cabell County School Employees	Huntington	19.5	10.6
Tin Mill Employees	Weirton	16.4	11.1
WISCONSIN			
Royal	Eau Claire	158.7	10.1
Westconsin	Menomonie	97.8	9.7
Wisconsin Axle	Oshkosh	86.0	9.9
Kimberly	Kimberly	83.6	9.4
Antigo Co-Op	Antigo	70.7	20.1

Name	City	Assets (in $ millions)	Capital ratio† (percentage)
WYOMING			
Warren	Cheyenne	$ 48.8	15.9%
Uniwyo Employees	Laramie	28.7	9.7
Wytel	Cheyenne	19.9	10.3
Natrona County School Employees	Casper	12.8	10.3
Sunlight	Cody	9.1	10.3

SOURCE: The Bauer Group, Coral Gables, Florida; data as of 12/30/90.

* This is a four-star institution.

† This is the capital ratio before deductions for bad loans and repossessed assets. Bad loans and repossessed assets have been factored into the capital ratio when assigning ratings.

≋ 6 ≋

THE REAL RISKS IN
MONEY-MARKET FUNDS

No One Has Ever Lost a Penny ... Yet

MONEY-MARKET-FUND sponsors like to brag that no investor has ever lost a cent in a money fund. They proudly point out that, unlike other investments which can be on top one day, down and out the next, a money fund has never taken a dive.

Enticed by that seemingly flawless safety record, yields that put bank savings accounts to shame, and the convenience of check-writing and withdrawing your cash with a telephone call, millions of investors have poured their savings into these funds. By early 1991, the assets of the nation's almost seven hundred money funds spread over some twenty million shareholder accounts totaled more than $549 billion—that's right, half a trillion bucks, more money than there is in all passbook savings accounts in this country. Today, everyone from thirty-something yuppies looking to squeeze a few extra bucks out of the meager savings they have left after their profligate spending, to older, more conservative savers who were weaned on passbook accounts and CDs, have now begun to think of money funds as a souped-up version of a bank account, practically as safe as an insured bank deposit but with the added advantage of a tantalizing yield.

But the money funds' highly touted safety record isn't nearly as pristine as the fund companies make out. By the end of the 1980s, the same disease that afflicted Michael Milken and his band of jolly junk bondsters began rubbing off on formerly mild-mannered money funds. The disease is "high yield-itis," and its chief symptom is a dangerously irrational pursuit of obscenely high interest rates, usually accompanied by the delusion that one can earn these greedy returns without taking on additional risks. The disease reached epidemic proportions during the all-gain-no-pain eighties and, unfortunately, many people on Wall Street still suffer from the malady even today.

As high yield-itis spread, the idea of giving investors a decent, safe return suddenly was no longer good enough. The yield had to be big and fat and preferably in the double digits. Why? Oh, the fund sponsors would say they chased high yields because bigger returns benefit fund shareholders. But the real reason is that fund companies know a high yield is the aphrodisiac that lures new investors into a fund. And more investors means more money in the fund. And because the fund is paid by taking a percentage of assets under management, more money in the fund means higher fees for the fund company. It's that simple. So, no longer content to stick to the highest-quality securities and offer money-fund investors a reasonable return, money-fund companies began to take more risks and dip into a whole slew of lower-grade investments and CDs issued by foreign banks. The result of this aggressive pursuit of high yields by money funds has been a number of close calls—the financial equivalent of near midair collisions—over the last few years in which investments held by money funds have gone sour and money-fund investors have only narrowly escaped a loss. These near misses have prompted savvy investors, not to mention the Securities and Exchange Commission, to take a closer look at the purported unassailable safety of this most popular form of mutual fund. If you are one of the many investors who has been lulled into a false sense of security by money-fund sponsors' marketing pitches that suggest money funds are guaranteed by the U.S. government or are otherwise virtually immune from loss, you will have to completely reevaluate the way you think about these funds. "People have to understand that no money-market fund is guaranteed by the federal government like a bank account is," says Mary Novick, a financial analyst who rates the safety of money funds at Standard & Poor's, the nation's premier financial research and ratings company. "While money funds have much less risk than many other investments, they are not completely without risk. It *is* possible to lose money."

122   Fortunately, by sticking to the safest money funds that limit themselves to secure, high-quality investments, it is also possible to reap the

superior yields of money funds and avoid taking unnecessary risks. In fact, you're almost always better off putting your cash in a safe money fund than you are in the bank's version of a money fund, a money-market deposit account. Money funds routinely beat the yield on the banks' money-market deposit accounts by anywhere from one to three percentage points annually. And when it comes to comparing the yield on money funds to those offered in traditional bank savings accounts, there's no contest. The money funds win hands down. True, money funds aren't federally insured—but *if you stick to the safest money funds around,* you will not be putting your savings at any significant additional risk and you will be earning a much higher return. The key to doing this, however, is choosing the right—that is, safest—money funds. And the best way to do that is to follow the advice on money funds in this chapter as well as in chapter 7 and chapter 8. To make the most of that advice, however, you first need to understand a bit more about how money funds work, what they invest in, and what risks those potential investments pose.

THE NEAR MISSES BECOME HITS

The idea of investors taking a loss in a money fund had always been considered only a remote possibility, about as likely to occur as Saddam Hussein winning the Nobel Peace prize. But, suddenly one summer, this abstract theoretical possibility became a frightening reality. In June of 1989, Integrated Resources, a financial services firm that peddled insurance, mutual funds, and an unconscionable number of real-estate limited partnerships to investors, became one of the first casualties of the real-estate slump and defaulted on about $1 billion of its short-term debt known as commercial paper. Normally this kind of event would be of little interest to anyone except creditors owed money by Integrated, its army of salesman who were depending on commission checks, and, of course, those poor unfortunates who sank their money into the company's partnerships, thereby making the salesmen's commission checks possible (or nearly possible, given the company's precarious condition). Certainly nothing for money-fund investors to worry themselves about. But this was different. Two money funds—Value Line Cash and Liquid Green Trust—together actually owned more than $30 million of the commercial paper welched on by Integrated (or *Dis*integrated as the company became known after filing bankruptcy). This left 123 the funds with a major problem: How do you tell investors who put their cash into a fund with the understanding that its net asset value would remain stable that the fund was looking at a loss? Rather than broach this embarrassing subject, the sponsors of the funds decided to dig into their pockets and absorb the hit. Value Line Cash's parent paid the fund almost $23 million for the Integrated commercial paper in the fund's portfolio, and Unified Management Corporation, the investment adviser to Liquid Green, shelled out $9 million to its fund. Money-fund investors had dodged the bullet.

Immediately fund sponsors pooh-poohed the Disintegrated default as an aberration, a freak accident, and assured money-fund investors that the funds were still extremely safe and that defaults like this weren't likely to occur again anytime soon. But just when the furor over Disintegrated was dying down, boom! Another default. These aberrations were beginning to look uncomfortably like the norm. This time, Mortgage Realty Trust, a real-estate investment trust located in Elkins Park, Pennsylvania, and then listed on the New York Stock Exchange, defaulted on $150 million or so of its short-term debt. It seems that just when Mortgage Realty Trust went to draw on its bank lines to make interest payments on its commercial paper, its bank pulled the line of credit out from under it. Without the banks backing the company, nobody wanted to own its commercial paper, so the funds couldn't sell it. And Mortgage and Realty Trust didn't have the cash to redeem the paper. Add up those two facts and they spell l-o-s-s. This time ten money funds held an estimated $75 million of Mortgage Realty and Trust's defaulted debt. Among the firms bagged was T. Rowe Price, whose Prime Reserves money fund held $42 million of the bad paper. But again, the fund sponsors stepped in front of their investors and took the bullet; and, again, no one (T. Rowe Price excepted) lost a cent.

Why, you may legitimately ask, did the fund sponsors act so gallantly? Perhaps out of a sense of fair play? Fiduciary duty? Altruism? If you go for any of those reasons you probably also don't flinch when your doctor says, "This won't hurt a bit." The truth is, money funds have absolutely no legal obligation to pay their investors back for losses. Nor are they bound by law to keep the fund at a one-dollar net-asset value. The reason the fund parents took the hit is simple: The very foundation of the money-market-fund business is that a fund's net-asset value should never "break a buck"—that is, the net-asset value should never dip below a dollar a share. True, the potential losses were small—Value Line Cash fund investors might have seen their investment dwindle by about 4 percent without the rescue operation, making each share worth

96 cents—but, if you are counting on bulletproof security, *any* loss is upsetting and, if you are investing money you simply cannot risk, unacceptable. In other words, the fund sponsors knew that if word got out that money funds weren't as safe as their marketing brochures and advertisements made them out to be and that people had actually *lost* money, chances are that fund investors would bail out of these funds as fast as their little fingers could dial a phone. While that may not be the end of the world for investors (though they might wind up with lower returns by going back to bank accounts), it would come pretty damn close to Armageddon for the money-fund investment managers who earn an estimated $1.5 billion a year or so in management fees from money funds. So much for altruism.

Given the fund sponsors' willingness to dig into their own pockets, the money funds' oft-quoted sacrosanct record of no investor ever having lost a penny is still secure—even if a bit misleading. But some people within the money-fund industry suspect sponsors may not be as quick to shield investors in the future. "I don't think the industry will continue to absorb losses because that would be like saying we not only manage the funds, but insure them like banks do," says Stan Egener, president of the New York City investment advisory firm Neuberger & Berman, which manages three money funds. "I don't think the industry is willing to do that." In other words, shareholders may no longer be able to depend on the largess of strangers to make them whole in the future. That means that conservative investors who prefer to see their savings grow rather than shrink even a little must be more vigilant than ever before about the latent risks in these funds. The first step toward protecting yourself is to understand what you're really buying when you invest in a money fund. If you don't know what's in the fund's portfolio, there's no way you can know how much of a risk you're taking with your money. Before you invest a single cent in any money fund—for that matter, *any* type of mutual fund, you should read the prospectus. This document tells you what kind of investments the fund manager is allowed to buy and how large an investment advisory fee the manager takes. The prospectus also informs you of any other kinds of sales charges you must pay to the fund manager, sponsor, or the person who sold you the fund. (All money funds charge a management or investment advisory fee, which is what they charge for choosing the investments for the fund. That fee is a flat percentage charged against the fund's assets and usually ranges from 0.25% to 0.5% each year. A sales charge is something different. That goes to the person, usually a broker or financial planner, who sells you the fund. It's like an insurance sales-man's commission on a life-insurance policy. Most money funds do *not* have sales charges, which are also known as "loads," although many other types of mutual funds do. To avoid sales charges, stick to what are known as "no-load" funds.)

Failing to read the prospectus before investing in a money fund is kind of like buying a house sight unseen and, instead, relying solely on the real-estate broker's description of it. Prospectuses are so excruciat-ingly boring, however, that most investors don't bother. On the off chance, however, that you will at least take a peek at the prospectus, here's a quick explanation of the different types of investments that money funds typically invest in and that are likely to be mentioned in the fund's prospectus.

JUST WHAT DO MONEY FUNDS INVEST IN?

You can pretty much divide the investments money funds buy into three broad categories—regular stuff, exotic stuff, and weird stuff. The funds that want to provide their investors with a reliable, steady, safe yield pretty much stick to the regular stuff. But fund companies know that nothing lures new investors to a money fund (and generates man-agement fees) faster than a big percentage sign with an even bigger number next to it, preferably in the double digits. So to pump up their yields, some funds delve into exotic stuff, and the most aggressive funds dabble in weird stuff. Before describing just what regular, exotic, and weird stuff is, however, I want to warn you a little more about another favorite ploy funds use to juice their yields, namely waiving management fees. The scheme goes like this: Instead of charging its usual annual management and administrative fees of .5 percent or so, the fund graciously decides to forego them. As a result, while other funds might be yielding 8 percent, one waiving fees might yield 8.5 percent. Many money funds employ this marketing gimmick to lure new investors. In the April 1991 "Fundwatch" section of *Money* magazine, for example, the sponsors of twelve of the fifteen highest-yielding money funds listed were waiving all or some of their management fees. Is this a good deal for you? Yes—for as long as it lasts. Sooner or later, though, the fund will begin charging expenses and your yield will fall. The funds aren't required to publicize the fact that they've begun charg-ing management fees again and, of course, they're hoping you don't notice. While this doesn't affect the safety of your investment, it may be a shock if you've been depending on the fund's higher yield to squeeze out a bit more income from your savings. To make sure your fund's yields haven't fallen behind the rest of the pack, check magazines such as *Money* and *Changing Times* as well as the business newspaper *The Wall Street Journal*, all of which follow money funds regularly. Or you can check your local newspaper, which probably reports money-fund yields weekly in its financial section.

Now, let's get back to what money funds actually invest in:

Regular stuff: The absolute safest investments in this category—and for that matter any other—are Treasury bills. T-bills, as they're more commonly known, are short-term securities (they mature, or come up for repayment, in one year or less) that are sold by the U.S. Treasury and backed by the full faith and credit of the U.S. government. Nothing is safer. Unless you think there's a good chance a hostile foreign power will wrest control from the U.S. government, there's no way Uncle Sam will default on Treasury securities. You can buy T-bills directly from the Treasury or through a bank, which is even safer than owning them in a money fund. The catch: You must buy at least $10,000 worth. Owning T-bills through a money fund is plenty safe and much more convenient. Many funds also invest in U.S. government agency securities, such as those issued by the Federal Farm Credit Bank. Agency securities are not directly backed by the U.S. Treasury. They are considered to be moral obligations of the federal government, however, so the chances of not getting paid back are about zero. While many funds buy a sprinkling of T-bills and U.S. agency securities, most stock their portfolios with the other investments described below. Usually, only money funds that specifically call themselves U.S. government funds invest primarily in government-backed securities.

Bank certificates of deposit are also a mainstay of money funds. These are much like the CDs you buy for yourself, except a money fund usually buys them in far larger denominations. These CDs are subject to the same FDIC deposit-insurance rules as the CDs you invest in. In other words, the amount of a CD over $100,000 is not federally insured.

By far the most popular investment for money-fund managers is commercial paper, which is basically an IOU issued by corporations. In 1990, roughly half of the almost $500 billion worth of savings in money funds was invested in commercial paper. Ideally, commercial paper works very simply. The fund buys it from the company, which could be
anyone from household names like IBM and Coca-Cola to companies

that you probably never heard of and haven't the slightest interest in hearing of again, such as Square D Co., a Palatine, Illinois-based manufacturer of circuit breakers and switch gears. The company pays interest to the money fund on the IOU and, when the IOU comes due, usually within nine months, the company pays it off. The risk is that the company, like a friend or relative who welches on a debt, won't be able to pay off the IOU when it matures, which is what happened with Disintegrated and Mortgage Realty Trust. In that case, the fund is holding a piece of paper of dubious value. To help fund managers separate the dogs that are likely to default from the purebreds that pay their bills as promised, credit-research agencies like Standard & Poor's and Moody's Investors Service give ratings to commercial paper. S&P's top commercial-paper rating is A-1, while Moody's is P-1. S&P's next notch down—but still investment quality—is A-2; Moody's is P-2. Money funds are not allowed to invest in commercial paper rated below A-2 or P-2. Following these ratings is by no means a guarantee against defaults—both Disintegrated and Mortgage Realty Trust were rated A-2 at the time the funds bought them. The ratings do, however, help fund managers weed out some of the junkier commercial paper floating around Wall Street in the wake of the wild eighties.

Exotic stuff: To inflate their yields, some funds, such as Fidelity Spartan Money Market and Dreyfus Worldwide Dollar, have gone beyond the mundane world of T-bills, regular bank CDs, and commercial paper into murkier investments in overseas banks. Two favorites: Eurodollar CDs, which are certificates of deposit issued—in dollars, not foreign currency—by foreign branches of U.S. banks; and Yankee-dollar CDs, which are CDs sold by U.S. branches of foreign banks. While foreign banks these days are often sturdier than U.S. banks, these investments subject money-fund investors to a new type of risk, known as sovereign risk. To get an idea of just what that means, check out the Dreyfus Worldwide Dollar fund's prospectus, which says, "The Fund will be subject to additional risks which include possible adverse political and economic developments, possible seizure or nationalization of foreign deposits, and possible adoption of governmental restrictions which might adversely affect the payment of principal and interest on the foreign securities or might restrict payment of principal and interest to investors located outside the country of the issuer, whether from currency blockage or otherwise." (Now you see why nobody can bear to read a prospectus.) Loosely translated, this sentence, which only a securities lawyer could write, says, "Look, folks, foreign governments can do pretty much anything they want with this money, and if they decide to keep it, there's not much we can do about it. So beware." The funds point out that the chances of a government seizing or freezing this money are pretty remote. And they're right; it's not that likely. But, as *Barron's* pointed out in a 1990 article outlining the new dangers in money funds: "In these parlous economic times, the unexpected seems to have a rude habit of coming to pass."

Weird stuff: As if Eurodollar and Yankee Dollar CDs aren't enough, aggressive fund managers have found even more creative—i.e., risky— ways to pump up their yields. Amazingly, some funds are actually buying pieces of bank loans and sticking them in their portfolios. These so-called bank participations are particularly dicey because the bank isn't guaranteeing repayment and if the bank fails (always a possibility nowadays) the fund may have no claim on the assets backing the loan. The fund just joins the lines of the bank's creditors. Isn't it wonderful the way Wall Street wizards have found a way to drag money funds into the banking crisis?

Unfortunately that's not the only link. There's another you probably won't believe. You know how some people won't leave home without their credit cards and, in fact, they're always rushing around town charging lavish vacations, expensive VCRs, and other basic necessities on plastic? How would you feel about investing in the debt these people create? You might already be doing it. Today, some funds invest in what are called "floating-rate renewable credit-card participation certificates"—a fancy term for credit-card bills. The risk in these securities (the word security hardly seems to apply here, does it?) is that the value of the certificate could drop precipitously, the fund might not be able to sell it immediately for cash, and could even have to wait as long as eleven months to get all its money back. Somehow, the fact that the brain trust at Citibank developed this plastic-backed security doesn't instill much confidence. After all, it was Citibank's corporate parent, Citicorp, which had to turn to an Arab sheik this year for cash to bolster its badly depleted capital base.

DEFAULTS AREN'T THE ONLY RISKS

But the possibility of former high-flying companies like Disintegrated Resources and Mortgage Realty Trust going into a nosedive and defaulting on their debt isn't the only danger lurking out there. Money-fund investors face another risk, even in funds that stick to the most secure investments in the world. This second risk is known as interest-rate or maturity risk. The fund companies don't have to worry about investors getting upset about this risk for several reasons, the biggest one being that most investors don't know what interest-rate or maturity risk is. In fact, understanding this risk isn't all that difficult and, because you'll find the same risk in other types of investments, especially bonds, it's worth taking a few minutes to go over it.

Let's start with an example that may initially seem a bit off base. Assume that today you buy a $1,000 newly issued thirty-year Treasury bond that pays an interest rate of 8 percent. (While Treasury *bills* require a $10,000 minimum purchase, Treasury bonds are sold in $1,000 denominations.) As long as the federal government can either tax us or print money, you're assured of getting $80 a year interest on that bond, plus your money back after thirty years. Now, let's say that the day after you bought your bond, the government issued more Treasury bonds but to get investors to buy them, the Treasury had to pay a higher rate of interest of, say, 9 percent. Someone who bought a $1,000 bond the day after you bought yours would get $90 a year—$10 more than you. Thinking that it would be nicer to get $90 a year instead of $80, you come up with the great idea of selling the bond you bought that pays 8 percent and buying one that pays 9 percent. Nice try, but it won't work. When you go to sell your 8 percent bond, you'll find nobody will give you $1,000 for it. After all, why would anyone give you $1,000 for a bond that generates $80 annually when they can spend $1,000 and get $90 annually, right? You can't change the amount of interest the bond will pay. The interest rate on Treasury bonds, as with most bonds, is fixed. (That's why you'll often hear people call bonds "fixed-income" investments.) So there's only one way to convince someone to buy that bond—lower the price. In this case, you'd have to lower the price about 10 percent to $900, which means the person paying $900 and getting $80 a year interest is earning the same yield as the person buying a new $1,000 bond paying $90—9 percent.

All this is a long way of saying that if you buy an investment that pays a fixed amount of interest, *and interest rates go up*, the market value that investment would fetch if you sold it now *goes down*. The opposite occurs if interest rates go down. When interest rates fall, people are willing to pay more for those investments issued before interest rates went down. This relationship—namely, that the value of fixed-interest-rate investments moves in the exact opposite direction of interest rates—is true whether the investment is a bond paying 8 percent or an investment you'd find in a money fund such as commercial paper paying 7 percent or a Treasury bill paying 6.5 percent. This explains the "interest rate" part of the risk we're talking about.

Now for the "maturity" part of the risk. You know that rising interest rates will push down the value of investments like bonds, commercial paper, and T-bills. But exactly how *far* the value of a fixed-interest-rate investment goes down depends largely on the maturity of that investment—that is, how long before you get your principal back. When you think about it, this makes sense. If I buy a thirty-year bond at 8 percent and interest rates go up to 9 percent the next day, I'm stuck with a low interest rate—and less interest income each year—for thirty years. I have to cut the price of that bond pretty substantially to convince someone to accept those smaller payments for three decades. But what if I buy a corporate IOU from IBM that pays me a 7 percent annual rate of interest and is repaid not in thirty years but in just thirty days? If interest rates jump up the next day, the market value of IBM's IOU, or commercial paper, certainly falls, but not by very much. You're only locked into that lower rate of interest a few weeks, so the price cut you have to take isn't nearly as steep as the price cut on a thirty-year bond. In other words, while the direction of interest rates determines whether the value of a fixed-interest-rate investment goes up or down, the *maturity* of the investment determines how *far* up or down the market value goes.

Okay, so what does all this have to do with money funds? Simple. If interest rates go up enough, the investments like Treasury bills and commercial paper in the fund's portfolio can suffer a loss and the money fund's value can decline—and you can lose money. Now, this isn't as likely to happen as with a bond because the investments money funds buy have extremely short maturities, anywhere from a few days to around a year. The best way to tell how vulnerable a fund is to swings in interest rates is to ask for its "average weighted maturity" (most people drop the weighted and just call it the "average maturity"), which, as the term implies, tells you the average maturity of all securities the fund holds. Thus, if a fund held $100 million in commercial paper with ten days until it matured, $100 million in T-bills with fifty days until maturity, and $100 million in Eurodollar CDs with a 120-day term, the fund's average maturity would be sixty days. Most newspapers and 131 magazines that follow money funds list a fund's current average maturity. (It can change from day to day since money funds are constantly buying and selling securities.) The fund's sponsor should also be able to tell you the current average maturity of the fund and give you a range of what that maturity has been over the past year or so. In chapter 8 you'll get some tips about how to use a fund's average maturity in picking a safe money fund.

Many fund companies scoff at the idea of money funds losing money because of rising interest rates. An interest-rate spike high enough to cause a loss in a money fund, they argue, would have to be so huge and happen so quickly that it's virtually impossible. That explanation makes sense, except for the fact that the impossible has already happened—at least one fund *has* taken a loss because of spiking interest rates. In the autumn of 1980, Institutional Liquid Assets, a money fund run by the First National Bank of Chicago and sold by the Wall Street firm Salomon Brothers, bet that interest rates were heading down and, to lock in some juicy yields before interest rates headed south, stretched the maturity of the fund to more than seventy days—a long maturity, but hardly reckless. But the fund manager guessed wrong. Interest rates went up, up, up, and the value of the fund went down as investors hightailed it out of the fund, forcing the manager to sell securities at a loss to pay off the deserting investors. So much for the notion that rising interest rates can't cause a loss in a money fund. True, the loss was relatively small—about 1 percent—but even 1 percent is too much in an investment that sells itself as a place to stash your cash when you want a virtually risk-free return.

THE SEC TIGHTENS THE SCREWS

After the Disintegrated and Mortgage Realty Trust scares, everyone was beginning to get a bit jittery and wondering what freak accident or impossibility was going to occur next. Things were looking so bad and people were so nervous that even the Securities and Exchange Commission, which, to put it mildly, doesn't have the greatest reputation for protecting individual investors, began looking for ways to tighten up the rules money funds play by. To their credit, money-fund sponsors also backed the SEC's efforts to make the funds safer. Of course, it was the sponsors themselves who started all the trouble by buying dicey investments in their aggressive pursuit of double-digit yields they could emblazon on advertisements and marketing brochures, so let's not get carried away in commending them. Both the SEC and the funds realized that some new ground rules weren't a bad idea and that, in fact, everyone could benefit—money-fund investors would be somewhat less vulnerable to losses, the SEC would look like the individual investor's friend and protector, and, most important, the fund industry would be forced to abandon some of the reckless investing practices that could wind up killing the goose (nearly $550 billion in money funds) that each year lays a golden egg (about $1.5 billion in management fees).

So after discussing several proposals and soliciting comment from the money-fund industry—in other words, the usual bureaucratic huffing, puffing, and posturing—the SEC finally passed new regulations designed to make money funds safer. Here is a rundown on the most important of these new regulations, which became effective June 1, 1991:

A Warning to Investors: The front page of every money-fund prospectus must now carry this message: "The shares of this money market fund are neither insured nor guaranteed by the U.S. Government and there is no assurance that the fund will be able to maintain a stable net asset value of $1.00 per share." You can think of it as the SEC's version of the surgeon general's warning. Translation: Don't even *think* the federal government stands behind a money fund and, remember, it is possible to lose money.

More diversity: To lower a fund's exposure to loss from defaulted securities, the new regulations make the fund spread its investments around more (a variation on the old don't-put-all-your-eggs-in-one-basket rule) and limit the amount a fund can invest in less-than-top-quality securities. For example, a fund cannot hold more than 5 percent of its assets in the securities of one company or issuer. In addition, no more than 5 percent of a fund's holdings can be invested in securities of less than the highest quality. That means 95 percent of a fund's assets must be in securities rated A-1 by S&P and P-1 by Moody's and only 5 percent can be in securities rated A-2 by S&P and P-2 by Moody's (funds are not allowed to invest in securities rated A-3 or lower). And if a fund chooses to invest in A-2/P-2 securities, no more than 1 percent of the fund's assets can be held in the A-2/P-2 securities of any single issuer.

A shorter average maturity: To provide a bit more protection 133
against rising interest rates, a fund cannot have an average maturity of

more than ninety days. Previously, fund managers could stretch the average maturity out as far as one hundred twenty days.

These new regulations will reduce, *but not eliminate*, the risks in money funds. For one thing, an average maturity of ninety days hardly immunizes a fund against a loss if interest rates make like the space shuttle and shoot straight up. Remember, ILA lost value when its average maturity was a little over seventy days—that's a long way from ninety.

As for restricting the funds from lower-quality investments, the funds can still stash up to 5 percent of its holdings in lower-rated securities. What's more, while the risk of a default in the highest-rated securities— those with A-1/P-1 ratings—is certainly low, it's not exactly impossible. In fact, some funds already shy away from the commercial paper of certain companies with the top A-1/P-1 rating. Not because they think the company will go bust tomorrow, but because they feel a bit more uneasy about these companies than other top-rated companies. As an extra measure of safety, therefore, they don't buy the commercial paper of these companies even though the new regulations certainly allow it. What would happen if an A-1/P-1 company did default on its debt? For one thing, unlike previous defaults, that of a top-rated company would probably affect many, many more funds since high-quality paper is more widely held. What's more, if a company with the highest rating did default, Neuberger & Berman's Stan Egener believes the fund sponsor might be less likely to reimburse the fund's loss to protect investors. Says Egener, "It's one thing to stand up because you own lower-grade paper. You may feel obligated. But if you buy top-quality paper and a lot of funds get hit, the management company that runs the fund might not feel so obligated because it followed the rules. Management companies are not the FDIC." But is a default by an A-1/P-1 company possible? "I don't think it's likely, but I do think it's possible," says Egener. So far, no A-1/P-1 rated security has defaulted. But, then again, before Disintegrated fell apart, a money fund had never had a security in its portfolio go into default. *Never* is a dangerous word.

YES, YOU CAN LOSE MONEY IN U.S. GOVERNMENT FUNDS . . . AND NO, THEY'RE NOT GUARANTEED

134   Speaking of dangerous words, I'd like to end with a warning about a very dangerous one: *guaranteed*. Money-fund sponsors *love* this word.

That's because they know that, next to high yields, investors crave safety most of all. So the funds like working *Guaranteed* into advertisements, brochures, and marketing literature, especially in BIG TYPE so you can't miss it. Usually the words *U.S. Government* immediately precede it, as in "U.S. Government Guaranteed." This is an especially popular technique with funds that invest in Treasury bills and other U.S. government securities. Oh sure, the new SEC regulations require the funds to disclose on the front page of the prospectus that the fund is "neither guaranteed nor insured by the U.S. government." But the simple truth is that you could print in huge red type across a prospectus, "THIS INVESTMENT IS A REAL DOG AND WILL EAT UP ALL YOUR HARD-EARNED MONEY AND LEAVE YOU DESTITUTE," and investors would still buy the fund. The reason: most investors just don't read the prospectus. Besides, the funds get the safety message across in their ads by saying that the *securities* the fund buys are U.S. government guaranteed. Most people jump to the erroneous conclusion that the fund itself is guaranteed. Let's make no mistake about this: No shares of any mutual fund are guaranteed in any way by the U.S. government no matter what the ad copy says, no matter what the fund representative says, and no matter what the broker peddling the fund says. The securities themselves—T-bills, for example, may be backed by the U.S. government's full faith and credit (which we know, of course, is Uncle Sam's ability to tax us and print money), but the actual shares of the fund are not. That might seem like nitpicking, but the distinction is important.

Here's why: Let's say you have a money fund that invests solely in U.S. Treasury bills, as many funds now do. The chances of a default in that fund are zero. The U.S. government pays its bills (well, you do, but it amounts to the same thing). But what happens if the average maturity of an all-Treasury-bill fund is ninety days and interest rates suddenly head for the stratosphere? Well, if interest rates jump by two percentage points, the value of that fund falls by .5 percent; if rates soar by four percentage points the fund's value drops 1 percent. Have interest rates ever done this? Not often, but we saw such wild swings in interest rates during the early 1980s. In other words, even if you own a fund that invests solely in U.S. Treasury bills—the safest investment on earth—it is possible to lose money in that fund. "If interest rates go up far enough," says Gene Gohlke, the associate director of investment management at the SEC, "the value of a U.S. government fund can go down. It can happen." From a tight-lipped organization like the SEC, 135 that's about as close as you'll get to a warning that, though unlikely, it's possible to lose money even in a U.S. government money fund.

Still, U.S. Treasury funds are far and away the safest kind of money funds around. And, fortunately, it's relatively easy to substantially eliminate even the small risk of losing money in this type of fund by sticking to Treasury funds that keep their average maturity short—sixty days or less is safest—and that really do invest only in T-bills. (See chapter 8 for lists of the safest money funds and for rules on choosing the safest Treasury and other types of money funds.) Of course, you may have to, though not always, sacrifice a bit of yield for added safety. But at least you'll have the comfort of knowing that there's no danger of losing what you thought you had earned.

7

THE SPECIAL DANGERS IN TAX-FREE MONEY FUNDS

Gimme Shelter—The Amazing Growth of Tax-Exempt Money Funds

NEXT to sports, and betting on sports, America's favorite pastime is evading taxes—legally, illegally, and, most of the time, by resorting to some ploy that falls into that large gray area in between. Each year, as the Ides of April draws near and once again we're faced with the prospect of filling out one, two, four, fifteen, twenty, tax forms and, horror of horrors, sending off a check to the Internal Revenue Service, the natural tendency to search for ways to keep more of what you earn by keeping it out of the hands of local, state, and federal tax collectors becomes a mania, an all-consuming passion. That magnificent obsession has led investors into some pretty perilous investments in the past— jojoba bean plantations, oil- and gas-drilling ventures, and, of course, enough real-estate limited partnerships to create millions of square feet of unused office space around the country and play a significant role in bringing both the banking and commercial real-estate industries to their knees. As often as not, investors in these dubious schemes would have been better off sticking to sound investments and paying their fair share of taxes on what they earned instead of turning to tottering tax shelters and winding up with a lousy investment to boot. Many investors who plowed their cash into cattle-breeding operations, for example, found that there was probably more bull in the broker's sales presentation than there was on the farm.

137

But when Congress cracked down on abusive tax shelters with the tax reform bill of 1986, investors did not go quietly into the hands of the IRS. Instead they looked for new ways to shelter their earnings from the taxman. And who was there to help them—i.e., milk this insatiable demand for tax-exempt income and generate some nice management fees in the process? The money-market-fund companies! This time with a tantalizing new offshoot to regular money funds, namely *tax-free* money-market funds. The theory is pretty straightforward: you invest in a money fund that limits itself to short-term securities issued by state and local governments and the fund pays you interest that is free from federal taxes and, sometimes, state and local taxes as well. As the people who sell and manage these tax-free funds (or municipal or muni funds, as they're also known) tell you every chance they get, by freeing you from the drag of taxes, a money fund that invests in the securities of municipalities can dramatically increase your return. For example, a muni fund paying just 4.2 percent—about the going rate in early 1991— but that is free from federal taxes is the equivalent of a 6.1 percent before-tax yield to a taxpayer suffering under the highest federal tax rate of 31 percent. (Actually, though the tax tables don't say this, you can get soaked with a federal tax rate as high as 34 percent by the time you work through all the cutbacks in deductions and exemptions in the five-year $500-billion budget deficit Congress passed in 1990. Consult a tax adviser to figure out your exact marginal tax rate.) There are also "double tax-free" and "triple tax-free" muni money funds that, by sticking to the securities of a single state, escape federal, state, and any local taxes. So a fund paying 4.2 percent that escapes not just the federal bite but that levied by state and local politicians, can translate to an even higher yield, especially in tax-hell states such as New York, Massachusetts, and Maryland. (*Never* automatically assume you'll earn more in a tax-exempt money fund than in a taxable one. Sometimes you come out with more interest income buying the higher-yielding taxable money and paying the taxes. The decision of whether to go taxable or tax-exempt will depend on the rates both types of funds are paying and the combined federal, state, and local income-tax rate you pay. Even if you come out slightly ahead in a tax-exempt fund, you must decide whether the extra income is worth the extra risk. At the end of this chapter, after you've had a chance to become better acquainted with the real risks in tax-free money funds, we'll look more closely at whether you're better off opting for the tax-free-fund option.)

138

Tax-free income is nothing new, of course. Brokerage firms have been hawking municipal bonds for years and investors have been collecting tax-exempt income on those bonds. But there's a major difference between buying muni bonds and tax-free muni money funds. The longer maturity of bonds means that their value can nosedive if interest rates go up. But by investing in very-short-term securities, tax-free money funds have been able to pay tax-free interest *and* sustain a stable value of one dollar per share. So far, anyway.

With that winning combination—tax-free interest and safety of principal—muni money funds have become all the rage among investors. In 1986, there were only 109 of these funds and they held about $36 billion in assets. By early 1991, their ranks had swollen to more than 250 funds with almost 1.2 million accounts holding assets of just over $91 billion, or roughly 20 percent of the near $550 billion held in all money-funds, taxable and tax-free.

THE ILLUSION OF SAFETY?

You would be making a huge mistake, however, to assume that there is safety in numbers. The mere fact that savers anxious to shield their interest payments from the tax collector's bite have rushed into muni money funds is hardly proof that they're safe. In fact, if history is any guide, the mad, lemminglike rush of savers into investments designed to escape taxes has usually ended in disaster. Witness the more than 500,000 investors languishing with losses or potential losses in real-estate limited partnerships.

Though the companies that hawk tax-free funds aren't about to tell you this, the truth is that tax-exempt money funds are not nearly as safe as money that's stashed in a good, solid bank. What's more, they're not as secure as conservative well-run taxable money funds and *nowhere near* as safe as money funds that invest solely in U.S. government securities. As a result, some investment advisers have been cautioning people to stay away from tax-free money funds, especially those that limit themselves to the securities of a single state. In July 1990, for example, James Lynch and Christine Carter Lynch, the editors of *Municipal Bond Fund Advisory*, a newsletter that tracks tax-free investments, flatly told their clients to bail out of tax-free money funds. "We think they're more risky than other money funds and that they're just too complex for individual investors to evaluate," says Christine Lynch.

Why the concern? For one thing, just as banks and S&Ls got caught up in the spend-now-pay-later mentality of the freewheeling eighties, 139 so, too, did state and local governments. They spent as if they had a never-ending supply of money flowing into their coffers. But when federal and state aid began to dry up in the late 1980s and tax receipts and property-tax revenue also slowed in the face of the 1990 recession, many municipalities found themselves in horrible fiscal shape. In a survey by the National League of Cities, 54 percent of the municipalities surveyed said they would be spending more than they took in during 1990. Overall, state and local governments faced a combined total budget deficit in 1990 of an estimated $30 billion—the biggest they've faced in forty years. Some came precipitously close to bankruptcy. Ratings agency Standard & Poor's lowered its rating on Philadelphia's securities to the junk level—CCC, or just one notch above the default category.

You may not really care what goes on in the city of Brotherly Love (make that Brotherly Need), but its problems, as well as the financial woes of other municipalities, could have a direct effect on the holdings of tax-free money funds. The reason: muni money funds invest primarily in debt issued by or through cities and states or their agencies. If the states' and cities' financial woes prevent them from paying back their debts—i.e., they default—money-fund investors could end up picking up the tab.

That's not the only danger in these funds. You see, a city or state doesn't even actually have to default for some of its securities to go down the tubes. That's because even though the securities muni money funds invest in are issued under the aegis of a state or local government, not all are backed by the full faith and credit of the state or municipality. (Those that do have direct backing are usually called general obligation securities.) Much of the short-term debt that finds its way into tax-exempt money funds are notes that are used to fund projects such as schools, hospitals, housing projects, even water and sewer systems. The owners of the securities—that's you, if you own shares of a tax-free fund—depend on revenue from those projects for repayment, which is why these are often called revenue bonds or notes. If money from those projects dwindles to a trickle and can't make the interest payments on the securities held in the money fund, the state or municipality may not be legally obligated to kick in the shortfall. And if a municipality is already reeling from interest payments on debt for which it is legally on the hook, chances are it will weasel out of any obligation it can.

140 What's more, through convoluted letter-of-credit arrangements,

many of the securities issued by states and municipalities and bought by tax-exempt money funds are ultimately backed by banks. That extra level of security would be nice—if only we weren't already in the midst of a banking crisis. So what we've got, essentially, is a system that looks to troubled banks to bail out troubled municipalities. That's a bit like a daredevil circus trapeze act whose safety net is stretched out nice and tight, except it's only attached to the support poles with thumbtacks. It's there, all right, but who knows what will happen if someone actually falls on it?

So it's especially important that you don't confuse tax-free money funds that invest in securities issued by local governments in any way with money funds that invest in securities of the *federal* government. One way or another, the feds can always repay their debts, even if it means running the printing presses night and day. But not one state in this country has the power to print money to pay off its debts. Instead, the cities and states have to squeeze it out of you through taxes—which can take time. As a result, there is simply no comparison in the levels of safety between tax-free funds and government funds. If you truly want the greatest assurance that your money will be there when you want it, look to U.S. government funds.

RULES? WHAT NEW SEC RULES?

As if all this doesn't add up to enough risk, there's one more thing that makes tax-free money funds inherently more risky than other funds. Starting in June 1991, a new set of Securities and Exchange Commission regulations went into effect that will substantially reduce, although not eliminate, the risk of investing in money funds. Essentially the new regs limit the amount of lower-quality securities the funds can invest in, make fund managers diversify their portfolios over a wide range of issuers to prevent a default of the securities of one issuer from mortally wounding the fund, and require the funds to limit their average maturity to no more than ninety days. This last requirement will prevent rising interest rates from zapping the value of a fund. (For more details on the SEC regulations, see page 132 in chapter 6). Overall, the new SEC rules added a much-needed dimension of safety to a type of investment that appeared to be on a collision course with more and more defaults.

All this would be great news to people who buy tax-free money funds but for one thing—none of the new rules, with the exception of the shorter average maturity, apply to tax-exempt money funds. They only apply to regular money funds and U.S. government funds. (The SEC was considering new restrictions for tax-free funds but as of fall 1991 had not adopted tougher standards.) The reason the SEC didn't make the new rules apply to tax-free money funds is quite funny, at least to anyone with an appreciation for macabre humor. It seems that many tax-free funds wouldn't be able to meet the stringent new rules. That's especially true for the ones that shoot for double- and triple-tax-free income by restricting themselves to the securities of a single state and municipalities within that state. In investment terms, that means many of these funds are not diversified, which is a fancy way of saying they have too many eggs in too few baskets. So essentially the SEC is saying that one group of money funds, because of safety concerns, has to meet a very strict set of new regulations. Then we've got another set of money funds, the tax-frees, which arouse even greater cause for concern on the safety front, but the SEC says they are exempt from the bulk of those strict rules because they wouldn't be able to meet them anyway. Irrational? Perhaps, but the SEC has decided that for now, at least, it's okay to have a tough set of rules for some funds and a laxer set for others. This is just one more reason to be wary of tax-free funds, regardless of how tantalizing those double- and triple-tax-free yields might seem.

To really appreciate just how different this breed of money fund is, let's take a look at what goes into the portfolios of tax-exempt money funds.

WELCOME TO THE WORLD OF TANS, RANS, BANS, VARDOS . . . AND SYNTHETIC FLOATERS

The very notion of investing in a money fund that buys something called "synthetic floaters" seems somehow ridiculous. You just know an investment with a name like that has got to be bristling with risks. In fact, once you start shining a light into the depths of the portfolios of tax-exempt money funds, it's like scouting the deepest parts of the ocean floor. You find all sorts of strange slithery creatures that many investors never knew existed. In the previous chapter, I divided the holdings of taxable money funds into three categories: regular stuff, exotic stuff, and weird stuff. I'll take the same approach here with one change: we can dispense with the first two categories because pretty much everything tax-free money funds invest in is weird stuff.

142

TANs, RANs, and BANs: Have you ever been in a position where you know you're going to have money coming in next week—let's say a friend is paying back $100 he borrowed—but you need some cash *right now*? So maybe you take a cash advance on a credit card or hit up a friend for a small loan to tide you over. Well, cities and states are almost always in that somewhat uncomfortable position. That's what they mean when they say they're having "cash flow" problems. And when municipalities face such a cash-flow crunch, they issue short-term securities to raise money. One way to do that is to issue TANs, or tax anticipation notes. When a local government issues a TAN, it is basically saying it wants to borrow money today and pay it back with property taxes or sales taxes or income taxes that will be collected sometime in the future. Alternately, the state or city might float a RAN, or revenue anticipation note, which depends on revenue from a project like a bridge for repayment, or a BAN, a bond anticipation note, which is relying on proceeds from a future bond sale to pay off the short-term debt. When you invest in a tax-exempt money fund, chances are you are buying into TANs, RANs, and BANs.

These arrangements usually go off without a hitch. But there are potential pitfalls, especially now that the budgets of many states and cities are strained to the breaking point. Let's go back to the example of someone borrowing from a friend or a credit card to get some cash to tide him over until another friend pays him back a $100 loan. Now, what happens if the day comes when the friend is supposed to repay that hundred bucks, but it turns out he doesn't have the money. Maybe he lost his job or owed someone else money and they got to him first. How do you repay the credit-card advance you took out or the money you borrowed and expected to pay off with that $100? You can always ask for another cash advance, but that might be a problem if you've already hit your credit limit—a situation some municipalities are approaching. Maybe you'd go to yet another friend for a loan to repay the first friend. That would work, but you might have trouble rousting up another loan if word got out that you were having trouble paying off the first loan. You get the idea. Well, that's exactly the risk investors face with TANs, RANs, and BANs. The property or sales taxes a city was counting on to repay a tax anticipation note, for example, might come up short of the amount needed because property values or retail sales fell and didn't generate as much revenue as expected. In the winter of 1991, for example, New York City's sales-tax revenue dropped $55 143 million, or almost 9 percent from the previous year, as shoppers spent less in the face of a recession. Similarly, a city might be planning to sell a bond issue to repay a bond anticipation note. But if a mammoth budget deficit suddenly looms and the city's debt rating is downgraded, it may have trouble getting investors to buy those bonds.

Whole lotta Vardos: A far more popular—and complicated—investment for money funds are VRDOs, variable-rate demand obligations, or what are known as Vardos. Some funds have as much as half their assets invested in these instruments. The term itself sounds like the name of a vampire in a Bela Lugosi horror film and, in fact, they're pretty scary in their own right. Vardos are a lot like long-term bonds, but not quite. You see, no money fund is allowed to invest in any security that comes due in more than two years. But Vardos get around this two-year restriction with a neat trick: the fund can demand repayment from the state or municipality issuing the Vardo, usually by giving one to thirty days' notice. Hence the term *demand obligations*. And to make sure the funds get an interest rate in line with current market rates, the rate on most Vardos is reset every seven days, which is where the term *variable rate* comes in. Funds also invest in what are known as "put" bonds. This means that the fund can "put," or sell, the bond back to the city or state at certain times. This supposedly assures the money fund that it can sell these bonds if, for example, they need cash to meet redemption requests for shareholders getting out of the fund.

So far, it's all very ingenious—variable rates, demand features, put bonds, all ways to give people like you and me safe, tax-free income. But the more you look into Vardos and put bonds, the worse many of them look. Because these instruments are very complicated, it's nice to have an independent agency like Standard & Poor's analyze them and give them a rating. This way the fund manager—and fund shareholders—have an independent valuation of the ability of the Vardo or put bond to pay off. But, to get the high-octane yields that attract shareholders, some funds also invest in unrated issues. One of the highest-yielding tax-exempt funds, Calvert Tax-Free Reserves Money Market, for example, had more than 25 percent of its holdings, or some $315 million, in unrated Vardos in early March 1991. Similarly, Nuveen Tax-Free Reserves had 19 percent of its near $460 million in assets stashed in unrated Vardos during that same period. While unrated issues might be of comparable quality to rated ones, there's no way for shareholders to tell. They are relying solely on the judgment of the fund

144

manager and (we hope) a staff of credit analysts. But even rigorous analysis by the fund isn't quite the same as that by an independent rating agency. Why? Simple. You have to remember that money funds earn their management fees by taking a percentage of the assets they manage. The more assets—i.e., shareholders like you and me—the fund brings in, the more it earns. In other words, it is clearly in the fund's interest to attract new investors. The way fund managers do that is by offering higher yields—and the way they do that, often, is by taking a bit more risk. In other words, a fund that wants to post high yields to woo new investors, consciously or not, might be more apt to take additional risks in the pursuit of high returns than would a ratings agency that has absolutely no stake in what a fund yields.

But even rated Vardos and bonds have another problem. Just as people who've borrowed too much and are considered bad risks, many states and municipalities also are not credit worthy enough to get a top rating from credit-rating agencies such as Standard & Poor's or Moody's. So to get that rating—which lowers their borrowing costs—the city or town gets a bank to agree to, in effect, guarantee repayment. The bank does this by issuing a letter of credit, which is the bank's promise—for a tidy fee—to cough up the money if the issuing city, town, or state can't. That's all well and good, except banks themselves are having trouble paying the bills these days—so their word isn't always reliable. Oddly enough, the biggest players in the letter-of-credit game have been Japanese banks, which have been turning out letters of credit faster than Sony churns out camcorders. In 1990 alone, Japanese banks issued more than $6 billion in letter-of-credit guarantees. Meanwhile, rising interest rates and other economic problems in Japan have eroded the profitability of many Japanese banks, resulting in lower credit ratings for some from Standard & Poor's. In fact, Japanese banks are already facing some big problems in letters of credit. According to a 1991 article in *Financial World* magazine, Japanese banks are already having to make good on more than $1 billion worth of letter-of-credit guarantees on U.S. student loans. If such losses continued, the banks could eventually have trouble coming up with the cash to make good on their letter-of-credit guarantees. The bottom line: the loss-shield provided by those letters of credit isn't as bulletproof as it seems.

In fact, the whole letter-of-credit system has already suffered one breakdown that proves they're not foolproof. The case involves tax-exempt industrial revenue bonds issued by the Prime Motor Inn motel chain. What in the world, you may ask, does a private company have to do with tax-exempt bonds? Simple. In the mid-1980s, many municipalities tried to spur economic development by allowing private companies to borrow under the aegis of the city. This arrangement was supposed to create jobs for the city and, by using tax-exempt bonds to finance development, lower interest rates for the private company. With a bank willing to issue a letter of credit to back the whole thing—for a nice fee, of course—everybody was happy. That all changed in October 1990, though, when Prime Motor Inns filed for bankruptcy. When that happened, the bank letters of credit were supposed to pay off the Prime Motor Inn tax-exempt industrial revenue bonds. (Several money-fund sources assured me that at least one and possibly more tax-exempt money funds allegedly held these Prime Motor Inn bonds, but no fund ever publicized that fact). But the bondholders got a big surprise. Prime Motor Inn asked a bankruptcy judge to stop the letter-of-credit bank from paying off the bondholders because that move, in effect, would replace cheap low-interest-rate tax-exempt bonds with high-interest-rate funds from the bank letter of credit. This would mean even higher interest costs for Prime and put them in even worse shape. The judge agreed and prevented the letter of credit from paying off the bonds. Not to worry, the bonds still had a "put," which gave the bondholders the right to sell the bonds back to the company. Ah, but the fine print in the bond documents said that all bets as far as the "put" were concerned were off if the company filed for bankruptcy. This left the bondholders in a horrible position. They owned the long-term bonds of a bankrupt company—and had almost no way of getting rid of them, or at least not without taking a big loss. Any money fund holding these bonds was in an especially precarious position: it is illegal for a fund to hold bonds with a maturity of more than two years. Fortunately the judge in this case came to his senses and reversed his decision. But the Prime Motor Inn incident sent a long chill down the spine of any tax-exempt-fund manager smart enough to realize that the whole supposedly failsafe system of letters of credits and puts and demand features really could go awry.

Synthetic floaters: No, synthetic floaters aren't a new L.L. Bean duck-hunting decoy or a new plastic bath toy. Rather, they are the latest, not to mention one of the strangest, tax-exempt investments to come along in some time. Here's how they work: Investment bankers buy long-term municipal bonds and strip the bonds of their interest-payment coupons. Using these coupons, which are the rights to a series of tax-free interest payments, the investment banks then manufacture a new security which promises to pay the tax-free money fund the going rate of interest for short-term tax-exempt securities. As with our old friend Vardos, the fund has the right to periodically sell the floater back to the issuer. What synthetic floaters boil down to then are a neat way of turning long-term muni bonds—an investment that tax-free money funds are prohibited by law from owning—into short-term tax-exempt notes that the fund can legally own. Not only does this give muni money funds more things to invest in, it gives them more *higher-yielding* things to invest in. That's because long-term bonds pay a higher interest rate (because they're more risky) than short-term securities like TANs, RANs, and BANs.

So what's the hitch? There are several. For one thing, it's still unclear whether these floaters are really exempt from taxes. The floaters are only derived from municipal securities—a municipality didn't actually issue them. If Congress or the Treasury Department decides one day that floaters definitely are not tax-exempt, shareholders in funds that bought floaters could wind up having to pay taxes on what they thought was tax-free income.

There's another way synthetic floaters could backfire. Although the fund has the right to sell a floater back to the issuer, that right might be tough to exercise. For example, a fund might have trouble selling the floater back if its credit rating is downgraded or if its tax status changes. In other words, just when the fund really needs to sell the floater, it may not be able to. Because of these risks, some of the more reputable fund groups, such as Vanguard, avoid synthetic floaters altogether. Given the potential dangers, you, too, should steer clear of them by shunning funds that put a substantial percentage of their assets—say, any more than 5 percent—in these untested hybrids.

ARE TAX-FREE FUNDS WORTH THE EXTRA RISKS?

Before taking the plunge into a tax-exempt money fund, you've got to decide whether you are being adequately compensated for shouldering the extra risks in such a fund. After all, you could simply park your cash in a CD at one of the safe banks listed in chapter 4, or you could duck into a fund that invests only in U.S. Treasury bills. In both cases your money would be safer. But would you have to settle for a mediocre or even lousy return by moving from a tax-exempt to a taxable investment? Let's take a look.

Assume for a minute you are a resident of the city of New York.

147

Aside from many other dangers and problems, living in the Big Apple means you could be beleaguered by a combined city, state, and federal tax rate of as high as 40 percent. (Assuming the highest rates as of early 1991). Now, if you wanted to completely avoid all those taxes, you could invest in a triple-tax-free fund such as Fidelity New York Tax-Free Money Market Portfolio, which was yielding 3.81 percent in early March of 1991. So if you invested, say, $10,000, you would earn $381 in annual interest and no one, not the IRS, the state taxman, or the city tax collector could take a dime of it. But . . . you could also put that $10,000 into a taxable money fund like Alex Brown Prime, which was yielding 6.3 percent at that same time. In that fund, your $10,000 investment would give you $630—but you would have to hand over roughly $252 in combined local, state, and federal taxes. That would leave you with $378 or about $3 less than the triple-tax-free fund. But, for a measly $3 a year on a $10,000 investment, is it really worth worrying whether New York City will survive its fiscal slump? I don't think so.

In fact, there's an even better, *even safer*, place to put your money *that may beat the returns on both these options*—namely a fund that invests solely in U.S. Treasury bills. Had you put that $10,000 into the Benham Capital Preservation Fund (a pure T-bill fund) that was paying 6.19 percent in early 1991, you would get $619 in interest. The IRS would grab 31 percent of that or $192. But that's it! Interest from Treasury bills is generally exempt from state and local taxes. So after paying off the IRS, you would have $427 left over—$46 more than if you'd invested in the far, far riskier Fidelity triple-tax-free fund and $49 more than if you had invested in the Alex Brown Prime fund.

This is what is known in common parlance as a no-brainer decision. When you get more money for taking less risk, you grab it, quick. Unfortunately it's not always that easy. The difference between interest rates on tax-free and taxable money funds widens and narrows at different times, sometimes making tax-frees a better deal, other times making taxables the wiser choice. Even more important is your actual income-tax rate, which will vary depending on how much you earn and where you live. Among the questions you must ask yourself: Are you in the top federal bracket or is your income low enough so you pay a far lower rate than 31 percent? Do you face a state income tax? If so, how high is the rate? How about local income taxes? The size of these taxes will largely determine whether it's worth trying to avoid them. After all, why bother avoiding a piddly little tax bill, especially if you have to take on added risk in the process? Clearly, there are too many unknowns for anyone to give a single easy-to-follow rule for when to invest in tax-free funds and when to stick to taxable ones. But keep this guideline in mind: The lower the income tax bracket you're in and the bigger the interest-rate advantage taxable funds have over tax-free funds, the more likely you'll be better off just sticking to taxable funds and possibly even those that invest only in U.S. Treasuries and other government securities. To tell exactly whether you're better off, go through the same exercise I just did for the hypothetical New York City resident above — that is, find out what taxable money funds are yielding after you pay the taxes on them and compare that to what you earn on the tax-free money fund. Of course, you'll substitute the actual income taxes you face, rather than use the confiscatory rates imposed on poor New Yorkers (like me). If you're unsure what your federal, state, and local income tax rates are (maybe you're luckier than New York City residents and you don't have to pay local income taxes to support a crumbling infrastructure), a tax preparer or accountant should be able to provide you with the appropriate rates. Keep in mind, though, that you really shouldn't be taking the tax-free option, unless you're getting a *higher* after-tax return with the tax-exempt fund than with the taxable fund. And even then you shouldn't do it unless that extra return is large enough to make it worth the extra risk.

THE CRUCIAL DIFFERENCE BETWEEN NATIONAL AND SINGLE-STATE TAX-FREE FUNDS

If you are already one of the more than one million shareholders in tax-free money funds—or you're thinking of joining their ranks—it's especially important that you understand the difference between the funds that invest in the securities of many states—what are called national tax-free funds—and those that restrict themselves to one state—the single-state funds. One of the most important ways of reducing risk in investing is to diversify—that is, buy a variety of different investments. In the case of tax-free funds, that means holding securities with varying maturities. This diversification—again, a highfalutin term for putting your eggs in many baskets—is particularly important today, when some parts of the country may be in recession while others are prospering and many cities and states are as wobbly as some of our banks. Why? Because divvying up the portfolio prevents economic problems in one state or city from dragging down the entire fund. A well-chosen national tax-exempt money fund can easily protect you against financial Armageddon in one state or city by picking and choosing among the short-term debt of fifty states, hundreds of cities, and thousands of towns across the country. If one city defaults or its debt is downgraded and loses value, at least the impact is limited to a small portion of the portfolio. You might suffer a loss, but it would be small, probably small enough that the interest earned on the rest of the portfolio would wipe out the loss in well under a year.

But a single-state fund is inherently *not* diversified because it limits itself to the securities of one state and municipalities within that state. If something happens to that state or those municipalities—their tax collections slow down, their debt is downgraded, or they actually default on their debt—a single-state money fund's value could go down faster than the *Titanic*. This risk is real, not just an interesting little hypothesis. In 1990, two Fidelity single-state funds—Massachusetts Tax Free Portfolio and Spartan New Jersey Municipal Money Market Portfolio—both bought out-of-state securities because the fund managers were having trouble finding an adequate supply of high-quality securities in those states. The bottom line is this: Gauging the riskiness of single-state tax-free money funds is extremely difficult for independent ratings agencies such as Standard & Poor's and virtually impossible for savers and individual investors. Though no one is predicting China Syndrome–like meltdowns in these funds, they are definitely more risky than national tax-exempt funds and far more risky than the best taxable funds. If you are a conservative saver or cautious investor and are dealing with money you simply cannot afford to take a loss on, you are better off steering clear of single-state muni funds. If the yields on single-state funds become especially attractive, and you're willing to take a bit more risk with some of your savings, fine. Otherwise, go with safe national tax-free funds, following the guidelines and lists of funds listed in chapter 8. Even then you should only go with the national tax-free funds if they're offering a better equivalent return than the highest-quality taxable funds and U.S. government funds. If you're not getting paid enough for taking that extra risk, stick to the taxables.

8

THE SAFEST
MONEY-MARKET FUNDS

Safety Plus Competitive Returns

NOW that you know all money funds are not created equal when it comes to safety, let's turn to the task of finding safe-harbor funds where you can stash your cash without worrying whether the fund manager is investing it in some kind of funny paper like synthetic floaters or credit-card bills. In other words, funds whose managers don't suffer from the dread high yield-itis, that dangerous obsession for chasing high yields accompanied by complete amnesia concerning the inevitable risks of that chase. Keep in mind as you read this chapter, however, that using a safe savings strategy with money funds means you sometimes might have to sacrifice a bit of yield. You can be sure that almost any time someone is offering an investment with a higher return than all others, it's because the higher-yielding investment is riskier. Money-market funds are no exception—a higher yield usually translates to a higher risk, despite fund salesmen's claims to the contrary. So if you're desperately seeking safety, you probably won't be the person at the cocktail party bragging between gin and tonics—or glasses of seltzer, if your drinking habits parallel your savings instincts—that your money fund was recently advertised in *The Wall Street Journal* as the top-yielding fund in the Western World. Then again, you also won't be the person nervously scanning the financial pages every time a bank fails or a company goes bankrupt and its commercial paper goes down in flames with it.

Fortunately, though, you don't have to give up much in the way of return if you decide to stick to safe money funds. For example, Standard & Poor's rates money-market funds for safety much the same as it does bonds and insurance companies. To get S&P's top rating—AAA—a fund must meet a variety of strict investing rules concerning the quality of investments the fund can buy, the average maturity, and how quickly the fund can come up with cash to pay off investors who want to get their money out. Unfortunately, S&P doesn't rate very many funds, largely because the funds have to pay an annual rating fee of roughly $12,500 and then agree to let S&P come in from time to time to make sure the fund continues to follow S&P's stringent investing guidelines. Nonetheless, some ninety-six money funds got S&P's triple-A rating as of mid-1991, although some of these funds are limited to large institutional investors and require minimum investments of $1 million or so. (At the end of this chapter, I've included a list of S&P's AAA-rated funds that are available to individuals). But the reason I bring up the S&P safety ratings is not to plug the company's mutual- and money-fund rating service, but to make this important point: Even after meeting extremely tough safety rules that restrict the fund to high-quality investments and prevent the manager from taking big risks to juice up the fund's yield, S&P's AAA funds are usually at or above the average in performance. A number of AAA funds, such as Scudder Cash Investment Trust and Kidder Peabody Premium, have consistently beaten the average return for all money funds. And top-rated funds even occasionally turn up at the top of lists of the top-performing money funds. In October 1990, the Benham Government Agency Fund was the second-best performing government-only fund listed in IBC/Donoghue's *Money Fund Report*, a weekly newsletter that tracks the performance of money funds. So while safe investing makes it unlikely your funds will be in the Top 40 Hit Parade week after week, you certainly don't have to settle for dinky yields to obtain the comforting security of a safe money fund.

Here's how the rest of this chapter will work. I'll start by giving you guidelines, tips, and some caveats about choosing safe funds in a variety of fund categories. So that you'll know how each category relates to another in terms of security, I'll start with the absolutely safest funds—those that invest in Treasury bills—and work my way down in descending order of safety until I get to the ones with higher risks—the tax-exempts. As I proceed through these categories, I'll tell you how to choose the safest funds within that group. This will tell you what you

152

need to know to choose money funds on your own and also help you evaluate the safety of funds you may already own. After giving you these guidelines, I'll end the section on each category with a list of safe funds for that group. To set the guidelines for choosing these safe funds and to come up with the lists themselves, I turned to Walter Frank, the chief economist at the Donoghue Organization, and his colleagues at Donoghue's for help. The Donoghue Organization is the guru when it comes to money funds. Along with the funds themselves at the end of the discussion of each category, I'll also give the criteria Donoghue used to come up with the list of safe funds.

There's one exception to this incredibly well planned and meticulously thought-out modus operandi. And that's the tax-exempt funds. In the section on these funds, I can't, and therefore won't, give you general tips for choosing safe tax-exempts because the investments they buy are too complicated for any useful guidelines that individuals can apply. I will, however, detail and explain the criteria the Donoghue Organization used to come up with the list of safe tax-exempts in the table. If you already own another tax-exempt fund that didn't make my list and you're reluctant to flee that fund, at least you can talk over these criteria with your fund's customer-service representative to get an idea of why your fund didn't make the cut.

Of course a money-market fund is no safer than the investments in its portfolio. The fund's prospectus—a document you should always read before sending a money fund a cent—will spell out what kind of investments the fund is allowed to buy. But the prospectus usually gives a fund wide leeway, and the mix of investments the fund holds can change day to day. That means it is possible that the risk level of a fund can change over time. To make sure that a fund that you chose for its security hasn't become more aggressive and risky, you must occasionally monitor it. Once you own a fund, you will receive semiannual and annual reports and, possibly, quarterly statements. Since these reports list the fund's holding at the end of the quarter, it's a good, easy way for you to keep track of what the fund manager is doing with your money. If you see an investment that strikes you as strange—say, a $1 million CD with the Nationalized Bank of the People's Republic of Albania—call the fund to see if it has adopted a more lenient investment strategy.

Between these reports, you can keep tabs on your fund by checking its yield in the financial section of your local newspaper. Typically, newspapers list the yields of major money funds and also list the average yield for all money funds. Many newspapers also list the average maturity of each fund and the average for all funds. If your money fund has suddenly changed its position—maybe it was in the middle of the pack in yield and average maturity, but now has zoomed up to the top in both yield and maturity—that may be a sign that the fund is taking on additional risks. If you bought the fund directly from a fund company, call their customer-service representative and ask why the fund has increased its yield or average maturity. If you bought the fund through a broker or financial planner, call him or her for the explanation. If the fund company or your broker or planner trails off into a series of "Well, uh, you see, I'm not exactly sure, but I think . . ." and obviously doesn't know what's going on, you may want to consider looking for another fund.

Another way to stay on top of what's going on in the mad, mad world of money funds is to subscribe to magazines or newsletters that follow them regularly. Both *Money* and *Changing Times* cover mutual funds in every issue. *Barron's* also writes about money funds from time to time, although the articles in this iconoclastic weekly newspaper may be a bit daunting for a money-fund neophyte. And *Barron's* is usually better at pointing out problems than at suggesting solutions. Besides newsletters that largely go to fund managers, the media, and others who closely follow money funds, the Donoghue Organization offers two publications that are useful to money-fund investors. The *Donoghue Money Letter* is a monthly newsletter that can help keep you abreast of news pertaining to money funds as well as other types of mutual funds (Cost: $109 a year, 24 issues). Donoghue also publishes an annual money-fund hand-book, *IBC/Donoghue's Money Fund Directory*, which includes fund telephone numbers, information on services offered by the funds, and ten-year performance figures on more than seven hundred money funds (cost: $27.95). For a subscription to either or both of these publications, call 508-429-5930 or write the Donoghue Organization, Box 8008, Holliston, MA 01746-8008). There's one other newsletter, *Income and Safety*, published monthly, which also assigns safety ratings to 148 money funds (cost: $100 per year). For a subscription to *Income and Safety*, call 800-327-6720 or write the Institute for Econometric Research, 3471 N. Federal Highway, Fort Lauderdale, FL 33306. By consulting a combination of these sources—and keeping in mind the guidelines and tips in this chapter as well as the information about funds in chapters 6 and 7, you should be able to settle on a fund that's just the right level of risk for you and monitor it so you don't wind up with any nasty surprises. Now let's get to picking funds.

U.S. TREASURY FUNDS—THE SAFEST REFUGE

To get the highest level of protection possible in a money fund—and still earn competitive returns—you should stick to pure Treasury-bill funds. This way you are investing in what is generally considered the benchmark for risk-free investing—U.S. T-bills. But whatever you do, *do not* confuse *Treasury* funds with *U.S. government* funds, which invest in Treasuries but also throw in varying amounts of securities issued by federal agencies whose debt may only be indirectly backed by the U.S. government. These two types of funds are slightly different and U.S. government funds, though also ultrasafe, aren't quite as free from risk as T-bill funds. (I'll tell you why and point out some other shortcomings of U.S. government funds when we get to the section devoted to this type of fund.)

Besides their unparalleled safety, T-bill funds have another big plus going for them—they are free of state and local income taxes in most states. Depending on how much the local politicians wring out of you in the way of income taxes, this can push the effective return on a Treasury-bill fund above that for riskier funds. In early March of 1991, for example, the Alex Brown Treasury Series fund, which invests only in Treasury bills, was yielding 6.1 percent. In a state like Oregon, where you can face a 9 percent state tax rate, that gives Alex Brown Treasury the equivalent of a 6.7 percent before federal taxes. That's higher than the 6.31 percent yield before taxes offered at that time by T. Rowe Price Cash Reserves, which you may recall (and T. Rowe Price would like you to forget) is the fund that was holding $42 million in Mortgage Realty Trust commercial paper when it defaulted. While there's no assurance that the yields on Treasury-bill funds will always beat those on riskier funds—in fact, the spread between different types of funds widens and narrows at different times—escaping the state and local tax bite amounts to a nice little bonus for conservative investors who would probably choose Treasury funds anyway.

WATCH OUT FOR REPOS AND LONG MATURITIES

Unfortunately, latching on to the security that comes with a 100 percent Treasury-bill portfolio is more difficult than it should be. One reason is that, in their zeal to inflate their yields and bring more money into their funds, many supposed Treasury funds don't invest entirely in T-bills and some don't invest in T-bills at all. That's right. Treasury Funds Without Treasuries—it almost sounds like a topic for an Oprah

Winfrey show. Of course, anywhere but on Wall Street playing up the safety of Treasury bills but not investing in them would be considered a bait-and-switch tactic. But in the financial world such shenanigans are known as smart marketing.

What then, you might ask, are Treasury-money funds investing in if they're not investing in Treasury bills? Repos. They're buying repurchase agreements, or what are better known as repos. Despite the implications of its name, the Treasury Cash Series fund, for example, had only 20 percent of its portfolio in Treasuries in early 1991—the remaining 80 percent was in repos. Similarly, Merrill Lynch's USA Government Reserves fund had 81 percent of its assets in repos and only 19 percent in actual Treasuries. Just what are repos? They are securities issued by brokerage firms or banks that are backed by Treasury bills. An investment firm, for example, might have lots of Treasury bills on hand and wants to turn them into quick cash without actually getting rid of them. So the firm will go to a mutual fund, sell them the Treasury bills, and, at the same time, agree to *buy the T-bills back* at a specified price. That deal is called a repurchase agreement. The yield the fund makes on it depends on the difference between the sale and buyback price. Repurchase agreements are popular with funds because they're a good place to park cash for as short as a day or as long as a month or so. But the important thing as far as money-fund investors are concerned is that the repos, while backed by Treasury bills, are not Treasury bills themselves and are therefore a smidgin riskier. In fact, you know they're riskier because the yield on repos is usually a bit higher than on T-bills (if T-bills are yielding 6 percent, repos would usually yield about 6.1 percent to 6.2 percent). While losses in repos are rare, they have occurred. The danger is that if the repo issuer—a bank or a brokerage firm, say—goes bankrupt, other creditors might try to claim the Treasury collateral backing the repo. This could prevent the fund from getting its money for the repo. Of course, this could never happen when the fund owns actual Treasury bills. The only way the fund wouldn't get paid then is if the U.S. government defaulted on its debts. If that ever happens, you'll have a lot more to worry about than the safety of your money-market fund.

There's another reason to avoid repos, though: the interest on repos is not exempt from state and local taxes as is interest from T-bills. As a result, you may have a rude surprise from the state taxman if you fail to pay taxes on interest from what you thought was a fund that bought

T-bills but actually invested in repos. This tax angle shouldn't matter, though, if you don't face significant state and local income taxes.

The easiest way to get the safety of T-bills is to stick with funds that invest only in Treasuries and eschew repos. But this is easier said than done. In fact, only a handful of funds limit themselves to Treasury bills all the time (For the names of these funds, see the list titled "100% Treasury Bill Funds" on page 159). The problem is that some pure Treasury-bill funds soup up their yields by stretching out the average maturity of the fund beyond the level acceptable to the most conservative investors. The reason safety-conscious investors should worry about a fund's average maturity is that the longer the average maturity, the greater the chance that a spike in interest rates could cause the value of a fund to drop and result in a loss, albeit only a small one. The Dreyfus 100 percent Treasury Money Market Fund, for example, has regularly kept its average maturity at one hundred days or longer. And the Strong U.S. Treasury Money Fund has gone out as far as one hundred twelve days in early 1991. As of June 1991, the effective date of the new Security and Exchange Commission regulations described in chapter 6, funds won't be able to legally push their average maturity beyond ninety days. While a ninety-day limit on average maturity certainly reduces the chances of rising interest rates eroding the value of a fund, some authorities consider ninety days a bit too liberal. Standard & Poor's, for example, won't give its AAA rating to any fund whose average maturity exceeds sixty days.

Ideally, then, you will get the highest level of security in a Treasury-bill fund that invests entirely or almost entirely in T-bills and also limits its maturity to sixty days or less. Getting this double level of security, though not impossible, is difficult. So you may want to settle for funds that at least tilt their mix in favor of Treasuries over repos and also keep short maturities. The following list of safe Treasury-bill funds culled from the Donoghue Organization's database fits that bill. To make this list, a fund had to invest at least 75 percent of its assets directly in Treasury bills (some were 100 percent in T-bills) and no fund could have an average maturity of more than seventy-five days (some were much lower). Given this tough set of rules, these funds qualify as among the safest, if not the absolute safest, places for money-fund investors to put their money. Note that the yields are as of early April 1991 and no doubt have changed since then. (As of mid-August, for example, Treasury-fund yields had dropped roughly one percentage from their yields in April.) I include them only to give you an idea of how these safe funds stack up against each other as well as against the average yield for all Treasury funds. As you can see, in many cases these funds beat the average yield for the category and no fund's yield lags far behind any other's in the group.

T A B L E   8 · 1

Safe Treasury Money-Market Funds

Fund name	Minimum Initial Investment	Percentage in Treasury Bills	Average Maturity	Yield	Telephone
U.S. Treasuries Cash Assets Trust	$ 1,000	92	44 days	6.52%*	212-697-6666
U.S. Treasury Trust	$10,000	100	72 days	6.31%*	800-225-8778 415-398-2727
Vanguard U.S. Treasury	$ 3,000	100	50 days	6.15%	800-662-7447 800-662-2739
Freedom Government Securities Fund	$ 2,500	100	57 days	6.04%	800-225-6258
Scudder U.S. Treasury Money Fund	$ 1,000	79	68 days	6.02%	800-225-2470
Alex Brown Treasury Series	$ 1,500	100	54 days	5.98%	800-767-3524
Prudential Government Securities/U.S. Treasuries	$ 1,000	100	70 days	5.89%*	800-225-1852
Short-term Income/U.S. Government	$ 5,000	76	62 days	5.87%	800-221-3079 212-370-1240
Fund for Government Investors	$ 2,500	100	59 days	5.81%	800-343-3355 301-657-1500
Neuberger & Berman Government Money Fund	$ 2,000	100	63 days	5.80%	800-877-9700 212-850-8300
Capital Preservation Fund	$ 1,000	100	52 days	5.75%	800-472-3389
U.S. Treasury Money Fund of America	$ 2,500	100	65 days	5.73%	800-421-9900

Fund name	Minimum Initial Investment	Percentage in Treasury Bills	Average Maturity	Yield	Telephone
Boston Company Government Money Fund	$1,000	79	52 days	5.70%	800-343-6324
Vision Treasury Money Fund	$1,000	76	54 days	5.68%	800-245-0242 412-288-1900
Calvert Money Management Plus/ Government	$2,000	100	51 days	5.41%	800-368-2748 301-951-4820
Average for all U.S. Treasury Money Funds			53 days	5.93%	

SOURCE: IBC/Donoghue. Data as of April 1991. Yield, percentage invested in Treasuries, and average maturity can change daily; check with fund before investing to make sure it still generally meets these criteria and read prospectus before investing a dime.

*These funds were waiving all or part of their investment advisory fee. Beware, since this *temporarily* boosts their yields.

T A B L E   8 · 2

100 Percent Treasury-Bill Funds

The following sixteen funds buy Treasury bills and only Treasury bills. That would make them the safest bet, except you'll notice that some stretch out their average maturity well beyond an ultraconservative sixty days to pump up their yields. As of June 1991, funds can't have an average maturity of more than ninety days, but even that is too long for truly safety-conscious investors. The absolutely safest funds are the ten marked by a # sign.

Fund name	Minimum Initial Investment	Average Maturity	Yield	Telephone
Alex Brown Treasury Series #	$ 1,500	54 days	5.98%	800-767-3524
Calvert Money Management Plus/Government #	$ 2,000	51 days	5.41%	800-368-2748 301-951-4820
Capital Preservation Fund #	$ 1,000	52 days	5.75%	800-472-3389
Dreyfus 100% U.S. Treasury Money Fund	$ 2,500	111 days	6.62%	800-829-3733
Fidelity Spartan U.S. Treasury Money Fund	$20,000	93 days	6.66%*	800-544-6666 617-523-1919

Fund name	Minimum Initial Investment	Average Maturity	Yield	Telephone
Freedom Government Securities #	$2,500	57 days	6.04%	800-225-6258
Fund for Government Investors #	$2,500	59 days	5.81%	800-343-3355 301-657-1500
Neuberger & Berman Government Money fund #	$2,000	63 days	5.80%	800-877-9700 212-850-8300
Prime Value Treasury Funds	$100,000	86 days	6.23%*	212-363-3300
Prudential Government Securities/U.S. Treasuries #	$1,000	70 days	5.89%*	800-225-1852
Strategic Treasury Positions	1,000	19 days	4.77%	800-527-5027 214-484-1326
Strong U.S. Treasury Money Fund	$1,000	112 days	6.52%*	800-368-3863 414-359-3400
USAA Treasury Money Market Trust	$3,000	93 days	5.77%*	800-531-8181 512-498-6505
U.S. Treasury Money Fund of America #	$2,500	65 days	5.73%	800-421-9900
The U.S. Treasury Trust #	$10,000	72 days	6.31%*	800-225-8778 415-398-2727
Vanguard U.S. Treasury #	$3,000	50 days	6.15%	800-662-7447

SOURCE: IBC/Donoghue; Average maturity and yields as of April 1991. Yield and average maturity can change daily; check with fund before investing to make sure it still generally mets these criteria and read prospectus before investing a dime.

*These funds were waiving all or part of their investment advisory fee. Beware, since this *temporarily* boosts their yields.

#These funds also appear on the Safe Treasury Money Market Fund list on Table 8.1.

U.S. GOVERNMENT AND AGENCY FUNDS

You may be able to eke out a slightly higher return—usually an additional .25 percent a year or so—while taking only an extremely small additional risk by going to a U.S. government and agency securities fund. These funds can invest in Treasury bills, but to increase their yields, they also buy the securities of government agencies such as the Federal National Mortgage Association, Government National Mortgage Association, and the Federal Farm Credit Bank. So if these are U.S. government agencies, why is the risk any different than that for U.S. Treasuries? Two reasons. First, the securities of many of these agencies are not directly backed by the full faith and credit of the United States. Some are indirectly backed or are considered a "moral obligation" of the U.S. Theoretically there's the chance the U.S. could walk away from some of these obligations, but as a practical matter the chances of Uncle Sam reneging on the debt of, say, the Government National Mortgage Association are about zilch.

There's a second potential danger that is worth considering, however. And that is known as "bad news" risk, which means there's the chance the price of an agency's securities could go down—and the value of the money fund holding those securities fall—if there's a rash of negative press about the agency. While such incidents are rare, a flurry of unfavorable articles about the Federal Farm Credit Bank a few years back did drive the price of that agency's securities down, even though there was no realistic chance of a default. The chances of an actual loss in a fund are pretty remote, however, and even if negative press does push prices down the likely loss will be small in a fund that spreads its money among the securities of many government agencies.

U.S. government and agency funds do suffer from a distinct tax disadvantage compared to Treasury funds, however. The interest on agency securities is not usually exempt from state and local taxes. If you face hefty state and local income taxes, you should check the return on a U.S. government and agency fund after subtracting the amount you would pay in state and local taxes and compare that to the return you would get on a pure Treasury-bill fund. If you're not netting more in the agency fund, you're better off remaining in the ultrasafe refuge of Treasuries.

As with Treasury funds, managers of U.S. government and agency funds will also try to plump up their yields by pushing the average maturity out toward ninety days. For conservative investors, that's too high. A seventy-five-day average maturity is better and a sixty-day average maturity is better still. If the fund regularly goes beyond the sixty-to-seventy-five-day range, you should consider switching to one that keeps below that ceiling. Many government agency funds also rely heavily on repos, although a small handful of funds—the Benham Government Agency Fund and the Lexington Government Securities Fund, to name two—do avoid them.

To come up with the group of safe U.S. government and agency funds listed on page 163, the Donoghue Organization went through all the funds in its Government and Agencies category and eliminated funds with an average maturity of more than sixty days. Donoghue chose the sixty-day criteria instead of the seventy-five-day standard used for Treasury funds to compensate for the fact that the assets in government and agency funds carry a tad more risk. Funds that bought repos backed by anything other than U.S. Treasury bills were eliminated. This gives an extra measure of safety since no collateral is as good as a T-bill. Almost half the funds on the list beat the yield of the average U.S. government and agency fund, and the rest weren't too far off. These yields, of course, change frequently. The reason they're given here isn't to turn this into a contest to pick the highest-yielding fund, but to give you an idea of how these safe funds stacked up against similar funds that did not make this list.

THE SAFEST NON–U.S. GOVERNMENT
MONEY FUNDS

Of course, most funds don't limit themselves to Treasury bills or the securities of government agencies. In fact, of the 741 money funds available to investors in the spring of 1991, only 134 were either Treasury or U.S. government and agency funds. The next biggest group, some 349 funds, are what are known as taxable funds. (The remaining 258 funds are the tax-exempt funds, which will be discussed a bit later.) They invest in certificates of deposit at U.S. banks as well as in more exotic Eurodollar or Yankee Dollar CDs. (Eurodollar CDs are certificates of deposit held in foreign branches of U.S. banks and Yankee Dollar CDs are certificates of deposit issued by U.S. branches of foreign banks. For more about the potential risks of these investments, see chapter 6.) Taxable funds may occasionally buy Treasury bills or government securities and even repos, but the bulk of their holdings are in commercial paper, or corporate IOUs.

You can sometimes get a higher return of anywhere from .5 percent to 1 percent a year by going to a taxable fund instead of a Treasury bill or a U.S. government and agency fund. The reason, quite simply, is that commercial paper is riskier than Treasury bills and other U.S. government securities. So you get a higher yield investing in it. Don't kid yourself that there's no difference in risk between government funds and regular taxable funds. Due to the profligate, pile-on-the-debt philosophy of the 1980s, the risk of a default in the commercial-paper holdings of a money fund is very real. Companies can welch on their IOUs—as Integrated Resources did in 1989 and Mortgage Realty and Trust did in 1990—and possibly leave money-fund shareholders with a loss.

But you *can* take advantage of the often higher yields in taxable funds

Safe U.S. Government and Agency Funds

Fund Name	Minimum Initial Investment	Percentage in Treasury Bills	Percentage in Repos	Yield	Average Maturity	Telephone
Benham Government Agency Fund	$ 1,000	15	none	6.49%*	48 days	800-472-3389
Vanguard Money Market Reserves—Federal	$ 3,000	16	17	6.36%	49 days	800-662-7447
The Galaxy Funds Treasury Fund	$ 2,500	64	none	6.31%*	37 days	800-343-6324
UST Master Government Money Fund	$ 1,000	3	44	6.27%	47 days	800-233-1136 / 213-488-0666
Centennial Government Trust	$ 500	14	24	6.11%	56 days	800-525-7048 / 303-671-3200
Cardinal Government Securities	$ 1,000	5	53	6.01%	49 days	800-282-9446 / 614-464-6817
Cash Accumulation Treasury National Government	$ 500	25	45	5.99%	22 days	800-628-1237 / 203-352-4900
UST Master Treasury Money Fund	$ 1,000	74	none	5.94%	31 days	800-233-1136 / 213-488-0666
Schwab Government Securities Fund	$ 1,000	5	56	5.86%*	28 days	415-627-7000
Cortland Trust Inc. U.S. Government Fund	$ 1,000	8	20	5.77%*	55 days	800-433-1918 / 201-342-5757
Government Cash Series	$10,000	6	73	5.75%*	40 days	800-245-2423 / 412-288-1900
Liberty Government Money Market Series	$ 500	7	61	5.71%	38 days	800-245-4770 / 412-288-1900
First Prairie Money Market Government Series	$ 1,000	17	75	5.54%	15 days	800-537-4938 / 718-895-1650
Massachusetts Cash Mgt. Trust Government Series	$ 1,000	60	1	5.45%	60 days	800-622-4273
Lexington Government Securities Money Market Fund	$ 1,000	22	none	5.31%*	32 days	800-526-0057 / 201-845-7300
Average for all U.S. Government and Agency Funds				5.95%	52 days	

SOURCE: IBC/Donoghue. Average maturities and yields as of April 1991. Yield, average maturity, and percentage invested in Treasuries and repos can change daily; before investing, check with fund to make sure it still generally meets these criteria and read prospectus.
*These funds were waiving all or part of their investment advisory fee. Beware, since this *temporarily* boosts their yields.

without significantly jeopardizing the safety of your money if you stick to conservative, well-managed, safe taxable funds. The new SEC regulations that prevent most funds from investing more than 5 percent of their assets in lower-quality investments will help lower the chances of a default handing you a loss. Conservative investors, however, may want an even higher level of safety. The first way to get it is to weed out funds that invest in anything but top-quality commercial paper. You can find out whether a fund you own or are thinking of buying buys lower-quality commercial paper simply by calling the fund's customer-service representative and asking if the fund holds A-2/P-2 commercial paper. Or you can ask if the fund limits itself to A-1/P-1 paper, which amounts to the same thing. Keep in mind that a fund may avoid lower-quality paper for a while and then go back to it. Ideally, therefore, you want a fund that either always restricts itself to top-quality investments or only strays on rare occasions. The funds rated AAA by Standard & Poor's and listed at the end of this chapter do not buy anything less than the highest-grade commercial paper.

You can also reduce your chances of a loss by investing in what the Donoghue Organization describes as Prime funds—these are funds that not only invest in top-quality commercial paper, but exclude investments such as Eurodollar and Yankee Dollar CDs. Again, the easiest way to find out if a fund you already own invests in these securities is to call the fund's customer-service representative and ask. Again, you should check the fund's average maturity. The longer the number of days average maturity, the more risk you take that interest rates could knock down the value of the fund. An average maturity of seventy-five days or less should give you adequate protection and an average maturity of less than sixty days virtually immunizes you from interest-rate risk.

The fifteen safe taxable funds listed below meet all these criteria. All were chosen from the Donoghue Organization's Prime category, which means they do not invest in lower-quality commercial paper or Yankee or Eurodollar CDs. Because of concerns about the credit quality of CDs in some U.S. banks, the Donoghue Organization limited exposure to potentially wobbly CDs by screening out funds that invested more than 5 percent of their assets in bank CDs. Finally, to make the list, all these funds had to have an average maturity of less than sixty days and beat the average yield for all funds in the prime category.

T A B L E 8 · 4

Safe Taxable Money-Market Funds

Fund Name	Minimum Initial Investment	Yield	Average Maturity	Telephone
Cash Assets Trust	$1,000	6.55%	39 days	212-697-6666
Riverside Capital Money Market Fund	$1,000	6.50%*	43 days	800-554-3862 614-899-4600
Flex-fund Money Market Fund	$2,500	6.49%*	55 days	800-325-3539 614-766-7000
William Penn Money Market Portfolio	$ 500	6.46%*	33 days	800-523-8440 215-670-1031
Washington Square Cash Fund	$1,000	6.41%*	39 days	800-333-6965 612-372-5507
Value Line Cash Fund	$1,000	6.41%	45 days	800-223-0818
Newton Money Fund	$1,000	6.35%*	46 days	800-242-7229 414-347-1141
Salem Money Market Portfolio Trust Shares	$1,000	6.33%*	34 days	800-326-3241 412-288-1900
MainStay Money Market Fund	$1,000	6.32%*	52 days	800-522-4202
Altura Prime Obligations Portfolio	$1,000	6.30%*	40 days	800-554-3862 614-899-4600
Churchill Cash Reserve Trust	$1,000	6.28%	49 days	212-697-6666
Princor Cash Management Fund	$1,000	6.27%*	49 days	800-247-4123 515-247-5711
PaineWebber Cashfund	$5,000	6.27%	51 days	800-762-1000 212-713-2000

Fund Name	Minimum Initial Investment	Yield	Average Maturity	Telephone
Calvert Social Investment Money Market	$1,000	6.24%*	58 days	800-368-2748 301-951-4820
Dean Witter/ Sears Liquid Asset Fund	$5,000	6.21%	58 days	212-392-1600
Average for all Prime funds		6.00%	47 days	

SOURCE: IBC/Donoghue. Average maturities and yields as of April 1991. Yields and average maturity can change daily; check with fund before investing to make sure it still generally meets these criteria and read prospectus before investing a dime.

*These funds were waiving all or part of their investment advisory fee. Beware, since this *temporarily* boosts their yields.

SAFE TAX-FREE MONEY FUNDS

You won't have any trouble finding a tax-exempt money-market fund. Knowing that many savers and investors are absolutely desperate for shelter from today's rising tax toll, money-fund sponsors have been churning out new tax-free funds at a frenetic pace. In 1990 alone, 41 of the 90 new money-funds launched were tax-exempt funds, bringing their ranks to some 258 funds—or more than a third of the 741 money funds in existence as of early 1991.

Finding a *safe* tax-free fund—at least one that parallels the safety of a bank account in a well-capitalized, secure, federally insured bank—is another matter. In fact, this is the category in which it is the most difficult to come up with truly safe funds. For one thing, the overwhelming popularity of tax-free funds actually adds to their riskiness. These funds attract so much cash from investors looking to escape the clutches of federal, state, and local tax collectors that the supply of investable funds has become larger than the supply of ultrasafe, conservative investments to buy with that money. It's a simple case of too much money chasing too few good investments—the very problem that made so many real-estate investments of the 1980s such a disaster. The deteriorating condition of our states and cities, which issue the securities tax-free money funds buy, has made this problem even worse by shrinking the supply of high-quality securities even more. The coup de

166

grace in this risky scenario comes from the fund sponsors and managers themselves. In a time of deteriorating credit quality in municipal securities, the funds persist in trying to outdo each other in posting high yields that will attract new investors and, ultimately, fatten the fund companies' coffers. In their quest for the aphrodisiac of high yields, fund managers are dabbling in a wide array of securities that bristle with risk and uncertainty, such as synthetic floaters, put bonds, iffy commercial paper, and the ever-popular Vardos, or variable-rate-demand obligations. (Those of you who flipped directly to the lists in this book might want to go back and read the section in chapter 7 that takes a more detailed look at the potential pitfalls in these investments. You won't earn extra credit, but you might wind up with a safer money fund.)

I said it before in the previous chapter, but it bears repeating: You should not be investing your money in these funds unless you are getting significantly more than you would in a high-quality taxable fund or a top-grade U.S. government and agency or U.S. Treasury fund. You are taking more risk in tax-free funds and you should only resort to them if you are getting paid decently for it. So before you invest a cent in a tax-free fund, sit down with a pencil and paper—or hire someone to do it for you—and figure out how much you will earn on a tax-free fund at current yields, and then compare that to what you will earn on taxable or government funds after paying taxes. That's the best way to tell whether you are being adequately compensated for shouldering the extra risk of these funds.

That said, let's get to the list of safe tax-free funds. When I asked the people at Donoghue to help come up with criteria for these funds, they reminded me of the difficulty of such an undertaking and then told me that they would only attempt it for *national* tax-free funds—that is, funds that can invest in the securities of *all* our states and cities, but are exempt only from federal taxes. The reason they insisted on national funds is that geographic diversity at least helps spread out the risks in these funds. If the securities of one state crash, they will represent only a small portion of the fund's assets and limit any possible loss. As a result, the funds on this list will be free of federal taxes. To the extent the fund holds securities in your own state you may also be able to shelter some of your income from state and local taxes. A tax adviser will be able to tell you more about your state's rules on this.

So starting with the 116 or so national tax-free funds available to individuals (the others are for large institutional investors like banks and trust companies), here's how we pared our way down to our safe list.

First we eliminated funds that had more than 20 percent of their holdings in municipal commercial paper. That's because much municipal commercial paper is what is known as "nonrecourse" debt, which the city doesn't back with its full faith and credit. So the city can weasel out of paying if it has to. We also did away with any funds holding more than 5 percent of their assets in bonds that could not be "put" or sold back to the issuer within six months. The reason: If the fund needed to drum up money quickly, it could have trouble unloading these bonds. Next we did away with funds that didn't have at least 50 percent of their holdings in variable-demand obligations that were rated by an independent agency such as Standard & Poor's or Moody's Investors Service. We then made the cut even harsher by eliminating any fund that had more than 20 percent of its assets in *unrated* demand obligations. The thinking here was that unrated investments should be kept to a minimum because it's nearly impossible to independently verify their safety. Finally, as an added measure of safety, we weeded out funds that had an average maturity of more than *fifty* days. We chose a more stringent standard in these funds than in the other categories because the types of securities held by tax-free funds can't be sold as quickly for top dollar as can the securities held by taxable and government funds. A shorter average maturity lowers the risk of a fund having trouble meeting shareholder redemptions should people want to get out of the fund for any reason. The following funds are the highest-yielding tax-free money funds that made it through our safety screens.

T A B L E   8 · 5

Safe National Tax-Free Money-Market Funds

Fund Name	Minimum Initial Investment	Percentage in Unrated Demand Notes and Commercial Paper	Average Maturity	Yield	Telephone
Municipal Cash Series	$10,000	10	34 days	4.63%*	800-245-2423 412-288-1900
Laurel Tax-Exempt Money Market I Portfolio	$1,000	6	38 days	4.47%*	800-323-9197

Fund Name	Minimum Initial Investment	Percentage in Unrated Demand Notes and Commercial Paper	Average Maturity	Yield	Telephone
Cortland Trust Municipal Money Market Fund	$1,000	5	43 days	4.46%*	800-435-1918 201-342-5757
Centennial Tax-Exempt Trust	$ 500	21	42 days	4.11%	800 525-7040 303-671-3200
Helmsman Tax-Free Obligations Portfolio	$1,000	18	41 days	4.42%*	800-338-4345
Daily Tax-Free Income Fund	$5,000	12	16 days	4.36%	800-221-3079 212-370-1240
General Municipal Money Market Fund	$2,500	6	40 days	4.36%	800-762-6620 718-895-1206
Boston Co. Tax-Free Money Fund	$1,000	none	45 days	4.35%	800-343-6324
Altura Tax-Free Obligations Portfolio	$1,000	9	43 days	4.32%*	800-255-9961 614-899-4600
Salem Tax-Free Money Market Portfolio	$1,000	2	45 days	4.31%*	800-326-3241 412-288-1900
Rodney Square Tax-Exempt Fund	$1,000	19	45 days	4.29%	800-225-5084
Princor Tax-Exempt Cash Management	$1,000	none	27 days	4.22%*	800-247-4123 515-247-5711
Pioneer Tax-Exempt Money Fund	$1,000	13	13 days	4.07%*	800-622-0181
Palm Tax-Free Money Fund	none	9	22 days	4.09%*	800-326-3241 412-288-1900
Hatteras Tax-Exempt Money Market Portfolio	none	18	36 days	3.97%*	800-659-1005 713-626-1919
Capital Reserves Municipal Money Market Portfolio	$1,000	4	15 days	3.96%*	800-544-6666 617-523-1919
Average for all National tax-free funds			50 days	4.27%	

SOURCE: IBC/Donoghue. Average maturities and yields as of April 1991. Yield and average maturity can change daily; check with fund before investing to make sure it still generally meets these criteria, and read the prospectus before investing a dime.

*These funds were waiving all or part of their investment advisory fee. Beware, since this *temporarily* boosts their yields.

SINGLE-STATE FUNDS—UNSAFE AT ANY SPEED?

We now come to the shortest list in this book. The list of safe single-state tax-free funds—that is, funds that invest only in the short-term debt of a single state. But this list is like the proverbial small town that's so tiny that if you blink as you drive by on the highway, you'll miss it. Well, you just passed the list of safe single-state tax-free funds. You see, there isn't one, because none of the experts I talked to believed there was any reasonable way of coming up with one. Aside from the near impossibility of gauging the real risks of many of the securities these funds invest in, single-state funds violate one of the cardinal requirements of safe investing—diversity. While a national tax-exempt fund can spread its investments around the fifty states and hundreds of municipalities, to get their double- or triple-tax-free status, single-state funds must limit themselves to the securities of one state. This means they are inherently nondiversified. Such lack of diversity would be the equivalent of General Schwarzkopf having put all the U.S. and Allied troops in one giant bunker, leaving the entire force vulnerable to a single SCUD missile. Well, in the case of single-state tax-free funds, deteriorating budgets, declining revenues, and mounting costs are the financial equivalents of a SCUD. And if all the fund's holdings are in one state, one SCUD can do an awful lot of damage. Even in good times, such a strategy is dangerous. And considering the poor fiscal shape many of our states and cities are in today, single-state funds are not good places for conservative investors to put money they can't afford to lose. Californians are in luck, though, since two tax-free funds for that state—Benham's California Municipal Money-Market Fund and Benham's California Tax-Free Trust Money Market Portfolio—earned a AAA rating from Standard & Poor's. Both are listed along with S&P's other AAA funds below. Given the strict investing guidelines funds must follow to get and keep S&P's highest rating, conservative investors should feel comfortable putting their money into these funds as long as they maintain their AAA status. Yes, it is unfair. And no, there isn't any cosmic justice. Californians have wonderful weather, a state brimming with natural beauty, *and* two top-rated single-state tax-free money funds, although it's unclear whether they really deserve any one of these things, let alone all three.

170

THE STANDARD & POOR'S STAMP OF APPROVAL

We end the money-fund section of the book with the list of funds rated AAA by Standard & Poor's. To get this top rating, funds must invest only in the highest-quality securities and maintain a short average maturity—no more than sixty days—to protect fund shareholders against the possibility of a loss due to rising interest rates. These funds pay Standard & Poor's a sizable ratings fee, about $12,500 a year, and then agree to submit to periodic S&P reviews. To keep the top rating, the fund must continue to meet Standard & Poor's strict investing guidelines. Not many money funds submit to this intense scrutiny—some because they don't want to shell out the fee, others because they know the fund's current investing guidelines wouldn't be up to snuff for an AAA rating. Considering the thoroughness of Standard & Poor's rating system and the strict guidelines rated funds must follow to get the highest rating, Standard & Poor's AAA-rated funds clearly rank as among the safest, if not *the* safest, money funds in the United States. They offer even the most safety-conscious investors not only a competitive return, but a safe harbor in a world that has become increasingly dangerous for money-fund shareholders.

T A B L E   8 · 6

Money Funds Rated AAA by Standard & Poor's

	Minimum Initial Investment	Telephone
U.S. Treasury and Government Agency Funds*		
Alex Brown Cash Reserve—Treasury	$1,500	800-553-8080
		301-727-1700
Benham Government Agency Fund	$1,000	800-472-3389
Capital Preservation Fund	$1,000	800-472-3389
Capital Preservation Fund II	$1,000	800-472-3389
Capital Reserves: U.S. Government Portfolio	$1,000	800-544-6666
		617-523-1919
First Prairie Money Market Fund—Government	$1,000	800-537-4938
		718-895-1650
Fountain Square U.S. Treasury Obligations Fund	$10,000	800-245-0242
		412-288-1900
Pacific Horizon Treasury Fund	$1,000	800-367-6075
		212-492-1600
Rodney Square Fund—U.S. Government Portfolio	$1,000	800-225-5084

	Minimum Initial Investment	Telephone
Vision Treasury Money Market Fund	$1,000	800-245-0242
		412-288-1900
Vista U.S. Government Money Market Fund	$2,500	800-367-6075
		212-586-0016
Wayne Hummer Money Fund Trust	$500	800-621-4477
		312-431-1700
Webster Cash Reserve Fund	$1,500	212-510-5351
Westcore Treasury Money Fund	$1,000	800-666-0367
		303-623-2577
Taxable Funds*		
AARP High Quality Money Fund	$500	800-253-2277
Alex Brown Cash Reserve Fund—Prime	$1,500	800-553-8080
		301-727-1700
Edward D. Jones Daily Passport Cash Trust	$1,000	314-851-2000
First Prairie Money Market Fund—Money Market Series	$1,000	800-537-4938
		718-895-1650
Freedom Cash Management Fund	$1,000	800-225-6258
Kidder Peabody Premium Account Fund	$25,000	212-510-5351
Lord Abbet Cash Reserve Fund	$1,000	800-426-1130
		212-848-1800
PaineWebber Cashfund	$5,000	800-762-1000
		212-713-2000
Scudder Cash Investment Trust	$1,000	800-225-2470
Tax-Free Funds*		
AARP High Quality Tax Free Money Fund	$2,500	800-253-2277
Benham California Municipal Money Market Fund	$1,000	800-472-3389
Benham California Tax-Free Trust Money Market Portfolio	$1,000	800-472-3389
Benham National Tax-Free Trust Money Market Portfolio	$1,000	800-472-3389
First Prairie Tax-Exempt Money Market Fund	$1,000	800-537-4938
		718-895-1650

SOURCE: Standard & Poor's. This list is limited to Standard & Poor's AAA-rated funds of August 1991, generally available to individual investors. Those AAA funds marketed primarily or solely to customers of a specific institution, such as a bank, those limited to institutional investors, and funds requiring a very high minimum initial investment have been excluded from this list. Before you invest, make sure the fund still holds Standard & Poor's top rating. To do this, you can call the fund's customer-service representative or call Standard & Poor's at 212-208-1527 for an updated list of AAA funds.

*Sorting of funds into Treasury and U.S. Government Agency, Taxable, and Tax-Exempt categories is based on IBC/Donoghue classifications.

≋ 9 ≋

INSURANCE COMPANIES: AN S&L DISASTER WAITING TO HAPPEN?

Beware of Falling Rock

NOT so long ago, an insurance company was a place you put your money when nothing short of rock-solid stability would do. It was a hallowed institution whose word you accepted without question. Whether it was the insurance company's promise to pay out life insurance policy benefits, make annuity payments right on schedule, or provide a risk-free refuge for retirement money that you might draw on ten, twenty, even thirty years down the road, you knew you could bank on it. It was *guaranteed.* You handed over your money and never lost a night's sleep worrying about its safety. In short, an insurance company was where you went when you wanted a piece of the rock.

That was exactly the image Miles Johnson, fifty-four, a mechanical designer for an electronics company in Aloha, Oregon, and his wife, Ann, fifty-five, a registered nurse, had of an insurance company. A place you put your money when you didn't want to worry about it. So that's what they did. They took $26,000, almost all the money they'd saved for retirement, and in 1987 invested it in an annuity, paying 9.65 percent, with the Pacific Standard Life Insurance Company. Then they forgot about it, secure in the knowledge that their investment was totally safe. But the Johnsons got a rude shock while attending a retirement planning seminar in April of 1990. One of the financial planners lecturing at the seminar told them that their insurance company, Pacific

Standard, had been taken over by the California State Insurance Department in 1989 because of losses in its junk-bond holdings. The couple was stunned. "I didn't even know the company was in trouble," says Miles. "Nobody ever contacted me."

Then came a worse surprise. When the Johnsons wrote Pacific Standard and asked to cash in their annuity, whose value by this time had grown to more than $29,000, the insurer told them they would have to wait six months. It seems the insurer had invoked a standard clause in most annuities that allows insurance companies to suspend withdrawals for up to six months. Still unsure whether they'd actually get their cash, the Johnsons patiently waited half a year. Then, just ten days before they were to get their money, Pacific Standard sent the couple a letter claiming that the Johnsons' request had been improperly filled out. Unless a correct form were sent within ten days, the insurer said it would consider the request invalid, which would trigger yet another six-month wait. Incensed at what he considered an underhanded attempt by the company to keep him from his money, Miles immediately sent the new form by certified mail.

Finally, on December 5, *seven months* after their original request, Ann and Miles Johnson got a check in the mail—but for only $26,938, not for the more than $29,000 in their annuity account. Why the shortfall? The company charged the couple a $2,600 penalty for withdrawing their money from the account prematurely. That's right. Even though it was the company's deteriorating financial condition that led the couple to seek a safer stash for their money, Pacific Standard still had the gall to hit the couple with a penalty known as a surrender charge. By that time, though, Miles Johnson felt lucky just to have his cash. "When I heard what bad shape the company was in, I wasn't sure we'd get anything at the end of six months," says Miles. "It was a scary experience that I hope I never have to go through again."

As it turned out, Miles Johnson may have been a lot luckier than he thought. For one thing, after he threatened legal action against the agent who originally sold him the policy, the agent gave him a promissory note to reimburse him for the $2,600 surrender charge. So, if the agent actually makes good on his promise to repay, Miles will wind up with all his money, minus whatever price you put on emotional wear and tear. But many other people who, like the Johnsons, trusted an insurance company with their retirement money may not be so lucky. Actually, hundreds of thousands of insurance-company customers are already going through a similar traumatic experience in the second-largest insurance-company collapse ever in the U.S. In April of 1991, the tottering $13-billion insurance empire of First Executive finally caved in under the weight of hundreds of millions of dollars' worth of defaulted junk bonds sold to the company by, you guessed it, the Prince of Los Angeles, Michael Milken, and his cronies at Drexel Burnham Lambert. First Executives's two largest insurance companies— Executive Life of California and Executive Life of New York—were both seized by their state insurance departments, which immediately restricted policyholders from cashing in their insurance policies and annuities. That left an estimated 350,000 or so people dangling in midair with no federal safety net below them, wondering how much, if any, of the money they entrusted to the company they would ever see again. To make matters even worse, the Internal Revenue Service then slapped a $643 million lien against Executive Life of California for back taxes, thus increasing the chances that policyholders might take a loss. California Insurance Commissioner John Garamendi then slashed monthly payments to retirees and other people receiving income from Executive Life annuities to seventy cents on the dollar. In other words, they were facing a 30 percent loss on what was supposed to be a safe, secure, guaranteed income. In early October, a complicated deal was in the works in which investors would buy Executive Life's battered junk-bond portfolio and resurrect the company under a different name. But even if this effort succeeds, it is uncertain how much of their money policyholders will ultimately get and how long it will take before they get it. Considering that people's pensions and retirement savings are at stake here, it's hard to see this rescue as much of a victory.

Though its self-induced—and, some might say, well-deserved—plight was the most highly publicized, First Executive was hardly the only major insurer wracked with problems. In the aftermath of the sleazo financial shenanigans of the eighties, the rock-solid stability of insurance companies had clearly begun to crumble. In July 1991, losses in real-estate loans and massive withdrawals by policyholders led to the largest insurance company collapse ever—Mutual Benefit Life, a Newark-based insurer with $13.5 billion in assets. After seizing the ailing insurer—which had an estimated 600,000 people covered by individual policies or annuities—the New Jersey Insurance Commissioner seized the insurer and froze cash withdrawals on individual policies for an indefinite period. And in May 1991, only a month before Mutual Benefit's downfall and a month after First Executive's demise, the California Insurance Department swooped down on another ailing insurer,

First Capital Life, freezing policyholder withdrawals, while insurance regulators from the state of Virginia seized Fidelity Banker's Life, an insurance company owned by First Capital Holdings, the corporate parent of First Capital. It seems that First Capital, like its Los Angeles neighbor First Executive, had become addicted to junk bonds and now had a severe case of financial DTs—that is, the value of its junk bonds had gone down, triggering a run as scared policyholders pulled out their money. When the hemorrhage hit $100 million in one day alone, the California Insurance Department ordered a freeze on all withdrawals, effectively preventing some 190,000 First Capital customers from getting at their money. And less than a year before First Executive's fall, the $32 billion Travelers Insurance Company had been forced to add $650 million in loan-loss reserves to shore up its deteriorating portfolio of real-estate loans. Seems the company had lent less than judiciously throughout Texas and the Southwest before the oil bust. Even the mighty Equitable Life Assurance Society of the U.S.—the nation's third-largest insurer with almost $99 billion in total assets and a brand-new cavernous Manhattan headquarters whose lobby is graced by huge murals by artists Roy Lichtenstein and Thomas Hart Benton—was facing possible losses from its above-average holdings of junk bonds and wobbly commercial mortgages.

All these troubled giants were symbols of an insurance industry beset by woes ranging from declining profitability and a shortage of capital to looming losses in high-yield (i.e., junk) bonds and real-estate loans that in many cases were either already in or heading for default. To give you an idea of just how badly things had deteriorated in this once solid industry, consider this: In the five years from 1986 through 1990, 102 life- and health-insurance companies failed. That's twice as many as in the previous five years and almost four times as many as in the five years before that.

Unfortunately the problems of the last decade may only be a harbinger of worse to come. A dire report issued in 1990 by IDS Financial Services, Inc., predicts that in a severe economic downturn as many as one-fifth of the major insurance companies in the U.S. could fail. Normally the insurance industry can brush off such ominous warnings as the ravings of crackpots or ill-informed and possibly dangerous consumer crusaders who just want to make insurance companies look bad. But this report came from a financial services industry that also happens to own an insurance company, IDS Life. Besides, none other than the respected independent ratings agency Standard & Poor's confirms that, indeed, while insurance companies overall may not be teetering on the precipice of total ruin, enough companies out there are close enough to collapse that it would be just plain stupid to look the other way. During the week that insurance regulators in New York and California were seizing both Executive Life insurance companies, Standard & Poor's pointed out in a press conference in its New York City headquarters that some 489 insurance companies had received below-average solvency ratings from S&P's insurance-rating division—a number S&P predicted would rise during the year. In other words, these companies were the financial equivalent of the walking wounded, many of whom would eventually stagger into insolvency and failure.

WHO CAN YOU TRUST?

As if insurers aren't suffering enough bad press, two more bombshells hit after the Executive Life fiasco. The Justice Department, uneasy about parallels between the insurance industry and the savings-and-loan debacle, announced it had assembled a special unit to investigate insurance fraud. And both John Dingell in the House of Representatives and Howard Metzenbaum in the Senate, staunch critics of state insurance regulators, unveiled proposals to create a new federal agency that, among other things, could set minimum solvency standards that would supersede those of some states. The very thought of a federal overseer sends chills up the spines of insurance-company executives and their lobbyists, who much prefer the inadequate patchwork of regulation administered, extremely poorly overall, by the states.

Given the recent dire problems of several major insurers, you can't help but wonder whether insurance companies are now following the footsteps of the S&Ls toward insolvency. Any number of insurance-industry associations such as the American Council of Life Insurers will testily point out that comparisons between insurance companies and S&Ls are uncalled for, inflammatory, irresponsible, etc., etc. In a letter to financial reporters, the American Council of Life Insurers even found a silver lining in the recent takeover of troubled insurance companies by state regulators, claiming this "is effective state regulation at work, protecting the interests of all policyholders." The letter went on to say that recent failures are "a normal process in a competitive, free-market environment." I wonder if the people who initially saw their pension payments drop by 30 percent see such an uplifting theme in all this. 177

But the insurance-industry apologists have a point. Despite its problems, the industry overall isn't in the dire shape S&Ls were in during the 1980s. Insurance companies have much more capital than the S&Ls and, though weak insurers will continue to fail and policyholders in those companies may suffer financial setbacks, it's unlikely we'll see S&L-style failures with thousands of insurance companies biting the dust.

Still, whether you believe the doomsayers who see Armageddon ahead for insurers or the optimists who claim the industry will weather its current problems without significant upheavals, it really doesn't matter. Enough companies are in bad enough shape that only a dunce would accept an insurance company's promise without thoroughly checking out the company's financial health through independent sources. The stakes are too high—retirement savings, pension payments, payments on life-insurance policies. And the downside is too great: If your insurer goes under, there is currently no federal cushion to break your fall. And the protection offered by state insurance commissions is notoriously flimsy.

And don't be too quick to assume you're not likely to be sucked into this mess. Chances are your financial future is more closely intertwined with the health of life-insurance companies than you think. Whether you own a life-insurance policy or you invested in a tax-sheltered annuity or your company savings or retirement plan buys insurer-backed guaranteed investment contracts, your finances are tied to the fortunes of one or more insurance companies. You may even be relying on insurance companies in ways you're not aware of. For example, some employers terminate their pension plans and, in effect, pay an insurer to take over the pension liabilities. The result: you are depending on the insurance company to make the payments on the pension you earned from your employer. Obviously, then, it is *crucial* that you evaluate the financial soundness of any insurance company you're already dealing with or one from which you plan to buy a policy or investment.

In order to accurately take the pulse of an insurer, it's important that you first understand how the basic nature of the industry radically changed during the financially licentious eighties. The personality transformation was so complete that the Rock of Gibraltar image you once associated with insurers has become a sad, ironic anachronism, kind of like comparing the egotistic, blow-hard, rich pre-real-estate-slump Trump to the egotistic, blow-hard, *poor* post-real-estate-slump Donald who is now dependent on the kindness of bankers and the bankruptcy laws. Given this scary new world of financial insecurity, it's equally critical that you realize that you simply cannot depend on the present state regulatory system to protect you from overly aggressive, incompetent, or even fraudulent insurers. Ostensibly they are there to protect your interests. But if there's any lesson to be learned from insurer insolvencies in the 1980s, that lesson is clearly and unequivocally this: You cannot count on the appointed state regulators to protect your money. Besides doing an overall lousy job, the state insurance commissions and their sister organization, the National Association of Insurance Commissioners, have been so soft on insurance companies that one can't help wondering at times whose interests the regulators are protecting—policyholders' or the insurers'. So the burden is on you to choose safe insurance companies and to monitor their soundness without help from the state regulators. This chapter and the one following will help you do just that.

INSURANCE COMPANIES' DR. JEKYLL AND MR. HYDE PERSONALITY

The best way to appreciate what happened to insurance companies in the 1980s is to think of them as the financial equivalent of Dr. Jekyll and Mr. Hyde. You see, like the character in the Robert Louis Stevenson story, insurers have always had split personalities. On the one side, there were the sales agents—aggressive, obnoxious, loud, willing to do anything to make a sale. On the other side were the analytic, plodding actuaries and investment managers who decided where to invest the money you trusted the company with. With the nerdy actuaries and money men balanced against the aggressive sales types, the two sides blended into a coherent personality and the organization stayed on an even keel.

But during the 1980s, the mild-mannered investment and actuary side began acting more like Mr. Hyde. And the aggressive side of insurers' personality gradually began to take over. Caught up in the fever for high yields, investment managers began putting their money in dicier investments they would have shunned before. One reason was that what you and other customers wanted from insurance companies changed. Instead of a plain vanilla life-insurance policy, you now wanted tax-sheltered annuities paying competitive interest rates. And to cater to the needs of companies that wanted a safe, secure investment for 401(k) and other employee retirement and savings plans, insurance companies began offering new investments such as guaranteed invest- 179 ment contracts, or GICs. Essentially these are like bank CDs except that, instead of federal insurance, you have the insurance company's guarantee of a fixed rate of interest for a period of one to three years and the promise that you will get your money back at the end of that period.

But there was another reason insurers became more Evel Knievel–like: greed. The companies realized that they could attract a lot more money from customers—and make a lot more themselves—if they offered higher interest rates. To do that, they had to delve into some schlocky investments, but, hey, this was the eighties and people believed strange things, like the notion that fad diets really *could* keep the pounds off and that The Donald really did know what he was doing.

No company exemplified this go-for-it attitude more than First Executive and its two big subsidiaries, Executive Life of California and Executive Life of New York. And no insurance-company executive was a better symbol of the gunslinger mentality toward investing than First Executive's chairman, Fred Carr.

FUN AND GAMES AT FIRST EXECUTIVE

In 1974, First Executive was a small, troubled insurance company operating out of Los Angeles. In an effort to revive the company, its founder and chairman, Otto Forst, turned to Fred Carr. During Wall Street's go-go era in the sixties, Carr had managed the high-flying mutual fund, The Enterprise Fund, but left just before its share price nosedived during a bear market. But Carr's less than brilliant career as a money manager didn't prevent him from coming up with a strategy that turned First Executive around (for a while anyway). In fact, Carr's experience in running the once-hot Enterprise Fund probably helped him come to the central insight that made First Executive an eighties success story and a nineties failure. That insight: that people will buy into almost anything if the return is high enough, the yield attractive enough.

So Carr began offering one of the stodgiest investments you could imagine—single-premium deferred annuities or SPDAs. Basically, SPDAs are like bank CDs. You give the insurance company a sum of money—usually $5,000 or more—and they pay you a fixed rate of interest on it—in 1991 that rate was about 7 percent or so. But because this is insurance companies we're talking about and because they've got 180 the most powerful congressional lobbying force ever to walk the hallowed halls of the Capitol, this 7 percent or so interest rate is free of taxes until you take your money out. (If you take the interest you earn on an annuity out before age 59 ½, you pay a 10 percent penalty to the federal government and, possibly, a penalty of as much as 10 percent to the insurance company in what's known as a surrender charge. But these are the features about annuities that the Dr. Jekyll sales types like to gloss over as quickly as possible in their sales presentations). All in all, that makes SPDAs not one of your most exciting investments. But Carr doled out his SPDAs with a twist—much higher interest rates than anyone else was offering. Sometimes the rates on his annuities were two or three percentage points higher than the competitors'. Which means that at some points during the eighties, First Executive annuities carried stratospheric interest rates of more than 14 percent a year. Offer somebody 14 percent a year and their first question is usually something like, "Where do I sign?"

Sign they did. Carr's sales force sold annuities to hundreds of thousands of mostly middle-aged and elderly people looking to get the best rate for money they were counting on for a comfortable retirement. But Carr didn't let his great idea end with annuities. Nope. It worked so well with annuities that he began using high interest rates as bait for other types of money. As company savings and retirement plans such as 401(k)s became increasingly popular during the 1980s, people were looking for a place to put their money where it would be safe and earn a competitive, reliable return. That opened the door for guaranteed investment contracts or GICs. The company savings plan hands over a lump sum to the insurance company—in this case one of the First Executive firms—and the insurer promises to pay a fixed rate of interest for a specific length of time—like a CD, although the insurance company usually offered a better rate. Bingo! Now First Executive was getting GIC money from corporate savings plans. He even sold GICs to states and municipalities. They raised cash by selling bonds and then bought First Executive GICs. Whether they'll retrieve any of those supposedly guaranteed investments now isn't clear, especially since the investor rescue plan, as originally proposed, makes no provision for these GICs.

Incredibly, Carr's sensitive nose for money led him to even more pots of cash. For example, if a company had a pension plan that was overfunded—that is, the value of the fund's investments was more than enough to pay out the money promised to the pensioners—the company would terminate the plan, skim the excess, and buy an annuity that would give the pensioners their monthly checks. The big question is, where do you buy that annuity? Since the company shutting down an overfunded pension is usually more interested in siphoning off as much cash as they can than in assuring that the retirees actually get what they're entitled to, they usually go to the insurer with the best price. More often than not in the 1980s, that turned out to be Carr's First Executive. Eventually Carr even got into what is known as structured settlements. For example, someone who loses a leg in a small aircraft crash and wins a $10 million lawsuit against the airline might agree to an arrangement in which he accepts $2 million up front and the rest spread out over ten years. This is known as a structured settlement. Instead of keeping that liability on their books, the airline would buy an annuity from an insurance company who would then pay the injured person. Enter Carr again. As a result, not only is the financial well-being of people in savings plans, life-insurance policies, and pensions at stake here, but so, too, are many accident victims and others who are due payments under a structured settlement.

Carr's and First Executive's ability to attract money is almost legendary. From less than $1 billion in assets in the early 1970s, First Executive ballooned to more than $13 billion in assets by early 1990. But the bigger issue—and the one that ultimately figured in his undoing—was this: What in the world do you invest in so you can pay those extravagant rates? But Carr had the answer there, too: junk bonds.

So as money came flowing in from SPDAs, from GICs, from structured settlements, from municipalities, Carr salted it away in junk bonds. Not just a few, but millions, billions of dollars' worth. At one point, upwards of 70 percent of First Executive's assets were invested in junk. In fact, First Executive became one of Drexel Burnham's and Michael Milken's best customers. Someone Milken could rely on to soak up almost any junk deal Drexel happened to be peddling. As a result, First Executive often wound up with the junkiest of junk. "They didn't just own junk," says Larry Mayewski, a vice president in the A.M. Best Company's insurance rating division. "They scraped the bottom of the barrel." At times, the relationship between Drexel, the junk-bond underwriter, and companies issuing junk bonds, and First Executive, the junk-bond buyer, turned into a seeming triangle of mutual back-scratching in the worst sense. For example: In 1986, Maxxam Group, Inc., headed by corporate raider Charles Hurwitz, launched a takeover of Pacific Lumber Company to grab its redwood forest holdings and the assets of its overfunded pension plan. To finance the $900 million transaction, Maxxam issued junk bonds through Drexel Burnham. First Executive, in turn, bought almost a third of those bonds, effectively helping Maxxam acquire the lumber company. But that wasn't the end of the relationship among these three companies. Maxxam wanted to shut down Pacific Lumber's pension fund and use some of that cash to pay off some of the takeover debt. So what did Maxxam do? They went to Drexel's wonderful customer First Executive and bought a $37 million annuity to cover the pension plan's liabilities. This immediately raises questions about a possible conflict of interest, morally if not legally. Even if there is no such conflict, Maxxam's purchase of an annuity from First Executive has the appearance of a payoff for abetting the takeover by buying Maxxam's bonds. The fact that First Executive would hardly be the first choice of a company truly concerned with making sure pension payments were absolutely secure only gives the entire deal more than a whiff of stench. A Maxxam spokesman firmly denies any conflict of interest and says the two transactions were completely separate. Nonetheless, the deal was great for Maxxam, because after paying for the First Executive annuity, the company was able to siphon off about $55 million of the pension fund's cash. The transaction was great for First Executive too, since $37 million flowed into its coffers. Was it great for Pacific Lumber pensioners? Hardly. The more than seventeen hundred people, both current and former Pacific Lumber employees, depending on that First Executive annuity for their pension could find themselves up the proverbial creek without a paddle if First Executive's junk-bond assets prove unable to back those pension payments. Had the company left the pension plan alone, the workers would have been covered by the Pension Benefit Guaranty Corporation, a federal agency. But by terminating the plan and funding it with an annuity, Maxxam effectively made the pensioners, some who worked more than four decades for the company, subject to the vagaries of the obliterated junk-bond market.

So where do the Pacific Lumber pensioners stand now? In April, their pension payments were cut by 30 percent by California Insurance Commissioner John Garamendi. He ordered the cut so that First Executive and its insurance subsidiaries wouldn't just flat run out of cash and leave the policyholders with nothing. So far, Maxxam has voluntarily made up the shortfall each month for the pensioners. And though a company spokesman says Maxxam will do everything it can to prevent the pensioners from suffering losses, the company insists it is under no legal obligation to do so. The U.S. Labor Department will try to convince a federal court otherwise. In June 1991, the U.S. Labor Department filed suit against Maxxam and another company, MagneTek, seeking to make the companies responsible for any losses suffered by their pensioners in First Executive annuities. The suit will have wide implications beyond those two companies. The reason: At least forty-seven other companies—including such well-known names as Revlon, Cannon Mills, and RJR Nabisco—have also purchased First Executive annuities.

THE JUNK HITS THE FAN

But First Executive's junk-bond strategy began falling apart when people realized, in the wake of junk bond whiz Michael Milken's guilty plea to multiple felony counts, that this wasn't a real market at all and that junk-bond prices were largely rigged. Even then, when the junk hit the fan, so to speak, First Executive was able to stay alive with the help of some lenient accounting rules for insurers. You see, insurance companies don't have to carry assets like bonds on their books at market value. They carry them at cost. That means a bond that originally cost $1,000 but might only fetch $750 if it were sold today can be carried by the insurance company at a $1,000 value, almost up until the bond actually defaults. This policy made First Executive's assets look more valuable than they really were, which allowed the company to carry on its charade even longer. At the end of 1990, while First Executive listed its bond portfolio's value at almost $10 billion, its market value was less than $7 billion. Eventually, as more and more First Executive customers became aware of just how devastated the junk-bond market was and just how far below water much of First Executive's junk portfolio had sunk, concerned life-insurance policyholders and people with annuities began pulling their money out of the company. During 1990, First Executive customers pulled out about $3.5 billion worth of insurance policies and annuities. And after First Executive announced that it had lost almost half a billion dollars in just the final quarter of 1990, the real rush for the exits began. In April, 260 redemption requests a day were coming in from justifiably anxious policyholders.

In mid-April 1991, the California Insurance Department seized Executive Life of California and the New York Insurance Department grabbed Executive Life of New York. Fred Carr's amazing run had come to an end, though not without one final tawdry incident. Apparently at the very time it looked as if First Executive wouldn't be able to make good on the promises it made to its own policyholders, First Executive set up a new company to guarantee roughly $11 million of deferred compensation to

184

Fred Carr and other First Executive employees. Even the regulators saw the basic inequity in this deal and said they would block the payments.

Adopting their damage-control mode, insurance-industry representatives began to downplay First Executive as an extreme, an isolated incident that had little bearing on the rest of the industry. While it's true that First Executive was a rogue insurance company, if you will, it's equally true that the company's investment policies had an industrywide effect. First Executive helped set a new aggressive tone for insurers in the 1980s. Once they began paying higher yields on annuities and other investments, other companies were almost forced to follow them in order to attract customers. So it escalated. Insurers got into a bidding war for business and, to offer those high rates, they had to buy riskier investments. For some that meant a big stake in junk bonds. While nobody got neck deep in junk like First Executive, many companies certainly waded knee-deep or higher into the heap. To give you an idea of how heavily invested in low-grade bonds some companies still are, take a look at this list of the fifteen companies with the highest percentage of their assets in junk bonds:

The Junk Meisters

Insurance Company	Percentage of Assets Invested in Junk Bonds
Executive Life of New York*	64
Executive Life (of California)*	62.7
Presidential Life	54.9
First Capital Life*	39.8
Fidelity Bankers Life*	36.9
United Pacific Life	32
Ohio Life	29
National Integrity Life	26.1
Capitol Life	24.9
American Franklin Life	22.6
Kemper Investors Life	21.7
Anchor National Life	21.7
Federal Kemper Life	21.2
CalFarm Life	20.3
North American Company for Life and Health	20.1

Source: Conning & Company; data as of April 1991.

* Under state supervision

Until recently, insurers' junk-bond holdings were actually *understated.* The reason: state insurance commissioners allowed insurance companies to classify some low-grade bonds as high-quality investments even though these bonds received noninvestment-grade or junk ratings from major rating services such as Moody's Investors Service and Standard & Poor's. That loophole allowed some companies to underreport their junk holdings by *half*! In other words, they were carrying twice as much junk as it seemed. Fortunately, however, under pressure from public-interest groups and a congressional committee looking into insurance problems, the National Association of Insurance Commissioners changed the rules to require insurers to report as junk any bonds considered junk by Moody's or Standard & Poor's. While closing this loophole won't increase the safety of those investments, this tighter reporting standard at least lets you know how deep the junk really runs in your insurance company's investment portfolio.

But insurers also shot themselves in the foot—some in the head—with lousy real-estate loans and investments. The worst offenders violated a cardinal rule of investing—diversify—and instead lent heavily in the oil patch in the early 1980s when it appeared Texas was on its way to becoming the center of the universe. The oil bust proved otherwise, and left banks and insurers with loans on properties that looked great, but had one problem: no tenants. Or at least not enough to keep up the mortgage payments.

Of course, competition can be healthy for companies and benefit policyholders. But in this case the competition was largely based on an illusion—the supposedly safe returns of junk bonds and higher-risk real-estate loans. So insurance companies were in much the same position as athletes who use steroids because they must compete against others who use steroids. And, just as steroid use eventually ruins your health, so, too, did insurance companies see their credit quality and financial soundness decline so that, by the end of the Milken era, the industry, though still healthy overall, was much weaker than it had been and many companies were in critical condition. Which makes it more important than ever before that you gauge the health of a company before you invest any of your money in it.

SO WHERE WERE THE REGULATORS?

186   But bad investments alone didn't reduce insurance companies to their state of penury. No, there were plenty of other villains to go around.

Although the year-and-a-half-long investigation into the insurance industry by the Subcommittee on Oversights and Investigations of the House of Representatives focused primarily on property and casualty insurers—that is, the people who insure your home and car and businesses—the problems they unearthed apply to life-insurance companies as well. Among the culprits contributing to insurance-company failures cited in *Failed Promises*, the report issued in 1990 by the House subcommittee were ". . . excessive underpricing, reserve problems, false reports, reckless management, gross incompetence, fraudulent activity, greed, and self-dealing." This laundry list is only a quick précis that appears on page 2 of a 76-page report that exhaustively details the ills afflicting the industry.

But perhaps the most dismaying part of this whole mess—the thing that really shakes whatever faith you might still have left in government regulators—is that the state insurance departments, the very people who were supposed to protect insurance-company customers, basically slept through the entire decade. Unlike banks, which are regulated by one or more federal agencies, and money-market funds, which are also overseen by a federal agency, the Securities and Exchange Commission, there is no federal regulator of insurance companies. No United States Insurance Commission, no Federal Insurance Corporation, no National Insurance Comptroller. Instead, insurance companies are overseen separately by each state, each of which has its own rules and regulations. Any reasonably intelligent person, of course, would see this nonsystem of varying, unevenly applied state regulation for what it is: cumbersome, inefficient, and just not very good at reining in problem insurance companies. But the insurers themselves love the state mishmash and lobby hard to keep it, largely because they can get away with a lot more under this system than they could under a responsible, strict federal overseer (if there is such a thing).

The simple fact is that while a few states do a decent job at regulating the insurers, many, if not most, seem more intent on protecting the insurance companies than the policyholders. In its *Failed Promises* report, the House of Representatives subcommittee had this to say about the state regulatory system: "The Subcommittee found numerous weaknesses and breakdowns in this system, including lack of coordination and cooperation, insufficient capital requirements and licensing procedures, failure to require the use of actuaries and independent audits, and improper influence on regulators." The report went on to mention 187 that "inadequate staffing and regulatory resources is also a serious problem, yet state governments collect twenty times more from premium taxes than they spend on insurance regulation." In other words, rather than using the tax money to provide tough regulation, state regulators have turned their insurance departments into nifty little profit centers.

Profitable or not, the record in some states is abominable. In Louisiana, for example, Doug Green, the insurance commissioner, was sentenced in July 1991, to twenty-five years in prison after being found guilty of mail fraud, conspiracy, and money-laundering activity that effectively funneled money from one of the insurance companies he regulated to his election campaign. And the California State Insurance Department wouldn't exactly win an Insurance Regulation Oscar for Best Performance in a Consumer Watchdog Role. During the yield-frenzied eighties, the California Insurance Department let Executive Life career toward insolvency with nary a warning to policyholders about the impending doom. According to an investigation by Senator Howard Metzenbaum's staff, Executive Life of California was actually $78 million in the red back in 1983 *and the California Insurance Department knew it.* A memo to Senator Metzenbaum from his antitrust staff amounts to a scathing indictment of the California Insurance Department. (The senator himself, by the way, had earlier fallen for the Executive Life sales pitch and bought a life-insurance policy with a death benefit of more than $1 million.) The memo reads: "The department failed to exercise responsible regulatory control to protect the policyholders and the public by allowing the company to experience spectacular growth even though the company's financial position endangered existing policyholders and its investment strategy was novel, unproven, and entailed high risk." In other words, despite their knowledge that the company was skating on very thin ice indeed, the supposed watchdogs for the public interest let Executive Life continue to sell its life insurance and annuities to the public, including many retired people, who were unaware of the company's shaky condition.

The current California insurance commissioner, John Garamendi, who took office in January 1991 (i.e., First Executive was already pretty much down the tubes by the time he took charge), as much as admitted the department had completely botched its official job. In a speech in April 1991 to the Los Angeles Chapter of the Health Underwriters Association, Garamendi said California's Insurance Department "just turned its back" on First Executive. The National Association of Insurance Commissioners (NAIC), the organization of state insurance commissioners, doesn't exactly have a reputation as a crusader for consumer rights either. One incident that is revealing of NAIC's competence—or lack of it—in protecting consumer interests occurred in December 1990, when the state of New Jersey demanded that First Executive make a $500 million deposit with the state or stop writing insurance policies in New Jersey. NAIC was outraged at New Jersey for acting alone. Fair enough. After all, New Jersey was, at the time, one of a few states that hadn't even taken the minimal step of setting up a guaranty fund to offer insurance policyholders at least a minimum of protection against failing insurers. (All states now have such funds; Washington, D.C., does not.) And grabbing $500 million from First Executive would effectively screw policyholders in other states. So NAIC's proclamation condemning New Jersey's action was justified. What *didn't* seem justified and was especially disturbing, however, was another part of the proclamation claiming that it was "the expert opinion" of a special NAIC committee "that the Executive Life Companies are in no imminent financial danger." This endorsement of First Executive's financial position came less than four months before the company announced a $466 million loss for the fourth quarter of 1990 and its own auditors, Price Waterhouse, said there was "substantial doubt" about the ability of the company to continue operating.

The NAIC's proclamation and the lack of warnings from state regulators about First Executive to the company's customers, raises one of the most frightening aspects of this whole issue: If your insurance company is in trouble, there's a good chance that you, like a cuckolded spouse, may be the last person to find out. "The regulators are *not* going to tell you if something's wrong," says Joseph Belth, an insurance expert and industry watchdog who publishes the monthly newsletter *Insurance Forum*. "The standard operating procedure if you inquire about a company is to tell you something like, 'The company is licensed to do business in this state and is in good standing.' That's what they'll tell you even if they're getting ready to take the company over in twenty-four hours." There's a reason the regulators are so tight-lipped: They—not to mention the insurance companies themselves—are afraid that if you get a whiff of bad news, you might pull your bucks out of the company and, in effect, start the equivalent of a run on the bank. So, seeking to avoid that possibility, the attitude of the regulators seems to be, "We'll work out these problems privately, so the customers won't have to bother their little heads about it." Aside from the fact that, had the regulators been more vigilant, maybe we wouldn't need a workout at all, this approach has two problems: First, these problems can't always be worked out, witness First Executive. Second, this approach usurps your right to make an informed decision based on the best information available. Fearful that your decision might be to take the money and run, the regulators seemingly go out of their way to downplay bad news and work with the company privately. When that approach backfires, the result is what happened at First Executive: some 350,000 people got stuck to varying degrees in a company with insufficient assets to make good on its guarantees.

If all this strikes you as familiar—inept regulators assuring you everything's under control while the evidence suggests deep-seated problems—it is. Though insurance companies are in far better financial shape than S&Ls were in the early 1980s, there are nonetheless striking parallels in the sleazy business practices both industries engaged in and in the way regulators mishandled the two industries. S&Ls were run into the ground by incompetents and looted by criminals and frauds. And, while fraud and embezzlement appear less widespread among insurers than among S&Ls, the insurance industry does have its share of incompetent executives and people like Fred Carr who could be accused of reckless endangerment of his customers' funds. And, in time, perhaps the Justice Department's ongoing insurance fraud investigation will show that insurers rank right up there with the best of the S&L scamsters when it comes to criminal activity. Fraud is at least enough of a problem that a Senate subcommittee on investigations was holding hearings on insurance fraud in the spring of 1991 and even the NAIC, in testimony before that committee, was calling for penalties of up to $1 million and thirty years in prison for crimes ranging from filing fraudulent financial statements, embezzling insurance-company funds, falsifying records in an attempt to defraud a company or its policyholders, and obstructing regulatory authorities' investigations.

Keep in mind, though, that there's another major difference between the crisis with the S&Ls and banks and the problems with insurance companies. In addition to having no federal regulation, there is *absolutely no federal backstop* for insurance companies. No federal deposit insurance, no FDIC, no Treasury Department backing. Nada. Which means that, even if the industry isn't in as much trouble overall as the S&Ls and many banks, the downside for policyholders is much greater. The FDIC can't bail you out.

190   The insurance companies will tell you that there *are* safeguards to protect you if your company goes bust, namely state insurance guaranty

funds. (The correct name is state guaranty associations, but virtually everyone inside and outside the industry calls them guaranty funds.) But these may be the biggest canard of all since those funds have no money in them, have a limited ability to raise money when they need it, and probably won't be able to raise enough to protect policyholders in the event of a major failure like that of First Executive. If these funds are supposed to be a safety cushion then it is so thin that no reasonable person would ever actually want to test it.

THE MYTH OF A SAFETY NET—WHY STATE GUARANTY FUNDS DON'T REALLY EXIST

Webster's New World Dictionary defines a fund as "a supply of money that can be drawn upon . . . a sum of money set aside for some particular purpose." The key words here are "supply of money" and "a sum of money set aside." It's pretty clear what the dictionary is getting at: to call something a fund it actually has to have money in it! Not a difficult concept.

But, in fact, the so-called state insurance guaranty funds don't have a cent in them. Not a penny. So why does the insurance industry insist on referring to them as guaranty funds? Maybe because the name conjures the notion of safety and security. It sounds good.

But these are not funds in the normal sense—like the FDIC deposit-insurance fund—but an association of state-licensed insurance companies who agree to kick in money to cover some losses to some policyholders if an insurance company fails.

Just how much money can be raised—and how quickly—is difficult to determine and varies with each state. In the event of a loss, most states can assess insurers 2 percent of the amount of life and health premiums written in the state for the previous year, although some states may assess as much as 4 percent and others as little as 1 percent. An insurance company can appeal the amount of the assessment or defer payment if making it would put them in financial distress. By the way, you, not the insurance companies, eventually pick up the tab for these assessments, since most states give insurers what amount to tax credits for any assessments they pay into the fund.

These phantom funds are a rat's nest of exclusions, qualifications, and other stipulations that make it exceedingly difficult to figure out exactly what and who is covered. As you might expect, coverage varies from 191 state to state. Typically, though, states cover life-insurance policies to a limit of $300,000 for death benefits and up to $100,000 for cash-withdrawal value of a life-insurance policy. Usually there's an overall limit of $300,000 in total coverage for any one person. The coverage on annuities can get tricky. An individual annuity you buy from a company is covered up to $100,000. But if your company shuts down its pension plan and buys an annuity from an insurance company to cover the pension payment, you will only be covered if you are named in the annuity policy. That doesn't always happen. Sometimes the company buys one group annuity that doesn't single out the individual employees. In such cases, the coverage would be minimal, usually $1 million to $5 million for all the people covered in the plan—not very much considering you could be talking about hundreds of employees. Unfortunately, once an insurance company takes over your pension, it's generally no longer covered by the federal Pension Benefit Guaranty Corporation either. Of course, if an insurer providing your pension goes bust, there's always the option of suing your company, claiming they didn't exercise due diligence with your pension bucks. But lawsuits aren't a quick and cheap remedy. They can drag on in the courts, and legal fees can soak up lots of money—not much of a solution if your pension checks aren't coming in in the meantime.

Finally, if your company savings plan invests in a GIC or guaranteed investment contract and the insurer issuing it goes under, you may not be covered. Some states, such as California, Hawaii, and Idaho, specifically exclude GICs. Others include them or cover GICs because court decisions force them to. Still, many states protect GICs to a maximum of only $1 million to $5 million—not much protection considering employee savings plans can easily hold more than ten times that amount in the GIC of one insurer.

For specifics about what is and isn't covered, write the insurance commissioner's office in your state (the head insurance honcho may go by another title, such as superintendent of insurance, in some states). The insurance department usually has an office, even if not its headquarters, in the state capital. Or, you can try A. M. Best Insurance Reports, a huge tome that can be found in many large libraries, which lists the names and addresses of all state insurance commissioners. The National Association of Insurance Commissioners (NAIC, 120 W. 12th Street, Suite 1100, Kansas City, MO 64105) can also give you the address of the insurance regulator in your state.

<u>192</u>   But the fact that your policy may qualify for coverage doesn't necessarily mean you'll get the money you're entitled to—or, if you do, get

it very quickly. It's extremely doubtful whether the guaranty funds can handle a failure the size of the Executive Life blowout. "The system might work for small insolvencies," says insurance expert Belth. "But for the biggies, no way." Even if the funds could handle the load, consider this: By the time they process your claim, assess members, and get around to paying you, you're looking at a few months at best. And if the loss is so big they have to assess companies more than once, you could be looking at more than a year.

Because of the fund's limited capacity and the difficulty in working with this piecemeal system, insurance companies have worked out other arrangements in the past. When Baldwin-United, a former piano maker turned insurance company (yes, former piano maker), failed in 1983, rather than go the slow and cumbersome guaranty-fund route, insurance companies and some of the brokerage companies that sold Baldwin-United annuities worked out a deal to make the insurer's customers whole. Though Baldwin-United annuity holders didn't lose money, they did have to accept lower interest rates than had been guaranteed them. But even worse than that, most of the 165,000 policyholders couldn't get their money out until 1987—a full *four years* later. If that's the havoc wreaked by the failure of Baldwin-United, a company with $3.4 billion in annuities at the time it died, you can imagine the industrial-size cleanup we could face when companies like First Executive, with an estimated $15 billion or so in liabilities, self-destruct.

Clearly, no safety-conscious saver—make that no sensible person at all—wants to find him or herself in the position of relying on one of these phantom state guaranty funds. Because when you get right down to it, no one knows exactly how they'll work—or whether they'll work at all. So the best thing you can do is avoid them completely. And the best way to do that is to seek out the safest, most secure insurance companies. In other words, those impeccable companies that have managed to come through the perilous eighties, and are most likely to make it well into the next century with their financial health, their reputation, and their customers' money intact. The following chapter will tell you all you need to know to find those companies.

≋ **10** ≋

HOW TO CHOOSE THE SAFEST INSURANCE COMPANIES

Why Safety Matters Most

I T'S amazing how little thought and effort most people put into choosing an insurance company. Usually an insurance agent or financial planner stops by the house and, over a cup of coffee, goes through a well-rehearsed dog-and-pony show complete with fancy cash-buildup projections based on dubious assumptions and glossy brochures that purport to show how much money you'll make if you buy the life-insurance policy or annuity offered by the company the agent rephpresents. After the agent soothingly reassures you of your Solo-monic wisdom in choosing this policy or investment, you sign on the dotted line.

But just think about this a minute. All you've really done is listen to one sales pitch from a person who usually stands to earn a fat commission—as much as 100 percent of the first year's premium on a whole-life policy and as much as 10 percent of the face amount of an annuity—and taken that person's word as if it were the opinion of a Price Waterhouse auditor. And you have just turned over a substantial amount of money—and control over your financial future—to an insurance company you probably know very little about, or at least not much beyond what the salesperson, who makes a living selling that very company's policies, has told you. Would you even think of buying a house like that, going out for one day with one agent and looking at a

194

single house. "Is this the best house I can get for my money?" you ask the agent. And after he assures you that this is a bargain and the perfect house for you, you say, "I'll take it. Where do I sign?" Of course, no reasonable person would look at just one house and buy it, based on one person's obviously biased advice. Surely you'd look at a number of houses and, before you bought any one of them, you would at least order a structural inspection and a title search.

Well, picking an insurance company demands *at least* as strict a standard as buying a house. For one thing, when you invest with an insurance company, you're making a choice that, like buying a house, will affect you for the very long term. For example, if you buy a whole-life-insurance policy at age thirty-five, you want to be sure the company can pay the death benefit to your beneficiary sometime way into the future—way, way into the future, you hope. If that policy builds cash value, as whole-life and many other varieties of insurance do, you may want to draw or borrow against it even sooner, so, besides the insurer's long-term health, you want to make sure the company can meet its short-term obligations too. The same goes if you buy an annuity. There, the whole idea is for you to give the insurance company a lump sum of money and have it either pay you a monthly income for the rest of your life or some other agreed-upon period. Or, to have the company invest the money for you so it builds without the drag of income taxes. Whichever type of annuity you choose—immediate or deferred—you are relying on the insurance company's promise to pay you your money today and, often, ten, twenty, thirty or more years into the future. When you get right down to it, it doesn't really matter what rate of interest or how big a monthly payment an insurance company promises you, if it can't deliver it. For conservative savers and investors, safety should come ahead of rate of return when choosing an insurer.

Of course, if you could quickly bail out of an insurance company at the first sign of trouble, then maybe your choice wouldn't carry so much weight. Ah, but the insurance companies specialize in attaching strings—actually they're closer to handcuffs than strings—to their policies. For example, if you terminate a whole-life-insurance policy within the first few years, you will have zero, or very little, cash value. The reason: virtually all of your premiums go to pay the agent's commission. Deferred annuities also carry heavy penalties, as much as 10 percent of the face amount of the annuity if you cash it in within the first few years. If you've bought an immediate annuity—for example, you gave the insurance company $100,000 and they agreed to pay you $700 a month 195 for the rest of your life, then you're really a captive. There's almost no way for you to get out of this arrangement. It's more permanent than most marriages.

Clearly, when you consider that you are investing long term and may have to pay ridiculously burdensome penalties to get out of an investment and throw on top of that the deteriorating financial condition of many insurance companies, the lousy job the regulators have done to monitor insurers' failing health and, finally, the fact that there is no federal backing to protect you, it is *crucial* that you gauge an insurance company's financial condition and limit yourself to dealing with the safest insurers.

THE DIFFICULTIES OF DIY INSURANCE ANALYSIS

So how do you separate the vibrant, healthy insurers that will be around well into the next century from those that are likely to be shut down in five or ten years, if not sooner? You start by realizing it's going to require a little legwork—and periodic monitoring after you've signed on with a company. This chapter will tell you exactly what you must do in order to choose the safest insurance companies—and, indeed, it includes a list of the *crème de la crème* of safe insurers as well as a table giving the safety ratings on the fifty largest insurance companies in the U.S. But it's also important to spend just a moment telling you what you can't do and probably shouldn't try to do—namely, try to take the pulse of an insurance company on your own by analyzing its financial statements. I know this is the age of self-help when intelligent, reasonable people are supposed to be able to sort out their psychic, physical, and financial lives on their own. But there are limits. And do-it-yourself analysis of insurance companies is definitely one of those limits for most people. Unless you are an MBA and a card-carrying member of the Texas Instruments Business Analyst Calculator Precision Drill Team, chances are you're not going to be able to wade through the number crunching necessary to really understand what shape an insurer is in. What's more, unless you belong to one of the agencies that rates insurers, it's extremely difficult to get up-to-date, accurate information on insurance companies. Even the regulators have trouble getting good information on a timely basis. As a result, trying to analyze an insurance company on your own is a bit like performing open-heart surgery on yourself; it's an operation whose chances of success vary between zero and less than zero.

196

So if you can't rely on the regulators and it's too difficult to do your own number crunching, who can you turn to? The best place is to the rating agencies such as Standard & Poor's, Moody's Investors Service, and A. M. Best Company, all of which assign safety ratings to major insurance companies. By turning to these agencies, you benefit from the judgment of seasoned financial analysts taking an independent look at these insurers. Even these organizations and their analysts aren't foolproof. For example, as recently as January 1990, both A. M. Best and Standard & Poor's had assigned their top rating to Executive Life— the insurance company seized in April 1991 by regulators in New York and California. Both organizations had downgraded Executive Life well before the regulators took over, so they did issue a warning to anyone listening, though the warning could have—and should have—come earlier. Mutual Benefit Life, which was seized by the New Jersey Insurance Commissioner in July 1991, also received apparently undeserved high ratings. A. M. Best gave the company its top rating until a week before its demise. Moody's gave the company its fourth-highest rating (Aa3) until May 1991, when it downgraded Mutual Benefit three more notches to A3.

In the wake of these incidents, the major ratings companies have been coming under sharp criticism and have been accused of being too lenient when grading insurers. The ratings agencies have defended their analysis, pointing out that in the case of Mutual Benefit Life, for example, the company was still solvent when seized by the New Jersey Insurance Department. It was panicked policyholders' rush to withdraw money—the equivalent of a run on the bank—that triggered the company's seizure. Such emotionally charged events are difficult, if not impossible, to predict. In any case, the rash of insurance-company failures and the public criticism that followed has apparently led the major ratings firms to reevaluate their analytical methods and toughen up their ratings.

No matter how strict these ratings, however, you should not think of them as a guarantee against failure. As in wearing a bulletproof vest, choosing insurance companies with high ratings gives you an extra measure of safety—but it doesn't make you invincible. To increase your margin of safety, I recommend you get the rating of three major rating agencies before choosing an insurance company. Had potential policyholders done that with Executive Life, for example, they would have found that one of the ratings agencies, Moody's, *never* gave Executive Life its highest or even second-highest rating. By using several ratings in combination, you can devise a stringent test that can provide a margin of safety far beyond what you would achieve by merely listening to the recommendations of an insurance agent who has a commission riding on the sale of a policy. Even after that, you should periodically check to make sure your insurance company upholds its rating—seventeen life and health insurers were downgraded last year by Standard & Poor's, for example—or at least ask the financial planner or insurance agent who sold you the policy to promise to notify you of downgrades. This will give you an early warning so, if necessary, you have a chance to get out before the regulators swoop in and prevent you from withdrawing your money.

A FEW RULES OF THUMB FOR EVALUATING INSURERS

Before we get into the ratings agencies and what they do and before we look at the ratings on major insurers, it's worthwhile to quickly go over a few rules of thumb about assessing the condition of an insurer. I'm not reneging on my recommendation that you shouldn't do this on your own. But taking a brief look at a few ratios the pros use when sizing up insurance companies can give you a bit of valuable insight into how the agencies arrive at their ratings. (The agencies can give you the information you need to calculate these ratios.) It will also help you better understand what's going on if your insurance company's name pops up in the news in connection with scary-sounding phrases like "technically insolvent" or "in receivership." Besides, if some insurance salesman tries to smooth-talk you into buying a policy with a low-rated company by claiming the rating agencies simply don't understand the company or are unnecessarily tough on it, you'll be able to ask a few simple pointed questions about the company's capital and asset quality. If the salesman hems and haws about the answers to these questions— or, worse yet, doesn't understand the questions—then it may mean the agent hasn't done his homework or knows you won't like the sound of the answers. Either way, this may be a tipoff to find both a new insurance company *and* a new agent.

The first and most important thing to look for is the company's capital cushion. As with banks and credit unions, this is a basic yardstick of comfort and is calculated by simply dividing the company's capital—also known as its statutory surplus—by its assets. (Sometimes you'll see its assets referred to as invested or admitted assets. That means these are all the assets of the company that back up things like insurance policies and some annuities. Often insurance companies manage money in separate accounts that are not included in their assets because these assets are not actually owned by the insurer.) So if the company has $500 million in assets and $40 million in surplus, then it has a capital ratio or capital cushion of 8 percent. This simple measure is crucial because it gives you an idea of what kind of safety margin the company has to absorb problems such as losses in its bond portfolio or defaults in the mortgages the insurance company holds. The more capital, the bigger the safety margin. To a lesser extent, capital also helps a company cope with unexpected policy redemptions and cash withdrawals. For example, if a movie theater had just one door that served as an entrance and exit, it could probably get by fine most of the time by strictly controlling when people go in and out. But if there were a fire and everyone rushed to get out at once, a theater with one exit would have serious problems. A large capital cushion, in effect, gives a company the advantage of multiple exits in the event many policyholders decide to cash out over a short period of time. It was precisely this problem—a scramble for the exits—that sealed Executive Life's and Mutual Benefit's fate.

In general, you should expect a sound company to have a capital ratio of 5 percent or more. The industry average is about 7 percent, although some well-heeled companies such as Guardian Life Insurance Company of America have capital in excess of 13 percent of its assets. A capital ratio of 5 percent doesn't necessarily mean a company is in trouble. Indeed, a few companies have earned very high ratings with capital ratios less than 5 percent, largely because they are in very conservative lines of business and have invested in high-quality assets. But, a capital ratio of under 5 percent should raise a warning flag. And if the company also has a low rating—anything under the top two or, stretching it, top three rating levels—conservative investors should probably avoid it.

Whatever you do, *do not confuse size with strength.* To sell a policy, a salesman may proudly point to the mammoth size of an insurer, its billions of dollars in assets, or hundreds of thousands of policyholders, as if to imply there is safety in big numbers. But if girth and strength were synonymous, then the "Today" show's Willard Scott would be the strongest man in the world and the Equitable Life Assurance Society of the U.S., with its $52 billion in assets, would be one of the safest insurance companies in the nation—neither of which is true. In fact, Equitable is huge, but flabby—weak on capital with a capital ratio of under 4 percent and out of shape from gulping down too many lousy real-estate investments, mortgage loans, and junk bonds. Remember, you are better off in a well-capitalized small company than a large one suffering from capital anemia.

The next thing to look at is the quality of the company's investments. This will tell you how much risk it is taking with your money. One telltale sign of a risky insurance company is one with a high concentration of junk bonds. Of course, they're not likely to be called junk bonds. Insurance companies prefer euphemisms like "high-yield" or "low-grade" or "noninvestment-grade" bonds. Whatever you call them, they have a higher risk of default than good old U.S. government bonds and high-quality corporate bonds. Another warning sign is a company with a high percentage of repossessed real estate and nonperforming real-estate mortgages—that is, mortgages with payments that are delinquent ninety or more days plus loans that have been foreclosed or are in the process of being foreclosed. These two important barometers—the capital cushion and asset quality—must be viewed together. Why? Because if junk bonds default or real-estate loans turn sour, the equity cushion can be deflated faster than you can spell i-n-s-o-l-v-e-n-c-y. That's why some analysts combine junk-bond holdings and nonperforming real-estate loans into one category called high-risk assets. If that combination of junk, repos, and bad real-estate loans is two or more times the company's capital—that is, 200 percent of capital or more—then a decline in the value of these assets could seriously jeopardize the company's capital. At the end of 1990, Executive Life's junk bonds alone were more than 1,200 percent of its capital—that's right 1,200 percent, or more than twelve times the value of its capital. While high-risk assets of more than 200 percent of capital doesn't mean such a company will necessarily go bust, conservative investors might just as well move on to a less risky insurer.

Financial ratios aside, you should *always* be suspicious of any company that offers a much better deal than its competitors. How, you should ask yourself, can this company offer annuities or life insurance policies with 10 percent yields when other companies are offering only 8 percent? Usually, the answer is that the insurance company is taking bigger risks, as Executive Life did when it sold annuities and life policies with tantalizing interest rates that were backed by junk bonds. So, along with your own analysis or a ratings company's safety rating, rely on common sense and healthy skepticism. If one insurance company is offering a much higher return than anyone else, 99 percent of the time it's because the company is subjecting you to a higher level of risk. The rest of the time it's because the policy has some other catch the company or agent hasn't fully explained to you. Either way, you're probably better off going to another insurance company.

MEET THE RATING AGENCIES

Essentially the rating agencies look at these and other factors in much greater depth to see how well the company can meet its obligations. But rather than rely on just a few simple rules of thumb—guidelines that have exceptions and can be misleading—these agencies examine the various types of business each insurer writes, assess the riskiness of it, and then compare that to the soundness of the company's assets. Most agencies also subject the insurance company to a kind of stress test, which gauges the company's ability to make good on its promises under a variety of tough economic conditions, ranging from mild to severe recessions. Finally, in the wake of the rash of recent insurance company failures caused by "runs on the bank," the rating companies are factoring investor confidence into their ratings. To do that, the agencies will look at the company's mix of business (its weighting in products, such as guaranteed-investment contracts, that investors can switch out of quickly versus whole life insurance policies in which policyholders tend to stay put) and balance that against the company's liquidity (its ability to sell investments to handle redemptions and withdrawals in a timely manner). Even though this process relies very heavily on number crunching, it also entails a lot of subjective judgment. Assumptions must be made about how likely policyholders are to die or cash in their policies and how stocks, bonds, and real-estate mortgages will perform in different economic scenarios. Which means there's no single answer or rating each agency comes to for each company. An insurer may win the top rating from one agency, but not from the other two, or vice versa.

A. M. Best, which has been rating insurance companies since 1900, has been at it the longest and currently gives financial strength ratings on 1,379 life and health insurers. But, just as grade inflation dilutes the true value of an A at colleges where professors hand them out indiscriminately, so too has A. M. Best's reputation for doling out its top rating of A + too liberally diluted the value of that rating. "It's absolutely clear it's easier to get the top rating from Best's than the other agencies," says Joseph Belth, an insurance professor at Indiana University and publisher of *Insurance Forum* newsletter. Still, A. M. Best ratings are the most widely available to the public and, even if not the most stringent, a good place to start your evaluation of an insurer. You can find *Best's Insurance Reports* (Life Health edition) in many major libraries (if they have it, it's hard to miss; it's a 2,500-page job). You can also get ratings on individual companies by calling BestLine at 900-420-0400. The charge is $2.50 a minute and you'll probably need at least two minutes, possibly more. To use that service, you must have the I.D. number assigned to the insurer by Best's or the company's I.D. number from the National Association of Insurance Commissioners (NAIC). You can find the Best's I.D. numbers in *Best's Insurance Reports* or you can order a copy of the *BestLine Quick Reference Guide* ($2.95; call 908-439-2200 or write A. M. Best Company, Ambest Road, Oldwick, NJ 08858-9988) which contains the I.D. numbers for all insurers rated by Best's as well as an explanation of their rating system.

Standard & Poor's and Moody's Investors Service, two companies that made their reputations rating bonds and stocks, also now assign financial strength or safety ratings to insurance companies. While neither company rates as many insurers as A. M. Best—Moody's rates 78 life and health insurers, while S&P rates 131—both companies are considered relatively stingy in handing out their highest ratings—AAA for S&P and Aaa for Moody's. You can get Moody's rating on an insurer by calling Moody's ratings desk at 212-553-0377. For S&P's rating, call S&P's insurance rating desk at 212-208-1527. You can also order S&P's written report on an insurer by calling 212-208-1524. Cost: $25. In April 1991, S&P unveiled a new service that assigns ratings to another nine hundred or so life and health insurers. But these ratings—which S&P calls qualified ratings—are not as comprehensive as S&P's regular safety ratings. While there are nine rating tiers under S&P's full-fledged rating system, S&P assigns only three qualified ratings: BBBq, above average; BBq, average; and Bq, below average. Unlike the company's full-fledged ratings, which include interviews with company management and an in-depth look at the insurer's accounts, the qualified or "barbeque" ratings are based exclusively on data provided to the National Association of Insurance Commissioners. That information is often dated and may not reflect the company's true health. Still, if your insurer doesn't have a full-fledged rating from one of the major agencies, the qualified rating can at least give you some idea of how the company stacks up. S&P's *Insurer Solvency Review* (Life/Health edition), which contains the comprehensive ratings on 459 companies plus the qualified ratings on another 900 or so, not to mention five years' worth of financial statistics on each insurer, costs $75 and can be ordered by calling 800-765-8362. That's a lot to spend for a limited rating. Truly conservative investors are better off simply sticking to companies that get a thorough going-over and are given the stamp of approval of a comprehensive rating.

There are one or two other prominent agencies that rate insurers and whose ratings you may wish to review, especially if the ratings from the three major agencies diverge, or if you are still unsure about a company's safety. Duff & Phelps, a Chicago company, rates sixty-one life insurance companies and subjects them to as tough an inspection as Moody's and S&P. But the company's ratings aren't as widely available as those of other major ratings services, although you can check with your insurance agent to find out if Duff & Phelps rates a given company and, if so, what that rating is. Weiss Research, in West Palm Beach, Florida, assigns 1,742 insurance companies a safety index number ranging from +200 to -200 and grades of A to F quarterly. To be classified as strong, a company must receive an index of at least 100. The ratings are based on a company's ability to withstand an average and a severe recession. Weiss's system has been criticized as relying too heavily on mechanical calculations and not interviewing the insurers themselves. Critics also contend Weiss's ratings are far too strict—in its March 1991, *Insurance Safety Directory* only four companies got the top rating, an A+, from Weiss—State Farm Life Insurance, Jefferson Pilot, Security Life of Denver, and United Insurance Company of America. Weiss representative Sue Ann Bailey staunchly defends the company's analytical approach and stinginess with its top ratings. "We are intentionally conservative," says Bailey. "And our track record speaks for itself. We've never given a good rating to a company that's later failed." In any event, Weiss does provide yet another source of information for assessing a company, especially small companies that don't get full-blown ratings from the other agencies. You can get Weiss's rating of A through F over the phone for $15. And if you want more information on your insurer, Weiss provides a brief report with financial information for $25 for each company and a far longer and more comprehensive report comparing the company to others in the industry for $45 (Call 800-289-9222, or write Weiss Research, N. Florida Mango Road, West Palm Beach, FL 33409.)

As you peruse the ratings of the different organizations, keep in mind that what looks like an impressive rating might not be as great as it seems. If you score an A on a test, you've got the top grade. But

Standard & Poor's best grade is AAA. To get to an A, you've got to go through AA+, AA, AA- and A+. So an A is five levels away from Standard & Poor's highest rating. Similarly, Moody's A rating is far down its ratings ladder, below Aaa, Aa1, Aa2, and Aa3. So, remember, that in the insurance ratings game, an A isn't a perfect score and is probably even below the level of safety the most conservative savers and investors should be looking for.

BELT, SUSPENDERS, AND SANSABELT APPROACH

No matter how thoroughly the ratings agencies do their jobs, there's always the possibility that they will err. No one's crystal ball is always crystal clear. To eliminate as much of that margin of error as is reasonably possible, I suggest you adopt what I call the belt, suspenders, and Sansabelt approach—that is, use the safety ratings of not one, not two, but all three major rating agencies. For the *highest* level of safety and comfort, you can choose a company that gets the top rating from all three agencies—an A+ from A. M. Best, AAA from Standard & Poor's, and Aaa from Moody's. But this test is so severe, so tough, that only nine companies passed it as of October 1991. These nine companies, the insurance company's equivalent to horse racing's and baseball's Triple Crown winners, are listed below.

T A B L E   1 0 · 1

The Triple Crown Club

Company	Safety Rating from			Telephone
	Standard & Poor's	Moody's	A. M. Best	
Guardian Life New York, NY	AAA	Aaa	A+	212-598-8000
Metropolitan Life New York, NY	AAA	Aaa	A+	212-578-2211
Nationwide Life Columbus, OH	AAA	Aaa	A+	614-249-7111
New York Life New York, NY	AAA	Aaa	A+	212-576-7000
New York Life and Annuity New York, NY	AAA	Aaa	A+	212-576-7000
Northwestern Mutual Milwaukee, WI	AAA	Aaa	A+	414-271-1444

	Safety Rating from			
Company	Standard & Poor's	Moody's	A. M. Best	Telephone
Prudential Insurance Newark, NJ	AAA	Aaa	A+	201-412-4345
State Farm Life Bloomington, IL	AAA	Aaa	A+	309-766-2735
Teachers Insurance and Annuity New York, NY	AAA	Aaa	A+	212-916-5317

SOURCES: Standard & Poor's, Moody's Investors Service, A. M. Best Co.

Fortunately, though, you don't have to limit yourself to these nine insurers to find a level of security that would satisfy even the most risk-averse person. There are other companies out there that, even though they aren't part of the Triple Crown Club, are nonetheless solid, secure companies. To help you in your search for the safest insurance companies, Table 10.2 lists the fifty largest insurance companies and their ratings, as of October 1991, from A. M. Best, Moody's, and Standard & Poor's.

As you can see, by loosening the Triple Crown criteria just a bit—still demanding an A+ from A. M. Best, but allowing a company to have a first- or second-tier rating from *both* Moody's (Aa1) and Standard & Poor's (AA+), you have more companies to choose from and still have an extremely high level of security. For example, sixteen of the fifty largest U.S. insurers meet this extremely stiff test. (They're the ones with a *Yes, Yes, Yes,* after their names in Table 10.2. Naturally, the Triple Crown companies are included in this group since they have top ratings from all three agencies.) And if you're willing to loosen up another notch—an A+ Best rating and a top or second-tier rating from Moody's *or* Standard & Poor's, you add another ten companies. (They would be the companies with a *Yes* in the first column and then at least one *Yes* in the next two columns.)

T A B L E 1 0 · 2

How the Fifty Largest Insurance Companies in the United States
Rate on Safety

Company Name	Highest Rating From A. M. Best?*	Highest or Second Highest Rating From	
		Moody's?*	Standard & Poor's?*
Prudential Insurance Newark, NJ 201-412-4345	Yes	Yes	Yes
Metropolitan Life New York, NY 212-598-8000	Yes	Yes	Yes
Teachers Insurance & Annuity New York, NY 212-916-5317	Yes	Yes	Yes
Aetna Life Insurance Hartford, CT 203-275-3777	Yes	No	No
New York Life New York, NY 212-576-7000	Yes	Yes	Yes
Equitable Life Assurance New York, NY 212-315-7021	No	No	No
John Hancock Mutual Life Boston, MA 617-572-6000	Yes	No	Yes
Northwestern Mutual Life Milwaukee, WI 414-271-1444	Yes	Yes	Yes
Travelers Insurance (Life Dept.) Hartford, CT 203-277-3966	Yes	No	No
Connecticut General Bloomfield, CT 203-726-6000	Yes	No	Yes
Massachusetts Mutual Life Springfield, MA 413-788-8411	Yes	Yes	Yes

Company Name	Highest Rating From A. M. Best?*	Highest or Second Highest Rating From	
		Moody's?*	Standard & Poor's?*
Principal Mutual Life Des Moines, IA 515-247-5111	Yes	Yes	Yes
Lincoln National Life Fort Wayne, IN 219-427-3640	Yes	No	No
Allstate Life Northbrook, IL 312-402-5156	Yes	Yes	Yes
Mutual Life Insurance of New York New York, NY 212-708-2000	No	No	No
Mutual Benefit Life # Newark, NJ 201-481-8356	No	No	No
New England Mutual Life Boston, MA 617-578-6398	Yes	No	No
IDS Life Minneapolis, MN 612-372-2581	Yes	Yes	Not rated**
State Farm Life Bloomington, IL 309-766-2735	Yes	Yes	Yes
Variable Annuity Life Houston, TX 713-831-5153	Yes	No	Yes
Jackson National Life Lansing, MI 517-394-3400	Yes	No	Not rated**
Executive Life # Inglewood, CA 213-312-1000	No	No	No
Connecticut Mutual Life Bloomfield, CT 203-727-6500	Yes	No	No
New York Life Insurance & Annuity New York, NY 212-576-7000	Yes	Yes	Yes
Nationwide Life Columbus, OH 614-249-7111	Yes	Yes	Yes

Company Name	Highest Rating From A. M. Best?*	Highest or Second Highest Rating From	
		Moody's?*	Standard & Poor's?*
Pacific Mutual Life Newport Beach, CA 714-640-3346	Yes	No	Yes
Equitable Variable Life New York, NY 212-641-8330	No	No	No
Transamerica Life & Annuity Los Angeles, CA 213-742-2137	No	No	Yes
Provident National Assurance Chattanooga, TN 615-755-1373	No	No	Yes
Transamerica Occidental of California Los Angeles, CA 213-742-2137	Yes	No	Yes
Aetna Life Insurance & Annuity Hartford, CT 203-275-3777	Yes	Yes	Yes
Hartford Life Hartford, CT 203-843-8216	Yes	No	Yes
Keyport Life Insurance Co. Boston, MA 617-457-1400	Yes	No	No
American Family Life Assurance Columbus, GA 404-323-3431	No	Not rated	Not rated**
Guardian Life New York, NY 212-598-8000	Yes	Yes	Yes
State Mutual Life Assurance Worcester, MA 508-852-1000	Yes	No	Yes
United Pacific Life Philadelphia, PA 215-864-5935	No	No	No

Company Name	Highest Rating From A. M. Best?*	Highest or Second Highest Rating From	
		Moody's?*	Standard & Poor's?*
Penn Mutual Life Philadelphia, PA 215-956-8104	Yes	No	No
Kemper Investors Life Chicago, IL 312-845-1701	No	No	Not rated**
General American Life St. Louis, MO 314-231-1700	Yes	No	No
Phoenix Mutual Life Enfield, CT 203-253-1179	Yes	No	Yes
Sun Life of America Los Angeles, CA 213-445-1748	Yes	No	No
Minnesota Mutual Life St. Paul, MN 612-223-4010	Yes	Yes	Yes
Northwestern National Life Minneapolis, MN 612-372-5432	Yes	No	No
American Life New York, NY 212-581-1200	Not rated	Not rated	Yes
Franklin Life Springfield, Il 217-528-2011	Yes	No	Not rated**
Unum Life Portland, ME 207-770-2445	Yes	Yes	Yes
Mutual of America Life New York, NY 212-399-6846	Yes	No	Yes

209

Company Name	Highest Rating From A. M. Best?*	Highest or Second Highest Rating From	
		Moody's?*	Standard & Poor's?*
First Capital Life # San Diego, CA 619-452-9060	No	Not rated	No
Continental Assurance Chicago, IL 312-822-5653	Yes	Yes	Yes

SOURCES: A.M. Best, Moody's Investors Service, Standard & Poor's. All data as of October 1991.

* Highest rating from A. M. Best is A+; Highest rating from Moody's is Aaa and second-highest rating is Aa1; rating from Standard & Poor's is AAA and second-highest rating is AA+.

** Companies listed "Not Rated" by Standard & Poor's may have received a qualified solvency rating from S&P. These ratings are not nearly as comprehensive as S&P's full-fledged claims-paying ability rating. To check a company's qualified rating, see Table 10.3, which lists all ratings, including qualified ratings, on the fifty companies above.

Under state supervision.

Of course, just because an insurer doesn't make it through one of these screens doesn't mean it isn't a solid company. Risk ratings are subjective, and you may feel perfectly comfortable with a company that has high—though not the highest—ratings with the agencies. In general, however, you should always get ratings from *at least* two ratings companies. And safety-conscious investors should be wary about signing on with a company that doesn't rate at least an Aa3 from Moody's and an AA from Standard & Poor's. (In no case should you rely only on A. M. Best's rating. If a company isn't rated by Standard & Poor's and Moody's, check out ratings from Duff & Phelps and Weiss.) For those interested in taking a look at the actual ratings of the fifty largest insurers, check the Table 10.3 at the end of this chapter. And to understand what those ratings mean, be sure to read the final tables of this chapter, which reprint the explanations each agency provides with its ratings.

Remember, too, that ratings can and do change. In 1990, for example, Standard & Poor's downgraded seventeen insurers and upgraded six. The number of downgrades in 1991 is likely to be higher. You

should periodically check your insurer's rating—once or twice a year at a minimum and certainly any time your company is described in news stories as having problems. You might also ask your insurance agent to inform you anytime your company is downgraded by one of the major rating agencies. If the agent keeps abreast of industry news—as good ones do—that shouldn't be a difficult job.

Before you buy any insurance policy, there's another risk you should also consider—what is known as lapse risk, or the risk that you simply won't keep up the payments on your policy, let it lapse, and, therefore, squander much of the money you paid in. "The lapse rate for insurance policies is close to fifty percent," says Glenn Daily, an insurance counselor in New York City. "And people lose millions of dollars every year in lapsed policies." In fact, you're more likely to lose money this way than by your insurance company going bust. There are a few companies who sell their policies directly and otherwise keep their commissions and fees very low. These are known as low-load insurers. As with mutual funds, the word *load* refers to the sales commission paid to the agent. Unfortunately, these low-load insurance companies are not among the industry giants and usually do not get the top ratings, if, indeed, they are rated at all. There are a few companies, however, that don't make it through the rigorous safety screens described above, but that, nonetheless, are considered secure companies. One low-load insurer, Lincoln Benefit Life, isn't rated by Moody's, but does get the highest AAA rating from Standard & Poor's, and another, Ameritas Life Insurance, gets a very solid A rating from Weiss Research. Insurance expert Glenn Daily considers both companies safe enough even for conservative investors. In any case, if you're considering buying an annuity or a form of insurance that also acts as an investment—whether from a low-load company or one of the insurers who meet the stringent safety criteria above—keep in mind that you are probably wasting money unless you plan to keep the policy for a long time—five years *at a minimum* and more likely ten or more years. If you realistically don't think you'll stick with it that long, buy term insurance—that is, insurance that only offers a death benefit and has no investment component—and put your money into another conservative investment such as a bank account or CD at a solid bank or a safe money fund.

Finally, don't forget a relatively simple yet still effective way of reducing risk—diversification. If you're thinking of buying a $100,000 annuity, instead of giving all your cash to one lucky insurer, spread it around to two or even three. This has several advantages. If you've chosen safe companies, the chances of one failing are small, of two going down the tubes tiny, and the probability of all three going bust are infinitesimal. There's another plus to this approach. If you need to cash in an annuity early, you may pay a surrender charge of as much as 10 percent of the face amount. That could be $10,000 on a $100,000 annuity. (Many policies won't impose a penalty large enough to eat into your original principal, though.) If you only needed, say, $30,000, you'd have to incur the entire penalty by cashing in your $100,000 annuity. But if you had split it up among three insurers, you could cash in just one and limit the penalty. While this theory also applies to life insurance, the policy fees you face would make probably make it too expensive to split $100,000 in coverage among two or more insurers. To prevent duplicate fees from eating you up, you need more like $300,000 or more in total coverage before it makes sense to split it among several insurers.

SHOULD YOU DESERT YOUR PRESENT INSURER?

If you're looking to buy an insurance policy or annuity, you can decide which level of safety you want and find a company that meets it. But what if you jumped into a policy or annuity years ago and, in retrospect, you realize you didn't do the legwork you should have done to assess the insurer's stability? Or maybe you've been hearing bad things in the newspaper lately about your company. Should you bail out and go to a new company—or hang in and hope for the best?

This is an especially difficult question because when you head for the exits you might not have much in the way of cash value to take with you. If you're concerned about the safety of your present insurance company, see how it stacks up according to the ratings agencies as if you were starting fresh with the company and decide whether the company meets your standards. Then, find out the cost of leaving. With a life-insurance policy, look at how much cash value you give up by leaving now compared to staying the next few years. With an annuity, check to see what surrender charges still apply. If it's a life-insurance policy you're considering cashing in, you should also consider what someone is likely to charge you for a similar policy now or, indeed, whether they're likely to give you one at all if you've aged or your health has changed for the worse since you bought your present policy. Even if you decide to give up your life-insurance policy to go with a more solid company, you should probably hold off leaving your present company until the new one actually issues your new policy. This way you won't be left in the cold without coverage.

212

In general, if your company is still rated Aa3 or higher by Moody's or at least AA by Standard & Poor's (or gets an equivalent rating from another ratings company), you're probably better off hanging in as long as you can. This way you'll get more cash value out of the policy and the surrender charges on an annuity are likely to decline. But if your company appears to be headed downhill fast—it's been downgraded several times within the last year and there's talk of regulators stepping in—you should seriously consider jumping, even if it means absorbing some penalties. If your company drops to the A level of Standard & Poor's or Moody's, you should also carefully monitor it. Though A seems like a good, solid rating—and it is—Moody's also adds in its explanation of the A rating that "elements may be present which suggest a susceptibility to impairment sometime in the future." Given that qualifier, conservative investors should probably flee if they can do so without incurring significant penalties. If staying for a short period of time—a year, maybe two at most—will take you beyond the surrender charges or dramatically increase your policy's value, then you can probably wait it out, as long as you keep a close watch on the company and are prepared to jump if it is downgraded below A. But conservative investors who want to stay in a policy for many years without worrying probably don't belong in a company only rated A by Standard & Poor's or Moody's. You may wish to stay briefly to lower the cost of exiting, but on a long-term basis, you probably want the security of that AA or Aa rating.

As if the decision of whether to stay or flee weren't complicated and agonizing enough, there are two more important caveats you should know about. First, there are unscrupulous agents out there trying to parlay policyholders' fears about insurers' safety into commissions for themselves. So beware of anyone who, under the guise of concern for your financial safety, points out how perilous your present company is and just happens to have the right policy all ready for you to sign. This supposed savior might even be the person who sold you the original policy and touted it as more reliable than Patriot missiles.

If you do cash in a life-insurance or annuity policy and you are under the age of 59½, you will have to pay income taxes on the earnings and a federal penalty of 10 percent of the earnings. To avoid the taxes and penalty and continue to have your money build tax-deferred, you must move the money into another life-insurance policy or annuity. The correct way to do this is through what is known as a "1035 exchange," which is the same way you can transfer money from one IRA account to another. Your new insurance company should be able to handle the 213 paperwork for the exchange.

HOW TO PROTECT YOUR RETIREMENT MONEY

When it comes to safeguarding your retirement and pension money that is invested with an insurance company, you unfortunately may have a lot less control than you might like. For example, when a company terminates its pension plan and buys an annuity from an insurer to make your pension payments to you, the company usually chooses the insurer. In cases where a company is terminating a pension plan so it can siphon off some of the assets, it's actually to the company's advantage *not* to pick the safest insurer it can find. Reason: The higher-rated insurance company probably will charge more for its annuity, which means the company will have less left over after buying the annuity with the pension plan's money. The problem is, if the insurer goes bust, as First Executive did, the money may not be there to make those pension payments. If you work for or are a retiree of a company that is considering terminating its pension plan and transferring its liabilities to an insurance company, one thing you can do is inform the company's management—as well as its board of directors—about your concern for the safety of your pension and request that the company set strict safety guidelines for choosing an insurer and inform you of those guidelines. The company does have a fiduciary responsibility for your pension money and is required to invest it in a prudent way. While you still may not have a direct say in what insurer management chooses—and as an individual you can't switch to another insurance company—at least you have informed your employer of your concerns, which could be important later on should the insurer fail and the company's retirees want to sue the company for lost pension benefits.

You're probably more likely, however, to have retirement funds invested in an insurance company through an investment known as a guaranteed investment contract, or GIC. GICs are *the* single most popular investment in company retirement and savings plans such as 401(k)s. About two of every three dollars going into a 401(k) goes into a GIC and somewhere around $150 billion or so of all the money in company savings plans is now invested in GICs. You may even have money in a GIC and not know it. Sometimes, instead of going by the arcane, plain old weird-sounding name GIC, this choice in a company savings plan is called the capital preservation account or even fixed-income account.

214 Whatever name it goes by, a GIC works much like a CD, except you get it from an insurance company rather than a bank. With a GIC, the

insurance company guarantees you a fixed rate of return for a specified period—usually one to three years—and promises that at the end of that period you'll get your interest plus your original investment back. The big difference between a CD and a GIC, of course, is that the insurer isn't federally insured. Which means you are relying on the insurance company to be healthy enough to make good on its promise when you want to take your money out. Banks, by the way, offer something like a GIC, but they call it a BIC, like the pen. Unlike GICs, BICs have generally been covered by federal deposit insurance. Congress, however, was toying with the idea of doing away with insurance for BICs. Your company benefits department should be able to tell you if your retirement savings plan buys BICs and whether they are insured. If they're not, make sure the company buys BICs only from banks with top ratings from Standard & Poor's and Moody's. Similarly, Congress was also considering eliminating federal insurance for CDs bought by pension funds. (For details on this, see chapter 3.)

While you have some control over a GIC—you can choose not to invest in that option—the company you work for, or an investment manager it designates, actually chooses the insurance companies whose GICs your company savings plan will buy. Remember, though, this is *your* money they are investing for you. So you shouldn't be shy about asking the company to explain what they're doing with it and, in so doing, perhaps nudge them toward greater safety. The Executive Life fiasco illustrates the potential risks. Several major corporations had invested their employees' savings in GICs issued by Executive Life. One company, computer giant Unisys, had 30 percent of its GICs in one employee fund invested with Executive Life. After California insurance regulators seized Executive Life in April 1991, Unisys froze the money in those GICs, preventing employees from withdrawing GIC money or shifting it to other investments. This raised the possibility that Unisys employees, as well as employees of other large corporations such as Honeywell and Xerox, could suffer losses in their retirement savings funds.

The best place to start checking out the safety of your company savings plan is with your employee benefits or personnel department. You can begin by simply asking them what specific written guidelines they have for choosing GICs. "Don't be surprised if they don't have any guidelines," says Paul Laughlin, a consultant who helps companies select GICs. "But it still pays to ask because if enough people do, the company is more likely to come up with a set of guidelines." While there's no magic formula that is the safest way to buy GICs, there are a few ways to greatly reduce the risk of loss due to a GIC issuer's default. The first layer of protection is sticking with highly rated insurance companies. Again, no strict formula here, but certainly the risk of facing a default is lower if your company savings plan or 401(k) stays with insurers that get the highest or second-highest rating from Standard & Poor's or Moody's. "Companies rated below that level may be safe," says Murray Becker, a GIC consultant in Teaneck, New Jersey. "But if they are downgraded, it's easier for them to slip below investment grade. With the highest-rated companies you've got a cushion."

You've probably already guessed that another way to insulate your retirement money from loss is through our old friend diversification—a high-concept word for the commonsense notion of lowering risk by spreading your investments around. Generally a company savings plan should invest in the GICs of at least seven and preferably ten to twelve insurance companies. This way, if one goes bust, only a small portion of the savings plan's cash is at risk. By the way, even if an insurer becomes insolvent, it's unlikely the savings plan would lose its entire investment in a GIC. In most cases the insurance company still has enough assets to pay off much, if not most, of the GIC obligation. But even if you had a meltdown where half the value of a GIC evaporated because the insurer self-destructed, your actual loss would only be 5 percent if the plan's assets were evenly spread among the GICs of ten different insurance companies (You'd lose half of 10 percent of the plan's assets, which equals 5 percent). So the benefits of a simple diversification approach are obvious and even the most lame-brained investment manager or employer in the world is capable of carrying out such a straightforward strategy. Since GICs are sold in $1 million lots or more, the savings plan of a small or medium-size company may not have enough cash coming in to buy GICs from seven or more insurers. In that case, the employer can look to invest in pooled GICs—essentially buying a share in a large portfolio made up of many GICs—or the employer can simply put more of an emphasis on highly rated insurers. Because of safety concerns about insurers, some company savings plans, such as the plan offered by Dow Jones, the company that publishes *The Wall Street Journal*, have also begun adding Treasury bonds to its GIC portfolio to increase its security. Clearly, then, there are a number of strategies that, alone or in combination, can greatly increase the safety of the GIC component of your company savings or retirement plan. If your company hasn't already thought out its own plan, now is the time to ask them, politely but firmly, to start.

In the meantime, though, if your company doesn't have an investment strategy for buying GICs or you consider it so inadequate that you believe your money is at risk, should you switch out of the GIC option? That depends. If you can immediately transfer your money into a money-market-fund portfolio—as some plans allow you to do—then switch away. But most corporate savings plans don't offer *both* a GIC and money-market-fund option. It's usually either/or. So the GIC is the most conservative investment the plan offers. Or, if the plan does offer both a money fund and a GIC, you're usually not allowed to go from the GIC to the money fund directly. You must transfer the GIC money to a stock or bond fund for a certain period, often six months, before you can go into the money fund. In making such a switch, you would probably be taking even more risk, since stock and bond prices fluctuate much more over the short term than almost any GIC's value. (Over longer periods of time, five years or more, bonds and particularly stocks outperform GICs, though. So don't exclude these investments altogether.)

Unless your savings plan's portfolio is brimming with GICs of poorly rated companies loaded with junk and defaulted real-estate loans, however, you're probably better off just sitting tight in the GIC rather than jumping to a riskier investment. But don't just bite your fingernails and worry. That's the time to begin applying pressure on your employer to start choosing safer GICs. After all, it *is* your money; your employer is only investing it for you. Since you're the one who'll suffer in the event of a loss, it makes sense to insist that your company take the same precautions you do to make your savings absolutely safe.

T A B L E   1 0 · 3

Safety Ratings
for the Fifty Largest Insurance
Companies in the United States

Below are the actual safety ratings for the fifty largest U.S. insurance companies from the three premier ratings agencies—A. M. Best Company, Moody's Investors Service, and Standard & Poor's. To understand just what each of these ratings means, turn to tables 10.4, 10.5, and 10.6, which give each company's explanation of its ratings.

	Safety Rating From		
	A. M. Best?	Moody's?	Standard & Poor's?
Prudential Insurance Newark, NJ 201-412-4345	A+	Aaa	AAA
Metropolitan Life New York, NY 212-598-8000	A+	Aaa	AAA
Teachers Insurance & Annuity New York, NY 212-916-5317	A+	Aaa	AAA
Aetna Life Insurance Hartford, CT 203-275-3777	A+	Aa2	AA−
New York Life New York, NY 212-576-7000	A+	Aaa	AAA
Equitable Life Assurance New York, NY 212-315-7021	A-	A3	A
John Hancock Mutual Life Boston, MA 617-572-6000	A+	Aa2	AAA
Northwestern Mutual Life Milwaukee, WI 414-271-1444	A+	Aa2	AAA
Travelers Insurance (Life Dept.) Hartford, CT 203-277-3966	A+c	A2	A+
Connecticut General Bloomfield, CT 203-726-6000	A+	Aa2	AAA
Massachusetts Mutual Life Springfield, MA 413-788-8411	A+	Aa1	AAA
Principal Mutual Life Des Moines, IA 515-247-5111	A+	Aa1	AA+
Lincoln National Life Fort Wayne, IN 219-427-3640	A+	Aa3	AA−

	Safety Rating From		
	A. M. Best?	Moody's?	Standard & Poor's?
Allstate Life Northbrook, IL 312-402-5156	A+	Aa1	AAA
Mutual Life Insurance of New York New York, NY 212-708-2000	A	Baa1	A
Mutual Benefit Life# Newark, NJ 201-481-8356	NA-10	Baa1	Rating suspended
New England Mutual Life Boston, MA 617-578-6398	A+c	Aa3	AA
IDS Life Minneapolis, MN 612-372-2581	A+	Aa1	BBBq
State Farm Life Bloomington, IL 309-766-2735	A+	Aaa	AAA
Variable Annuity Life Houston, TX 713-831-5153	A+	Aa2	AA+
Jackson National Life Lansing, MI 517-394-3400	A+	A2	BBq
Executive Life# Inglewood, CA 213-312-1000	NA-10	Caa	CC
Connecticut Mutual Life Bloomfield, CT 203-727-6500	A+	Aa2	AA-
New York Life Insurance & Annuity New York, NY 212-576-7000	A+	Aaa	AAA
Nationwide Life Columbus, OH 614-249-7111	A+	Aaa	AAA
Pacific Mutual Life Newport Beach, CA 714-640-3346	A+	A1	AA+
Equitable Variable Life New York, NY 212-641-8330	A-	A3	A

	Safety Rating From		
	A. M. Best?	*Moody's?*	*Standard & Poor's?*
Transamerica Life & Annuity Los Angeles, CA 213-742-2137	A	Aa3	AA+
Provident National Assurance Chattanooga, TN 615-755-1373	A	Aa2	AA+
Transamerica Occidental of California Los Angeles, CA 213-742-2137	A+	Aa3	AA+
Aetna Life Insurance & Annuity Hartford, CT 203-275-3777	A+	Aa1	AAA
Hartford Life Hartford, CT 203-843-8216	A+	Aa2	AAA
Keyport Life Insurance Co. Boston, MA 617-457-1400	A+	A1	A+
American Family Life Assurance Columbus, GA 404-323-3431	A	Not rated	BBBq
Guardian Life New York, NY 212-598-8000	A+	Aaa	AAA
State Mutual Life Assurance Worcester, MA 508-852-1000	A+	Aa3	AA+
United Pacific Life Philadelphia, PA 215-864-5935	A	Ba1	BBB
Penn Mutual Life Philadelphia, PA 215-956-8104	A+	A1	A+
Kemper Investors Life Chicago, IL 312-845-1701	A	A2	BBq
General American Life St. Louis, MO 314-231-1700	A+	A1	AA

	Safety Rating From		
	A. M. Best?	Moody's?	Standard & Poor's?
Phoenix Mutual Life Enfield, CT 203-253-1179	A+	Aa2	AA+
Sun Life of America Los Angeles, CA 213-445-1748	A+	A3	AA
Minnesota Mutual Life St. Paul, MN 612-223-4010	A+	Aa1	AA+
Northwestern National Life Minneapolis, MN 612-372-5432	A+c	A3	A
American Life New York, NY 212-581-1200	NA4	Not rated	AAA
Franklin Life Springfield, IL 217-528-2011	A+	Aa2	BBBq
Unum Life Insurance Co. Portland, ME 207-770-2445	A+	Aa1	AA+
Mutual of America Life New York, NY 212-399-6846	A+	Aa2	AA+
First Capital Life# San Diego, CA 619-452-9060	NA-10	Not rated	CC
Continental Assurance Chicago, IL 312-822-5653	A+	Aa1	AA+

SOURCES: A. M. Best, Moody's Investors Service, Standard & Poor's. All data as of October 1991.

#Under state supervision.

T A B L E 1 0 · 4

Comparing the Rating Scales

The table below gives the ratings, from the highest to lowest, for the three best-known ratings companies—A. M. Best, Moody's Investors Service, and Standard & Poor's. Keep in mind, however, that it is easier for a company to get a top rating from A. M. Best than from

Moody's and Standard & Poor's and, therefore, professionals within the insurance industry usually don't give equal weight to A. M. Best ratings. For a better understanding of just what these letter grades mean, turn to Tables 10.5, 10.6, and 10.7, which give each company's explanation of their ratings.

	A. M. Best	Moody's	Standard & Poor's
Highest Rating	**A+** Superior **A and A-** Excellent **B+** Very Good **B and B-** Good **C+** Fairly Good **C and C-** Fair **Not Assigned**	**Aaa** Exceptional **Aa** Excellent **A** Good **Baa** Adequate **Ba** Questionable **B** Poor **Caa** Very poor **Ca** Extremely Poor	**AAA** Superior **AA** Excellent **A** Good **BBB** Adequate **BB** Adequate/caution **B** High vulnerability **CCC** Highly question-able **CC** Vulnerable to liquidation
Lowest Rating		**C** Lowest	**C** Vulnerable to liquidation
Company in Default			**D** Under order of liquidation

T A B L E   1 0 · 5

A. M. Best's Insurance Company Ratings

The following are A. M. Best's own explanations of its insurance-company ratings. The ratings are listed from the highest (A+) to lowest (C and C−).

A+ (Superior):   Assigned to those companies which in our opinion have achieved superior overall performance when compared to the norms of the life/health insurance industry. A+ (Superior) rated insurers generally have demonstrated the strongest ability to meet their respective policyholder and other contractual obligations.

A and A− (Excellent):   Assigned to those companies which in our opinion have achieved excellent overall performance when compared to the norms of the life/health insurance industry. A and A− (Excellent) rated insurers generally have demonstrated a strong ability to meet their respective policyholder and other contractual obligations.

B+ (Very Good): Assigned to those companies which in our opinion have achieved very good overall performance when compared to the norms of the life/health insurance industry. B+ (Very Good) rated insurers generally have demonstrated a very good ability to meet their respective policyholder and other contractual obligations.

B and B− (Good): Assigned to those companies which in our opinion have achieved good overall performance when compared to the norms of the life/health insurance industry. B and B− (Good) rated insurers generally have demonstrated a good ability to meet their respective policyholder and other contractual obligations.

C+ (Fairly Good): Assigned to those companies which in our opinion have achieved fairly good overall performance when compared to the norms of the life/health insurance industry. C+ (Fairly Good) rated insurers generally have demonstrated a fairly good ability to meet their respective policyholder and other contractual obligations.

C and C− (Fair): Assigned to those companies which in our opinion have achieved fair overall performance when compared to the norms of the life/health insurance industry. C and C− (Fair) rated insurers generally have demonstrated a fair ability to meet their respective policyholder and other contractual obligations.

Not Assigned: Companies not receiving a Best's Rating (A+ to C− are assigned to a Rating "Not Assigned" classification (abbreviated NA) which is divided into ten classifications to identify the reason why the company was not eligible for a Best's Rating. NA-10, for example, means the company is not rated because it is under state supervision. For information on other reasons a company gets an NA rating, see *A. M. Best Reports* (Life/Health edition), which is available in many large libraries.

The following are excerpts from Best's Rating Modifiers:

"c"—Contingent Rating. Temporarily assigned to a company when there has been a decline in performance in its profitability, leverage, and/or liquidity results, but the decline has not been significant enough to warrant an actual reduction in the company's previously assigned rating. Our evaluation may be based on the availability of more current information and/or contingent on the successful execution by management of a program of corrective action. Our evaluation may also reflect situations involving matters of a more subjective nature.

"w"—Watch List. Indicates the company was placed on our Rating "Watch List" during the year because it experienced a downward trend in profitability, leverage, and/or liquidity performance, or other significant event affecting the operations of the subject company, but the decline was not significant enough to warrant an actual reduction in the assigned rating.

"x"—Revised Rating. Indicates the company's assigned rating was revised during the year to the rating shown.

T A B L E   1 0 · 6

Moody's Insurance Financial Strength Ratings

The following are Moody's Investors Service's own explanations of its insurance financial strength ratings. The ratings are listed from the highest (Aaa) to lowest (C). Moody's also applies numerical modifiers 1, 2, and 3 in each generic rating category from Aa to B. The modifier 1 indicates that the insurance company ranks in the higher end of its generic rating category; the modifier 2 indicates a mid-range ranking; and the modifier 3 indicates that the company ranks in the lower end of its generic rating category.

Aaa: Insurance companies rated Aaa offer Exceptional financial security. While the financial strength of these companies is likiely to change, such changes as can be visualized are most unlikely to impair their fundamentally strong position.

Aa: Insurance companies rated Aa offer excellent financial security. Together with the Aaa group they constitute what are generally known as high-grade companies. They are rated lower than Aaa companies because long-term risks appear somewhat larger.

A: Insurance companies rated A offer good financial security. However, elements may be present which suggest a susceptibility to impairment sometime in the future.

Baa: Insurance companies rated Baa offer adequate financial security. However, certain protective elements may be lacking or may be characteristically unreliable over any great length of time.

224 **Ba:**   Insurance companies rated Ba offer questionable financial security. Often the ability of these companies to meet policyholder obliga-

tions may be very moderate and thereby not well safe-guarded in the future.

B: Insurance companies rated B offer poor financial security. Assurance of punctual payment of policyholder obligations over any long period of time is small.

Caa: Insurance companies rated Caa offer very poor financial security. They may be in default on their policyholder obligations or there may be present elements of danger with respect to punctual payment of policyholder obligations and claims.

Ca: Insurance companies rated Ca offer extremely poor financial security. Such companies are often in default on their policyholder obligations or have other marked shortcomings.

C: Insurance companies rated C are the lowest-rated class of insurance company and can be regarded as having extremely poor prospects of ever offering financial security.

T A B L E   1 0 · 7

Standard & Poor's Claims-Paying Ability Rating Definitions

The following are Standard & Poor's own explanations of its insurance company claims-paying ability ratings. The ratings are listed from the highest (AAA) to lowest (D). Ratings from AA to CCC may be modified by the use of a plus (+) sign or minus (−) sign to show relative standing of the insurer within those rating categories. Standard & Poor's also issues qualified solvency ratings. Less comprehensive than the claims-paying ability ratings, the qualified ratings are based on public financial data taken from financial statements filed with state insurance regulators. The qualified ratings are BBBq, and BBq and Ba. Explanations of these ratings follow those of the claims-paying ability ratings below.

AAA: Insurers rated AAA offer superior financial security on both an absolute and relative basis. They possess the highest safety and have an overwhelming capacity to meet policyholder obligations.

AA: Insurers rated AA offer excellent financial security, and their capacity to meet policyholder obligations differs only in a small degree from insurers rated AAA.

A: Insurers rated A offer good financial security, but their capacity to meet policyholder obligations is somewhat more susceptible to adverse changes in economic or underwriting conditions than more highly rated insurers.

BBB: Insurers rated BBB offer adequate financial security, but their capacity to meet policyholder obligations is considered more vulnerale to adverse economic or underwriting conditions than that of more highly rated insurers.

BB: Insurers rated BB offer financial security that may be adequate but caution is indicated since their capacity to meet policyholder obligations is considered vulnerable to adverse economic or underwriting conditions and may not be adequate for "long-tail" or long-term policies.

B: Insurers rated B are currently able to meet policyholder obligations, but their vulnerability to adverse economic or underwriting conditions is considered high.

CCC: Insurers rated CCC are vulnerable to adverse economic or underwriting conditions to the extent that their continued capacity to meet policyholder obligations is highly questionable unless a favorable environment prevails.

CC and C: Insurers rated CC or C may not be meeting all policyholder obligations, may be operating under the jurisdiction of insurance regulators, and are vulnerable to liquidation.

D: Insurers rated D have been placed under an order of liquidation.

Standard & Poor's Qualified Solvency Ratings

BBBq: Results of S&P's quantitative tests on the insurer's past performance as disclosed in statutory financial statements are consistent with those of insurers offering *above average* security.

BBq: Results of S&P's quantitative tests on the insurer's past performance as disclosed in statutory financial statements are consistent with those of insurers offering *average* security.

Bq: Results of S&P's quantitative tests on the insurer's past performance as disclosed in statutory financial statements are consistent with those of insurers offering *below average* security.

AFTERWORD

The Need to Remain Vigilant

SAVING and investing money ultimately comes down to balancing our conflicting emotions of fear and greed. In the 1980s, greed got the upper hand as savers and investors reached for unrealistically high rates of interest. In the 1990s, fear already seems to be regaining dominance. The S&L crisis, rising bank failures, the collapse of large insurance companies—all have made us focus more on the safety of our money than on how much it earns.

It would always be wonderful to have the best of both worlds—a completely safe investment that also has the highest yield. But that never happens. But if you follow the guidelines I've laid out in this book, you should be able to get, if not the best of both worlds, the best that is possible: competitive returns on your savings with a high degree of safety.

You should remember that, sooner or later, heightened concern about the financial woes of banks and insurance companies will fade—and the need for safety will seem less pressing. Suddenly, bankers, brokers, and insurance agents will be back making their old pitch, trying to win you over with CDs or annuities or money funds that beat the competition's yields but supposedly have less risk. When that happens—when you find financial advisers making the kind of all-gain-no-pain claims that were common when junk-bond king Michael Milken was on top of the world (and not in prison)—that is the time when it is most important to remember the message in this book.

INDEX